Sexual Arrangements

Janet Reibstein is a psychologist and psychotherapist, and an Affiliated Lecturer in the Social and Political Sciences Faculty at Cambridge University. She has published widely on family and marital issues.

Martin Richards is Reader in Human Development at Cambridge University and Head of the Centre for Family Research. He is the author of, among other books, *Divorce Matters* (Penguin) and *Infancy* (Harper & Row).

D0610609

Also by M. P. M. Richards

The Integration of a Child into a Social World (editor). Cambridge University Press. 1974.
Infancy. The World of the Newborn. Harper and Row. 1980.
Children of Social Worlds (edited with Paul Light). Polity Press. 1986.
Divorce Matters (with Jacqueline Burgoyne & Roger Ormrod). Penguin Books. 1987.
The Politics of Maternity Care (edited with Jo Garcia and Robert Kilpatrick). Oxford University Press. 1989.

SEXUAL ARRANGEMENTS
Marriage and Affairs

JANET REIBSTEIN
and MARTIN RICHARDS

Mandarin

To my family
J.R.

A Mandarin Paperback
SEXUAL ARRANGEMENTS

First published in Great Britain 1992
by William Heinemann Ltd
This edition published 1993
by Mandarin Paperbacks
an imprint of Reed Consumer Books Ltd
Michelin House, 81 Fulham Road, London SW3 6RB
and Auckland, Melbourne, Singapore and Toronto

Copyright © Janet Reibstein and Martin Richards 1992

A CIP catalogue record for this title
is available from the British Library
ISBN 0 7493 1412 5

Printed and bound in Great Britain
by Cox & Wyman Ltd, Reading, Berks

Contents

Preface

This book is the product of a collaboration across disciplines and professional roles. While the first author draws on her experience as a therapist and a psychologist who has researched both psychotherapy and relationships, the second uses his background as a social scientist, particularly as a researcher on divorce and parents and children. We believe that our approaches are complementary and that the different knowledge, assumptions and experience we have each contributed have created a better argument than the simple sum of its two parts. Our writing was preceded – and followed – by long hours of discussion. One of us has taken primary responsibility for each chapter (J.R. the Introduction, 2, 4, 5 and 6, M.R. 1, 3, 7 and 8) but the final version embodies ideas from both of us.

We would both like to thank the many individuals and couples who have generously shared their accounts of their marriages and other relationships with us. They have provided an invaluable resource for our thinking and writing. We are also greatly indebted to all those colleagues, friends and students with whom we have discussed, argued and rehearsed our ideas. They have stimulated our thinking, extended our knowledge and helped us to clarify our arguments. Sally Roberts and Jill Brown have typed all too many versions of the manuscript and have moved between three word processing systems with great skill.

The first author's family, including her husband, Stephen Monsell, whose support and often wry insights were invaluable, and two young sons, Adam and Daniel Monsell, who adapted cheerfully to the sometimes unfair demands of that third child 'the book', merit profound and lasting admiration and gratitude.

The second author would like to thank Jane Elliott who has been his collaborator in his recent divorce research. Among other assistance, she was responsible for clarifying the concept of her and his divorce. He has always found the process of writing, and the reading and thought that precedes it, a lonely business and owes a special debt to the familiar voices of Billie Jo, Crystal, Emmylou, Holly, K.T., Nanci, Tanya, Wynonna and Naomi.

We would like to thank the following publishers, agents and authors for permission to quote from their work: Faber, Philip Larkin: 'Annus Mirabilis'; Virago Press, Curtis Brown Group Ltd, Jane Lazarre: *On Loving Men*; Jonathan Cape, Ann Oakley: *Taking It Like a Woman*; Routledge, Brian Jackson: *Working Class Community*; Oxford University Press, Inc., John Gillis: *For Better, For Worse*.

We are also grateful to Warner Chappell Music and Palace Music Co. Ltd for permission to quote from 'Three Steps to Heaven' by Eddie and Bob Cochrane. The excerpt from 'Remember You're Mine' by Mann and Lowe is reproduced by kind permission of Carlin Music Corporation, Iron Bridge House, 3 Bridge Approach, London NW1 8BD, courtesy of MCA Records Inc., courtesy of WEA International Inc. P. 1957. Collection Time Life Music 1990 and Warner Chappell Music Australia Pty Ltd.

We offer our apologies to any copyright owners who, despite our best efforts, we have been unable to locate.

Introduction

Do not adultery commit;
Advantage rarely comes of it.

> Arthur Hugh Clough (1819–1861),
> *The Latest Decalogue*

Accursed from birth they be
Who seek to find monogamy,
Pursuing it from bed to bed –
I think they would be better dead.

> Dorothy Parker,
> *Not So Deep as a Well*, 1937

For many months Sam was in love. Flashes of Ellen, her smile, her body, shivers of her scent and fragments of their days and nights together floated in and out of his day, inflating him with longing, with fondness and with desire.

Sam is forty-two. He is a successful investment banker. He surveys the world's money markets from a large mahogany desk on the top floor of an impressive building in a major financial centre. One might well have passed him, on his daily train commute, wearing his smart dark-blue suit and pure silk tie, or have observed him, trading jokes with colleagues or chairing meetings with solemn aplomb, and never guessed at the images of Ellen jostling for attention with banking figures in his brain. One would not have guessed because Ellen, powerful as she was for him, was a secret. For Sam is married – to somebody else. Like so many others who have affairs, Sam's with Ellen was secret. Now, years later, after Sam and Ellen have both put each other and their affair far away, it has remained secret. Sam is still married. He hopes his affair will *never* come to light.

Christina was also in love and sleeping with someone who was not her husband. She, too, watched over her secret, carrying it like a tune as she went through her day teaching dance classes, collecting children, doing the shopping, cooking the meals. But one day the carefully constructed walls around her romantic idyll split asunder: somebody knew and was threatening to tell. So Christina confessed to her husband, and overnight a passionate love affair turned into a tragic and painful mess. Two years on her husband's friendship with her former lover is forever destroyed; her marriage survives but remains shaken to the core.

Ursula and David are also having affairs. They, too, are married – to each other. Each knows about the other's affair, and each says that the other's affair enriches their life together. Ursula, too, lives as if with an extra sense, an ever-present sexuality now that she is sleeping with Sean. The image of herself as an 'adulteress' excites her, and for the first time since the beginning of their marriage she and David have had exciting, inventive sex. Meanwhile, David is feeling 'tingly', as he describes it, as well, from his latest 'crush' (again, his words). He is also in love and the feeling that he is alive with love suffuses the rest of his world with it. As he sees it, in large part because of their affairs, he and Ursula are brimming with sexuality together, and this despite a small town house teeming with three small and demanding children, two active careers, and a history of deep affection but unexciting sex.

And then there is Annie, who slept with a man other than her husband while on a self-improvement holiday. She was not in love. Indeed, she felt something like contempt for the man who had shared her bed. Or Sam, again, who once slept with a secretary provided for him on a business trip, and though he thought she was attractive had no interest in repeating the experience.

We could go on. Examples are rife in life and in literature, in films and on television. Indeed, everywhere there is a story of a marriage there could be a story of an affair. David, Ursula, Sam, Annie, Christina – they are all having or have had affairs. Yet, despite some similarities, their affairs are different, carried on for different reasons, inspiring different feelings, and leaving very different marks on the people involved.

If any of these people were our friends, colleagues or neighbours we would probably find ourselves shocked to discover their affairs. For affairs, in themselves, shock. They represent what we are not supposed to do. While preparing this book, telling colleagues and acquaintances the subject matter under study, as often as not we have encountered raised eyebrows, low chuckles and embarrassed silences. People tend to miss a beat before asking further questions. Affairs bring other people up short. Yet most people either know people close to them who have had an affair, have had one themselves, endured their spouse having one, or, before marriage, were the third party in one. If they fail to fall into one of these four categories, normally they do fall into a fifth: they have thought about having an affair, or, a smaller subcategory of this, have *almost* had an affair themselves. Still, despite their prevalence, despite people's fascination with affairs, we do not know how to understand them. We do not know why people have them – although we can tell you why they should not – or what they get from having them, or even what an affair is. Are David's and Ursula's affairs the same thing as Christina's? Should the two we've described for Sam really both be called 'affairs'?

To the best of our knowledge a large number of married people, both men and women, have affairs. Most of these people do not approve of their own affairs, believing in monogamy but not practising it. Affairs are difficult for researchers to study. People do not want to confess to them, for obvious reasons, since most are secret and if discovered might wreck marriages. Beyond that, most people feel embarrassed to confess, afraid that moral judgements will be passed upon them. There are also other factors making it a difficult area to research. Most studies have made do with samples which have become available to them: studies have recruited their samples through press advertisements, or through what is known as the 'snowball' method (interview one subject, and get them to nominate another person to be interviewed), or through

clinical samples, such as people in marital therapy or counselling. These are not representative samples; that is, they do not
accurately reflect the population at large, since they have been
self-selected, or selected in other biased ways. Any conclusions
drawn from them are therefore shaky, and we cannot necessarily apply them generally. The best way to study affairs would
be to take a random sample of married people. In such a
sample, some people will have had affairs. However, such a
method poses ethical and practical problems (who would own
up? Could the research damage the marriage?) and is unwieldy
and expensive. Questions about affairs stir up marriage. Privacy
and confidentiality are necessary, yet those very conditions can
provoke suspicions in spouses, or arouse guilt in those who
have had affairs. Moreover, most funding agencies do not want
to be seen as funding a study which could be construed as
invading people's privacy or, more pertinently, as sensationalist.
This is an unfortunate by-product of the titillation and embar-
rassment which accompanies the subject of affairs. However,
judging from the admittedly flawed studies which have been
done, we estimate that between 50 per cent and 75 per cent of
men and an only slightly smaller proportion of women have had
or are having affairs while married.

Few people have tried to take a dispassionate overview of
this phenomenon (or set of phenomena) which we are calling
affairs, but fewer still have attempted to explain it in its
psychological detail. We intend in this book not only to define
and to understand what an affair is, but also to examine why
affairs happen and to see what it is about marriage itself which
might push people into having affairs – despite most married
couples' avowed intent to be monogamous. In doing so we also
will focus on the secrecy which is a cornerstone of so many –
probably most – affairs, and we will dissect the difference
between men's affairs and women's. For one of the great
unexamined yet explosive areas of affairs is the influence of the
gender divide: man's world/woman's world; her marriage his
marriage; his affair/her affair.

A Definition of Affairs

In this book we are using the term affair for a sexual relationship between people who are not married to each other and when at least one of the partners in this relationship is married to someone else. Other authors have used different terminology to signify the same phenomenon. It has been called infidelity by some and adultery by others. Both of these terms carry a moral judgement which is not the purpose or message of this book. Adultery is forbidden in the Tenth Commandment. Infidelity means unfaithful; an infidel is one who breaks faith and a moral commitment.

The word affair does not carry these moralistic overtones but it does perhaps imply something frivolous. The difficulty of finding the appropriate terminology is, of course, related to both the difficult feelings aroused by affairs and by the many variations of affairs experienced. Some affairs are frivolous, unimportant in the larger scheme of the participants' lives, and sometimes short-lived – a 'best-forgotten few hours in a long life' as one person said in an interview. Others are serious, sometimes even life-changing, and sometimes virtually lifelong. Some are like parallel marriages, others intermittently important, others almost forgotten. Can a single word, or indeed a single concept, encompass all of these?

Just as there has been little agreement about what to call an affair among people writing on the subject, there has also been little consensus about how best to categorise these various relationships. Most current attempts have begun with the view that an affair only happens when something is lacking in the marriage – and that lack is shown up by the affair. The American psychiatrist and marital therapist Frank Pittman, in his recent book, *Private Lies* (1989), calls affairs adultery and expounds the view that the adulterer is acting as if 'sick'. The sickness, infecting a marriage, consequently, needs a treatment – therapy – which will 'cure' it. He says affairs can be one of four kinds. They might be 'accidental' ('it just happened'); or they might be of the 'philandering' sort which occur mostly in men, who in Pittman's description 'depersonalize both the woman at home and the woman in bed at the moment'). In this sort of affair, he says, in marital sex there is little relationship with the wife and this carries over into sex outside the marriage. Or affairs may be 'romantic': these are affairs which involve love or its near equivalents and which then compete with feelings for one's spouse. Or they can be 'marital arrangements': these are affairs within 'open' marriages in which sex outside is acceptable. Pittman's views are strong and guided by a fierce moral conviction. Affairs are wrong. Monogamous marriage is healthy. His classifications are forged by this moral severity and we think consequently too narrowly describe the variety of affairs which seem to exist.

Emily Brown, another American marital therapist, has a different classification of affairs in her book *Patterns of Infidelity and Their Treatment* (Brunner/Mazel, 1990), written for therapists who deal with them. There is the 'out-the-door' affair, in which the partner having the affair is really trying to end the marriage; the 'sexual addict affair', in which sexual commitment to one person poses a never-ending problem for the addict; and the 'conflict avoiding affair' and 'intimacy avoiding affair' which both divert energy away from the marriage (either away from conflict resolution or from the achievement of intimacy). Again, Brown takes a strong if less than moralistic view. For her, affairs are always a symptom of something amiss in a marriage, and therefore a good diagnostic aid to what must be done to save it, if possible. Affairs, she holds, carry a message. The message may be about the marriage itself or it may be about what the person having the affair needs or wants to get, but is not getting, from the marriage. Or it can be about what a person is diverting from the marriage. For instance, in the 'conflict avoiding' type of affair a woman who is very angry with her husband for not being loving enough may take up with someone else. She thus avoids venting her anger at her spouse both by pouring energy into an affair and also by getting attention elsewhere. Her affair cures her of feeling unnoticed and may thus diminish her anger. For Brown, affairs, although they may benefit the individual, like this hypothetical woman, cannot ever help a marriage. For marriages, affairs are not only bad news, but also represent the worm in the apple. Brown's view, that marriage ought to be monogamous because spouses ought to be able to give each other sufficient emotional and sexual sustenance to avoid affairs, limits her categorisation of affairs. In her classification affairs are always negative comments on marriages.

In her book *Adultery: An Analysis of Love and Betrayal* (1988), the British sociologist Annette Lawson classifies affairs as either 'romantic' (that is, an affair which encroaches on the romantic ideals which marriage is supposed to embody) or those which enact the 'myth of me' (that is an affair which signifies the participant has chosen his or her own personal development over the growth of the marital relationship). Lawson does not take a position on the morality or healthiness of affairs. Hers is a sociological analysis of what motivates people to have them. But her classification leaves out the differences men and women bring to their affairs as well as the psychological backdrop explaining why people might have them. Her classification avoids, too, a central issue in affairs: whether they are secret or open.

Individuals also classify their affairs in other ways. In interviews for this book we found that they they do so according to the importance of and satisfaction brought from affairs specifically in two areas: their emotions and the impact of affairs on them sexually.

On the emotional dimension: people classify their affairs as 'casual' or 'serious' – or somewhere in between. In addition they can tell you whether or not they considered themselves to have been in love with their affair partner, whether or not they liked him or her, and whether or not the emotions kindled by this partner had posed a real threat to their marriages. In Annie's affair with the man on her self-improvement holiday there was little emotional attachment, and none after the affair had ended, while Sam's attachment to Ellen was deep and intense, and posed a real threat to his marriage. Christina's affair felt threatening to her marriage only at its end, although she was in love with the man she was having an affair with. And in Ursula's there was affection but not love, and no threat to her marriage.

Another dimension in the way that people classify their affairs is that of time: both how long the affair lasted and how much time the couple spent together. This is usually related to emotion, although that relationship is not always simple. Often a casual affair is a brief one, or a one-night stand. Indeed, pointing out the briefness of an affair can become a strategy for minimising its effects: 'It was only very brief', or 'It was just a one-night stand'. This often does comfort the spouse because time robbed from the marriage is minimal and so implies the investment in the affair was insignificant. Yet sometimes brief affairs can be very traumatic. Diana, a mother of two in her early thirties who was married for twelve years, had a brief affair with her tennis instructor. Two years later she has still not recovered. The affair revealed to her that sex and romance can be more intense and deep than she had imagined; she now feels the lack of such intensity in her marriage and mourns its loss. Similarly, a long-term affair need not be emotionally important. Nick, a middle-aged academic with three sons has had a recurring affair, conducted once a year over the course of about ten years, with a foreign colleague. His is an intermittent long-term affair which is of modest emotional significance. However, some long-term affairs become a bit like alternative marriages, as we shall see in the case of Cathy and Bruce. Like marriages, such affairs have built-in rules, habits and customs. Especially if both partners have families and jobs, long-term affairs need to be well governed by rules and habits. For example; 'We meet Friday afternoons, except if the children are sick; I phone you at 9:30 Wednesday, unless there is an emergency, or my husband is around, in which case we will wait until your phone call to me on Thursday afternoon,' etc. In busy lives with potentially conflicting commitments there is not much room for unpredictability if an affair, as well as a marriage, is to endure over time. Of course, a long-term affair is often serious, demanding as it does time, attention, and the considerable energy it takes to maintain it.

In terms of the sexual dimension of affairs, people rate not only the degree of satisfaction and excitement an affair afforded but also whether or not they felt they had learned something about themselves sexually, and how central the sexual element was to the affair. Annie, whose first affair was with someone she had met at an evening class, knew that sex was the central attraction for it confirmed both her sexiness and appetite. Ursula felt that sex with Sean was not as satisfactory as with her husband David, yet because she was an 'adulteress' she grew sexier with David. In that sense sex was important in her affair, but not because she was enormously attracted to her lover.

Jacqueline, a dance instructor, had an affair with a man who was both her friend and her husband's. She says that the affair enhanced marital sex. She and the man became sexually involved (although no penetration ever occurred) during a theatre production in which they were both working. They spent hours together, sharing creative work. Her partner's passion for her was profound, and she was heady with it. Like Ursula, she was not transported by the actual sex, but being desired made her sexier with her husband. Similarly, Neil, an academic, married to Marie for seventeen years, had numerous affairs. One was with his GP. 'Sex with Marie is great,' he says. But when he tells about seducing his doctor his eyes light up. While sex with Marie might be great it can never be illicit, her seduction never electrified by the forbidden. Sex may or may not be the most important – or satisfactory – element of an affair, but it is a crucial one because, when such extramarital friendships become sexual, they cross the forbidden line.

These classifications begin to indicate some of the ways we can begin to understand affairs. But they leave out a lot of the really interesting material – particularly the difference in men's and women's behaviour and reactions – as well as people's ideas about marriage, the things which predispose people to have affairs and may make some people vulnerable to having them, and finally the all-important question of whether or not an affair is secret.

Main Themes

We don't want to oversimplify this rich and complex area of human experience, so we won't try to give a single 'theory' on affairs in this book. Instead we will look at all the issues – the gender divide, the models of marriage, the predisposing factors and the secrecy question – as ways of getting a better understanding both of affairs and of marriage.

When we began to think about writing a book on affairs, we decided that we had, first, to look at marriage – for without marriage there can be no affair. In the course of informally interviewing the men and women whose voices can be heard in the book, we came to believe that the kind of marriage most of us are familiar with – 'Western marriage' – contains within itself contradictory beliefs and pressures which could well propel individuals into affairs. Modern-day marriage, we will show, demands explicitly that husbands and wives are everything to each other – intimate, helpmate. It also demands that these marriages last till death do these spouses part. But nowadays both men and women are expected to be sexual as well as loving, and loving as well as sexual. Both are now expected in marriage – great sex and good love. Sex is something that both sexes now have the capacity to enjoy in itself – and intimacy is something we have grown to expect with sex. But is marriage a suitable lifelong vehicle for sex – and love? Married life can be mundane, the marital relationship can be a fragile one to contain these needs, over time. Sex in marriage can become routine – dulling both men's and women's appetite. And intimacy within marriage, especially when tied to sex, can similarly falter in the ups and downs of a long-term relationship.

Yet our ideas about marriage have not changed or adapted as we have found the experience of marriage failing to give us as much sex or as much intimacy as we need. Men and women, especially given the sexual sophistication both have reached, all too often feel the gap between the marriage they have and their 'ideal marriage'. Perhaps because of this gap and their sophistication over sex and intimacy, men and women have affairs. But they are not supposed to and they know it. They are letting down the marital ideal to which they still hold. Their affairs, therefore, have to be secret. And it is this secrecy, we will show, that erodes marriages as much as anything else. Undiscovered affairs – probably most of them – don't normally end marriages. But the quality of intimacy in the marriage can be dramatically eroded by the secrecy involved in such affairs. Moreover, when a husband or wife does discover a secret affair, they feel the whole basis of their marital trust is decayed.

Affairs: Posing a Challenge

Let us return to those men and women who opened this chapter. If these were our neighbours, friends or colleagues at work, why would we be shocked by Sam's or Annie's or Christina's or Ursula's and David's stories?

As we have already argued, affairs implicitly pose a challenge to our prevailing beliefs about marriage. As such, they shake our complacency. For a moment we have to think, 'could this be me?' or, 'why not me?' They further challenge our ideas that marriage is a partnership in which we own or possess our spouse, an implicit code by which most marriages are lived: '*my* wife/*my* husband'. Clearly, if one spouse can go to bed with someone else, that spouse is not possessed by the other. As we will argue in chapter 1, this possessiveness is particularly true for husbands, since modern Western marriage grew out of a patriarchy in which families themselves, including wives, belonged to husbands. The still-strong double standard, growing out of that patriarchy, makes having affairs a greater transgression for women than for men. Affairs also contradict the very vows which supposedly bind most marriages: thou shalt forsake all others, in sickness and in health, till death us do part.

Affairs are unsettling in other ways, too. We are not writing in this book about platonic friendships between men and women, or business partnerships, or non-sexual service relationships between the sexes. We are writing about sexual activities shared between men and women, with feelings attached. Sexual matters titillate. Breaking sexual rules shocks.

What We Are Not Looking at in this Book

This book focuses on heterosexual affairs. These are different from homosexual ones. For one thing, married people who have homosexual affairs may have them, at least in part, for different reasons. They may prefer to have sex with members of their own sex and their sexual frustration can therefore never be remedied with the marriage. Or, if bisexual, they may feel only partly sexually alive if they are only having sex with members of the opposite sex. Homosexual affairs may seem less competitive than heterosexual ones to those having them (but not necessarily to their spouses). That is, sexual relationships with members of one's own sex may feel so different that it may be easier to believe that they exist parallel to, rather than in conflict with, marriage. In addition, people impose secrecy in homosexual affairs for special reasons. Most married people who have homosexual affairs prefer to be seen publicly as heterosexual. Thus secrecy about homosexual affairs carries additional urgency. And the repercussions upon discovery of secret homosexuality, such as disgrace, stigma, deeper shock, and the need to recast the identity of the spouse having the affair, are additional to any in a heterosexual affair.

Similarly, we are not including visits to prostitutes as affairs. In these the basis on which sex is entered into is different. There is a clear exchange: money for sex. Admittedly, these are still sexual encounters outside marriage. However, even proverbial one-night stands normally include something more personal. Usually they are preceded by some conversational encounter in which both participants wish to be viewed as more than a set of genitals. Discovering that a husband has secret one-night stands can be much more unsettling to the marital status quo than discovery that he visits a prostitute. The wife can realistically wonder if there was something she was not providing – affection, for instance – which she will not worry about if her husband visits a prostitute. On the other hand prostitute visits currently pose a different sort of threat: the increased risk of contracting AIDS or other sexually transmitted diseases. They also often arouse suspicions that one's husband might not be sexually normal (and so is compelled to visit prostitutes for kinky or other disturbing reasons). For these reasons, visits to prostitutes can and often do disturb marriages profoundly. But they can also be more easily dismissed as 'just for sex'.

Some people consider themselves to have had an affair even when the involvement was emotional but not sexual. Most sexual affairs include some form of emotional involvement, even if minimal in duration and importance. The fact that they are sexual makes them different. What is problematic about our definition that an affair is sexual is the difficulty in defining what is sexual. Many people define an affair by the fact of penetration. Sex without intercourse is one way of accommodating the desire for an affair and the notion that one is still faithful, like a virgin, outside of marriage. The story of Paul and Emily underscores this point. Paul and Emily had an open marriage, but their contract excluded Paul's having affairs while Emily was pregnant or breastfeeding. But after the birth of their second child Paul found himself irresistibly drawn to Stephanie, a colleague at work. He confessed this to Emily, hoping to renegotiate their agreement, but she refused. His attraction to Stephanie did not wane, and they began to meet. Eventually, they became sexually involved, and if one uses Kinsey's measure, which is the number of orgasms achieved as a measure of sexual involvement, they certainly fit the definition. But penetration never occurred. This for Paul meant that he was honouring his marital agreement, and he did not define what he and Stephanie were doing as having an affair. All except two of the people who appear in this book had affairs in which full intercourse took place. Yet we would define Paul's and Stephanie's relationship as an affair. When there is substantial sexual involvement, and especially genital contact, it constitutes for us an affair.

Affairs and AIDS

Affairs mean an increased risk of contracting AIDS. The ultimate safe sex is monogamy. Strikingly in this book only two people spontaneously mentioned AIDS. One said that in recent years he has not had any casual affairs because of the risk. The other, in an affair with a bisexual man, said that this man had recently had an AIDS test which proved negative, so that she felt safe sleeping with him. Most had not been promiscuous and considered themselves to be in low-risk groups, and so did not take precautions to avoid any sexually transmitted diseases.

It is our impression that, as most of the current research on AIDS has shown, people who are not homosexual, bisexual, or intravenous drug users still do not consider AIDS to be a risk they are running, especially if they do not have many sexual partners. It is possible that there may be less activity at the more casual end of the affair spectrum. But people do seem to be continuing to have affairs. Certainly, affairs are now riskier than before. And the secrecy now rests on even shakier ground. If someone with whom you have had an affair turns out to be HIV-positive and you contract the virus there is nothing defensible about keeping that affair secret any longer. Yet even so, it is undeniable that enormous numbers of people find the temptation to have an affair irresistible.

This irresistibility, this fact that even despite the spectre of AIDS people are drawn in possibly increasing numbers to sexual liaisons outside of marriage, is what compels us to dissect affairs. What is it about them which so attracts? What are they like for men and women? How do some marriages accommodate them while others do not? *Why* affairs? And *what*, indeed, are they about? That is what we propose to address in this book.

1 The Making of Modern Marriage

That the man and woman were husband and
wife, and the parents of the girl in arms there
could be little doubt. No other than such a
relationship would have accounted for the
atmosphere of stale familiarity which the trio
carried along with them like a nimbus as
they moved down the road.

Thomas Hardy,
The Mayor of Casterbridge, 1886

The formula for heaven's very simple,
Just follow the rules and you will see.
And as life travels on and things do go wrong,
Just follow steps one, two and three:
Step one, you find a girl who you love,
Step two, she falls in love with you,
Step three, you kiss and hold her tightly.
Yer, that sure seems like heaven to me.
Just follow steps one, two and three.

Eddie Cochrane
'Three Steps To Heaven', 1960

It is often suggested that present-day marriages are much more
free and easy than those of our parents or grandparents.
Standards have changed, it is claimed, especially after the so-
called sexual revolution of the 1960s, and monogamy is no
longer seen as the basis for marriage. Change there has
certainly been, but it would be very misleading to see it simply
as a reduced concern with sexual exclusivity. This neither
accurately portrays contemporary marriage nor the complicated
route by which we have reached the present. Contrary to
popular belief, while we may take a much more liberal attitude
towards sexual relationships among the unmarried, monogamy

is now held to be a *more* important basis for marriage than at
any other time in the last century.

Questioned before marriage and in the early years of marriage, young people place 'faithfulness' among the most important characteristics they seek in a spouse. Whether or not
husband and wife live up to these ideals is, of course, another
matter, and one about which we will have much more to say.
However, the important point we want to establish is that the
ideal and stated intention for monogamy is now stronger than
it has ever been. Monogamy is part of the very high hopes of
marriage that most young people hold today. Marriage has
come to be seen as a relationship which, ideally at least, will
offer not just love, affection and a sexual relationship, but a
shared and private social world in which spouses, outside their
work (though sometimes there too), will spend most of their
time together. A spouse is not simply a lover and companion,
but a friend with whom everything – emotions, friends, hobbies,
chores, relations, holidays – may be shared.

This pattern of marriage, which social scientists call companionate marriage, has its origins in the middle-class domestic
life of the last century. In this chapter we will trace the evolution
of this pattern of marriage which has come to predominate, not
only in Britain, North America and Western Europe, but to
varying degrees in much of the industrialised world and
elsewhere.

Victorian Marriage

Industrialisation in the nineteenth century not only created an
army of factory workers who peopled the ever expanding
terraced housing of the manufacturing areas but also a middle
class who moved into the villas on the better side of town.
These were the owners of the smaller businesses, the managers
of larger ones, the architects, engineers, doctors and the many
others who directed, administered and organised the growing
industrial world. It is this Victorian middle class, who perhaps
first exerted its power and cohesion at the Great Exhibition of

1851, to whom we owe the origins of the contemporary companionate marriage.

The Victorian age was one of deep divisions; between rich and poor, worker and owner, men and women and, most importantly from our point of view, between the public world of work and the domestic world to which men could retreat at the end of the working day. While the work ethic was highly valued in Victorian Britain, for the successful man the roles of husband and father were as important as his position in the public world of politics and commerce. It was at home as head of the family and in the company of women that he would be refreshed and renewed for his return to the harsh and competitive world outside. Home and the family, as well as being the place for male recreation, were a symbol of his status and position. At a time of rapid social and economic change, such as the Victorian age, status and position become all important. The size and position of a man's house, the number of his servants and the social circle within which he moved were all indicators of his position. While he was out making his way in the world, it was the function of his wife to pay and receive calls, to entertain and to arrange social events of all kinds. Formality and etiquette were central to this Victorian social life in which appearances counted for so much. Complex rules governed such matters as who first called on whom, the time for calls and how they would be received. These rules expressed all the fine distinctions of class and status which were fundamental in a world of rapidly shifting fortunes.

Not surprisingly, marriage played a central part in this status-conscious age. As readers of Victorian novels will be well aware, for a man, a good marriage to someone of wealth and position was crucial for his career while for a woman it was almost her only chance to move away from her parental home. Marriage for middle-class men was delayed to the late twenties or early thirties by which time a man could have 'established' himself in his chosen profession. Without position and prospects he would not be seen as a suitable partner for a woman of social standing. Marriage, of course, was not simply a matter of the individual

choice of the two potential spouses but would be of considerable concern to the parents and relatives on both sides.
Choosing a son-in-law might, in effect, be the selection of a
future business partner while the right daughter-in-law could
mean an important injection of capital for a firm or a link with
a new trading partner. Given the importance of a good
marriage, the social world in which potential partners might
meet was carefully controlled and long before a man got to the
stage of asking a future father-in-law for his daughter's hand,
he and the family would have been carefully vetted.

Again, as readers of the Victorian novel will know, while love
was not always considered unimportant in these marriages, it
did not occupy the central place it has gained in more recent
decades. Love was certainly not enough if the two families did
not find the match acceptable, nor was its absence a bar to
marriage. For many women, all they might hope for was an
honourable man of good family whom they might come to trust,
and perhaps love, after the marriage when they came to know
him a little better. Despite the long engagements common at
this time, couples would have very little chance to spend much
time alone together before their wedding. Brief words at social
occasions and the exchange of letters was as much as many
would know of each other.

Motives for marriage were usually very different for men and
women. Emigration to the colonies, losses in imperial wars and
the high mortality of boys from the infectious diseases that so
dominated childhood, all meant that there were significantly
more adult women than men. Few acceptable occupations,
beyond the often dreary life of a governess, existed for middle-
class women, so this, combined with the relative scarcity of men,
meant that there was a very limited choice of men for women
who were brought up on the assumption that they were destined
for marriage – and few other options outside marriage. For men
with money, who could live a comfortable life looked after by
servants and having freedoms of every kind (most of which were
denied to women), married life seemed to have a lot less to offer,
beyond of course the possibility of children and heirs.

Victorian marriage was based on the double standard which accepted in men sexual conduct forbidden to women. This is well illustrated by the divorce law which was enacted in 1857 when regulation of marriage passed from the Church to the civil courts. All the grounds for divorce concerned sexual misconduct, but while a man might divorce his wife for a simple act of adultery, a woman could only take action if her husband's adultery was aggravated by circumstances such as incest, bestiality, sodomy or cruelty. Furthermore, for a mother, any sexual misconduct would usually mean the end of any contact with her children.

It was also assumed that a man, but not of course his wife, would have had sexual relationships before his marriage. These would most often be with a prostitute, a paid mistress or a servant; all women from a very different class than his own. Not surprisingly, for an age that went to great lengths not to discuss sexuality, reliable accounts of sexual behaviour are very rare. However, there is every reason to think that sex for money or by exploitation of their social position was freely available to middle-, and especially upper-middle-class men, and that many, if not most, took advantage of it. Prostitutes were numerous even in small towns and were largely young, working-class women who found the economic and social advantages of the 'gay' life more attractive than sweated labour or domestic service. Or they combined the two. They plied their trade in the streets, pubs and pleasure gardens as well as in the numerous brothels. Men who wished for a rather more permanent kind of arrangement could at little cost set up a mistress in an apartment. As well as those who earned their living primarily by prostitution, there was probably an even larger group of women, domestic servants and labourers, who by use of force, money or persuasion were, on occasion, made to provide sex for middle-class men.

Perhaps the most widely held stereotype about Victorian sexuality is the unresponsiveness of the middle-class wife who is supposed never to have enjoyed sex, submitting to her husband from time to time either from a sense of duty or to provide children, thinking, of course, only of England. Given the scarcity of source material, it is very difficult to assess the truth of the stereotype from this distance in time. But there are a few diaries and other such sources which suggest that there were certainly couples who enjoyed their sexual relationship. The basis for the claim about sexual unresponsiveness seems to be the writings of a few Victorian male doctors who were unlikely to have had much, if any, direct evidence and, from the general tone of their writing, were more interested in supporting an ideological position than in providing an accurate picture of married life in their time. The best known of such medical writers is William Acton, a genito-urinary surgeon who, in 1857, published his book entitled *The Functions and Disorders of the Reproductive Organs in Childhood, Youth, Adult Age and Advanced Life, considered in the Psychological, Social and Moral Relations*. In this he states:

> I should say that the majority of women (happily for them) are not very much troubled with sexual feelings of any kind. What men are habitually, women are only exceptionally . . . there can be no doubt that sexual feeling in the female is in the majority of cases in abeyance . . . and even if aroused (which in many instances it never can be) is very moderate compared with that of the male. Many men, and particularly young men, form their idea of women's feelings from what they notice early in life among loose, or, at least, low and vulgar women . . . Such women however give a very false idea of the condition of female sexual feeling in general . . . loose women (who, if they have no sexual feeling, counterfeit it so well that the novice does not suspect but that it is genuine) all seem to corroborate such an impression . . . it is from these erroneous notions that so many young men think that the marital duties they will have to undertake are beyond their exhausted strength, and for that reason dread and avoid marriage . . . the married woman has no wish to be treated on the footing of a mistress.

This is the great divide of Victorian sexuality: dangerous, exciting, illicit sex with working-class women and the carefully regulated and dutiful visits to the bedroom of the pure and unresponsive wife for the procreation of children. It is a world that was reflected in the pornography of the period. Very soon after Daguerre's invention of photography in 1839, the technique was used to create erotic and pornographic images of women. Expensively produced, these photographs were only available to a relatively rich buyer but many of them portrayed women dressed as servants and posed in kitchens and servants' quarters.

Whatever else may be said about the Victorian pattern of marriage, it was not a system that was particularly likely to lead to satisfactory sexual relationships. A man came to his marriage bed with a variety of sexual experience with women from a very different social background from his wife. These relationships, far from providing a model and learning experience for the marriage, were likely to become a source of guilt and anxiety which would be projected on to the relationship with his wife. Despite the great Victorian preoccupation with sex, there was a very strong taboo about discussing it, especially between middle-class men and women. So the marriage relationship was set up with every opportunity for men and women to misunderstand each others' needs and with no effective means of communication for reaching a better understanding. If all went well, it would be in spite of the attitudes and expectations that men and women brought to marriage. Not surprisingly, relationships were often far from satisfactory and men would continue to seek more open, and possibly satisfactory, relationships outside their own class.

Working-class Victorian marriages were very different. Indeed, there was often little expectation of marriage at all. The economic uncertainties of working-class life did not make for permanent marriage. There was often little expectation that a marriage would take place, as evidenced by the very high figure for births outside marriage which are only rivalled by those of the late 1980s. But even this comparison is somewhat misleading because while today cohabitation and births to single women are spread over the whole social spectrum, neither really existed at all for the Victorian middle class. Victorian

illegitimacy was an almost exclusively working-class phenomenon, at least so far as the mother's social class was concerned.
As we move towards the end of the nineteenth century we
begin to see the development of a working-class pattern of
formal marriage which increasingly adopts middle-class attitudes of marital respectability. At first this is largely seen among
the 'aristocrats of labour': the relatively well-paid workers, such
as skilled engineers and machine-makers who enjoyed relative
security of employment. As well as economic changes, the
increasing involvement of the state in family life encouraged
formal registration of marriages and drew a much stronger line
between the married and unmarried mother. The beginnings
of health and welfare provisions encouraged these trends. As
we move into the present century, matters such as pensions,
housing and subsidised medical care became available to some
women by virtue of their marriage to an employed man. These
growing social and economic encouragements, acting together
with changing values, led working-class couples to put increasing emphasis on having a 'proper' wedding and adopting what
had previously been more typically middle-class values of
marriage. Also of importance here is the spread of literacy
among the working-class population in the nineteenth century
with the development of state education. This new literate
population created a demand for newspapers and magazines
which were probably very important in promoting ideas about
love and marriage, not least through the romantic fiction which
featured prominently in their pages.

By the late nineteenth century it is possible to find descrip-
tions of working-class marriage which seem to be very similar
to those of the 1940s and 1950s such as portrayed in the classic
account of life in Bethnal Green by Michael Young and Peter
Wilmott in *Family and Kinship in East London* (1957). These are
characterised by very separate roles for men and women within
the household: man as breadwinner, uninvolved in any of the
household work, and woman as the one who was responsible
for housework and looking after children. Each had rather
separate cirlces of friends, men with their male clubs and pubs

and women with a network of female friends and relatives. The strength of the female: female relationship – mother and adult daughter living a few doors away from each other, having daily contact, sharing childcare, domestic work and gossip – echoes the earlier world of economic uncertainty when men came and went according to employment. At least among the 'respectable' working class, there was great emphasis on doing things 'properly' which in a number of respects parallels nineteenth-century middle-class marriage. Engagements were a matter for family approval on both sides and would be acknowledged by institutions like Sunday tea with the prospective in-laws. Weddings became important occasions. The couple and close relatives dressed up in formal wear, photographs were taken and subsequently remained framed on family mantelpieces, cars were hired and perhaps there was a week-long honeymoon by the sea.

Young men and women in this social world lived very separate lives. Each went around in groups of friends of their own sex. Courting was often done in groups. Boys and girls would pass one another,

> exchange a few words, and carry on. Yet at the very end of the evening the groups will meet again, break down into couples and the apparently casual exchange of words earlier turns out to be between boys and girls who have already fixed their wedding day. (Brian Jackson, *Working-Class Community*, 1968)

As a writer reporting on this period has argued, most of these working-class boys had no real experience of sex until their late teens or early twenties.

> It cannot be said that they had any real knowledge of women as women; and their notions of females were almost as idealized as the views that adolescent girls had about men ... This combination of fear and attraction produced a peculiar awkwardness that prevented intimacy beyond sex play with women of the same age and status. Early encounters were limited to symbolic gestures, and even later on

boys found themselves unable to express their feelings ...
The public sexual bravado compensated for feelings of
weakness men experienced in domestic settings. The swag-
ger and obscenity of street and shop floor were signs not of
sexual confidence but the lack of it. Such behaviour was a
bond among men and a barrier between them and women.
At home, while courting, and even in bed, neither men nor
women felt comfortable with their own sexuality. The love-
making was as inhibited as their conversation. (John Gillis,
For Better, For Worse, 1985)

But we are running ahead of our story; we need to return to
Victorian middle-class marriage. This pattern of marriage was
not without its critics, especially towards the end of the
nineteenth century. Many drew attention to the double standard
for men and women and this was often linked to issues like
prostitution and venereal disease. Many feminists of the time,
together with religious moralists, argued that men, like women,
should become chaste before and outside marriage. Great
emphasis was put on the danger of venereal disease, how men
could infect their wives and so pollute and destroy their
domestic haven. Both gonorrhoea and syphilis were indeed
common and doubtless many middle-class women and their
children did become infected. But as well as those who argued
for the 'levelling up' of the moral standards of men to those of
women, there were some, albeit a small minority, who promoted
'levelling down'; that is to say they pushed for sexual and social
freedom for all. Some presented marriage as a form of prostitution in which women exchanged their freedom for lifelong
economic support. Others agitated about the legal status of
women and their property within marriage for, on marriage, as
men and women became one, so did the property, which
thereafter became that of the husband. As women's employment in areas like education became more common, pressures
for change grew and resulted in a series of Married Women's
Property Acts which gave women at least a minimum of
economic independence in marriage.

Some reformers went a great deal further, not only in their

arguments, but in the practical steps that they were prepared to take to put them into practice. Communities of one kind or another were common in this period, especially in the USA, but also in Britain and parts of Europe. These usually had religious or political aims but in many cases explicitly provided alternatives to conventional marriage. One example is the Oneida Community which was set up by an itinerant preacher, John Humphrey Noyes, in Upper New York State in 1847. In its heyday, nearly two hundred men, women and children lived in their custom-built communal home, The Mansion House. Economically, the community was very successful, producing metal animal traps, and all property was held in common. Indeed, the name Oneida persists to this day as the title of a company manufacturing cutlery which is the direct descendant of the community.

Marriage was not permitted at Oneida. According to a pamphlet called *Slavery and Marriage* written by Noyes, the founder of the self-styled Perfectionists, 'Marriage is not an institution of the Kingdom of Heaven, and must give place to communism . . . The abolishment of exclusiveness involved in the love-relation is required between all believers in Christ'. All members were free to have sexual relationships with anyone in the community that they chose, but relationships were regulated. A man interested in a woman had to make the approach through a third party and a member always had the right of refusal. If a couple spent too much time with each other this was held to be socially divisive. If they persisted, they would be subjected to public group criticism. In extreme cases, if this did not work they were sent to a different branch of the community so that they had no chance to meet. Children were reared and educated communally. Like many communities of this kind, Oneida centred around a charismatic leader, in this case Noyes. The story goes that in his early days as a travelling preacher he married, but subsequently met another woman to whom he was attracted. At that point he began to promote an interpretation of the biblical injunction 'love thy neighbour' probably not intended by the gospel writer. The group grew and eventually settled to found the community at Oneida. As with all institutions with charismatic leaders, there was a problem of succession. Noyes groomed one of his sons to take over, but he was clearly not a leader and the community would not accept him after Noyes's death. After an uneasy period in which the community began to fragment, it voted to dissolve itself in 1881 and became the joint-stock company which was the forerunner of the present Oneida Silverware Company.

Not surprisingly, communities like Oneida provoked a good deal of criticism, if not persecution, from more conventional elements in the surrounding society. But social reformers were not slow to discuss the implications of such experiments for marriage, child-rearing and the position of women. These certainly fed into a stream of criticism which was having clear effects by the turn of the century.

The changes may be illustrated by looking at *Modern Marriage and How to Bear It* by Maud Churton Braby. This was a widely read marriage manual which was published in London just after the turn of the century and ran to several editions. The author suggests that people should marry 'for neither passion or convenience' but, setting aside romance, they should look for 'quiet, sober, beautiful and restful affection' and respect. Throughout the book the view is of companionate marriage, and the author constantly emphasises the need for mutual respect and friendship between spouses. She brings this same attitude to divorce, regarding it as a sad necessity which should be available to men and women on equal terms.

There are a number of respects in which this book, and others like it from the same period, present a view of marriage very different from that of the early Victorian period. For instance, it expresses the view that to be adequate partners for their men, women must be educated and know something of the world, and they also should be educated as sexual partners:

> No woman should wed until she understands something of life, has met a good number of men, has acquired a certain knowledge of physiology and eugenics and a clear under-

standing of what marriage really means. If girls were more reasonably trained with regard to matters of sex, there would be far fewer miserable wives in the world, and fewer husbands would be driven to seek happiness outside their home circle ... let us teach our girls to regard sex as a *natural* and *ordinary* fact, and the infinite evils which spring from regarding it as extraordinary and repulsive will thus be avoided. (emphasis in original)

By this date there were a number of books available which gave quite detailed physiological and anatomical information including those cutaway sections of the human body which remained the stock in trade of such instructional books right up to the 1950s. However, these books did not describe sexual intercourse. That had to wait until the end of the First World War with the publication of books like Marie Stopes's *Married Love* in 1918.

Beyond sex education, Mrs Braby advocates other preparations for marriage for women. In a chapter on the advantages of the 'preliminary canter' she argues for:

feminine wild oats, otherwise an ante-hymeneal 'fling' ... a woman – new style – who has knocked about one half of the world and sown a mild crop of the delectable cereal will prove a far better wife, a more cheery friend and faithful comrade.

She is quick to point out that feminine 'wild oats' are not the same as the 'licence generally accorded to men'. But she goes on to complain about the unfairness of the double standard applied to women who have 'sown real wild oats'. Because of the 'burning injustice that a woman should suffer ... for what would be absolutely disregarded in a man', she advises women 'not to confess their indiscretions'. And she goes as far as saying that:

a good woman who has surrendered herself to an ardent lover and has been deserted by him must necessarily have gone through such intense suffering that her character is probably deepened thereby and her capacity for love and faithfulness increased.

Mrs Braby does not expect men to keep their vows. 'When men are faithful, it is principally from lack of opportunity, or disinclination to do otherwise ... man is essentially a polygamous animal.' But 'fortunately a man is seldom so lacking in worldly wisdom as to let his wife discover his misconduct.' She argues that men should be more forgiving of women who do the same, although she believes that men are more jealous than women because they have 'had their own way since the menage in Eden and they resent having their belongings taken from them'.

In a long and interesting section of the book, Mrs Braby discusses various alternatives to marriage, including trial marriages, free love, polygamy and 'duogamy'. The latter is an idea of her own whereby each spouse has a second partner. Like several of the arguments she makes for arrangements other than conventional marriage, she uses the device of an imagined discussion between women, presumably to avoid being accused of directly advocating alternatives. This part of the conversation about duogamy captures the spirit of the argument.

> 'I have often felt I could make two men happy', said Isolda, 'some of my best points are wasted on Launcelot ... he never tires of the country and his beloved golf, but I do and when one of my fits of London longing comes over me I'd just run to town and have a ripping time with my London husband.'
> 'Without feeling you were doing anything wrong', supplemented Amoret, whose apparent experience of the qualms of conscience struck me as being rather suspicious.

In many respects Mrs Braby's view of 'modern marriage' is a good deal more liberal than any of the mainstream manuals written since the Edwardian period. Of course, no marriage manual presents a picture of what people do, rather it is the author's view of what people should do. However, when a book like *Modern Marriage and How to Bear It* runs to several editions and so is presumably widely read, we may at least assume that many readers read it because they liked what it said.

Later interviews with women married in the early years of the century at least suggest that Mrs Braby was not out of line with liberal middle-class opinion. Middle-class marriage was now very largely a matter of the individual's choice and love was a central, if not *the* central issue. The control exercised by families had weakened and their concern was likely to be as much for the suitability of the intended spouse in personal terms as it was for economic and social status. A general loosening of the rigidity of Victorian social life allowed young unmarried men and women to meet together much more freely. Leisure and recreational activities for young people developed rapidly in this period. Trains and charabancs provided excursions to the country and the growing seaside resorts. There was a cycling craze at the turn of the century which, interestingly enough, provoked criticism, or even alarm, from conservative elements in the older generation, including gynaecologists. Among their claims was that bicycling would excite sexual feelings in young women. Perhaps these irrational fears may be best understood as resistance to the new social freedoms that activities of this kind brought for young people. Couples were able to spend much more time together before marriage and a few of them, at least, spent some of this time in bed together.

The First World War served to accelerate the trends that were already underway. As did the Second World War in its turn, this war provided a much wider range of employment for women and made paid employment socially acceptable for women in all social classes. Women had more economic independence and the disruptions of the war served to widen social horizons. These changes inevitably influenced attitudes to marriage and relationships and, together with the separations caused by the war, led to a peak in divorce rates at the end of it.

For many who lived through the war, it later seemed a crucial turning point.

The Great War of European Disintegration had naturally, for the time being, a catastrophic effect upon English moral complacency. Perpetually faced by the cruder realities of life and death, the youth of the War generation began, to the horror of their elders, to call the facts of sex by their names. Released from sheltered dependence by war-work, and from the trivial cowardice of shame by the constant threat of disaster, young women, as we learn from the conversations of the heroines in the fiction of the period, did not shrink from admitting both to themselves and to their lovers the mutual character of sex-desire. As the conflict gradually extended from military to civilian ranks, the enormously curtailed expectation of life, combined with the rapid subterranean spread of birth-control information, produced in the young of both sexes a tendency to seize immediately such physical and emotional satisfactions as offered themselves, without waiting for the conventional blessings of Church, State, or family. (Vera Brittain, *Halcyon or The Future of Monogamy*, 1929)

The 1920s and 1930s

With the return to peace, there was a reassertion of traditional values for marriage and the family, emphasising the belief that a woman's place is in the home. This is evidenced by the bans on the employment of married women imposed in many professions. Opposition to birth control was widespread. In 1923, for example, two socialists were prosecuted for selling Margaret Sanger's book, *Family Limitation: Handbook for Working Mothers*.

But the post-war home to which women might have returned was very different from that of even a few decades earlier. Economic changes in the labour market led to a large decline in the availability of servants. Most professional couples had to make do with a 'home help' who would come in each day. With the advent of machines like the vacuum cleaner, which by now were widespread, much of the domestic work, including child care, was being undertaken by the wives themselves. Relationships with the daily help were likely to be very different from those which had existed with servants who, a generation earlier, had lived beyond the green baize door. The home help was often a working-class married woman with children, working while her children were at school. She and the housewife might work side by side at times. It certainly would not have been unusual for them to sit each side of the kitchen table and drink a mid-morning cup of tea. Catering to middle-class women of this period was a whole new generation of women's magazines like *Home and Garden* and *Ideal Home* which carried articles about cooking, shopping, sewing and the care of children.

There were further developments in leisure activities – the cinema, motoring, the dance hall and the tea dance – which both provided shared pursuits for husband and wife as well as meeting places for the unmarried.

Both inside and outside the home the lives of husband and wife became less separate. Evenings might often be spent on either side of the same fire before retiring to their twin beds in the same bedroom.

Books of the period for parents present a safe domestic world as in *Baby From Bud to Blossom* which was written by a midwife:

> In the quiet of the evening hour, when curtains are cosily drawn, the tranquil lure of hearth and home filling them with a sense of benediction, parents direct their thoughts to the future for the beloved little one ... They will desire that by careful pioneering and management their son shall be brought up in the English tradition of 'playing the game', some already visualise his career from a good preparatory school through a famous Public School to a University, while others have ambitions less expensive to attain.
>
> Or if it be a daughter they will wish her to be equipped for the Battle of Life in one of the splendid modern colleges, and armed with a training for a profession. They will desire to be prepared should she marry for the provision of her trousseau and her dowry. (Hewer, 1922)

Despite the opposition to publication of information about birth control, contraception was widely, if not almost universally, used by middle-class couples. Marriage manuals, as well as women's magazines, conveyed the message that a good sexual relationship was a basic element of a good marriage. Ignorance and lack of knowledge were seen as the great bar to a successful sexual relationship. Books like those of Marie Stopes were much more explicit than those of earlier decades: they described techniques of making love, if in somewhat mechanical terms. While by the ideals of the late twentieth century their approach would be criticised for portraying women as passive, they at least recognised women's needs for sexual satisfaction. Typical of this period is Helena Wright's *The Sex Factor in Marriage*, which was published in 1930:

> A woman's body can be regarded as a musical instrument awaiting the hand of an artist. Clumsiness and ignorance will produce nothing but discord, knowledge and skill evoke responses of limitless beauty.

Despite changing attitudes to male and female sexuality and relationships in the 1920s and 1930s, the double standard persisted. Men were considered more likely to indulge in pre- and extramarital sexual relationships. But these are likely to have had rather different characteristics from those of their Victorian fathers. The great armies of Victorian prostitutes were no longer on the streets. While men could certainly continue to find sex for sale, and many did, a great deal of the sex experienced before marriage was now between engaged couples. For an increasing number of men – and women – their sexual relationships began within their own social group. The great Victorian divide between marriage within your social class and extramarital sex outside it had now gone. Men incorporated eroticism within marriage rather than regarding it as something to pursue elsewhere.

An interesting insight into male sexuality of the period is given by the many letters which men wrote to Marie Stopes which have recently been analysed by Lesley Hall. As the title of her book *Hidden Anxieties* implies, male sexuality was often surrounded by anxieties. These were often attributed by the men themselves to early masturbation (which in advice books of this period was still sometimes portrayed as damaging), or early sexual experiences with prostitutes. Premature ejaculation was, as Marie Stopes herself remarked, 'distressingly prevalent' among middle-class men, 'quite apart from the ordinary haste and carelessness of which so many were guilty'. Liberals of the day believed that men required education in love-making. Havelock Ellis, for instance, who was a prominent writer on sex, believed that middle-class men

> have acquired the notion that sexual indulgence and all that appertains to it is something low and degrading, at worst a mere natural necessity and at best a duty to be accepted in a direct, honourable and straightforward manner. No-one seems to have told them that love is an art. ('Studies in the Psychology of Sex', Vol VI. *Sex in Relation to Society*, 1910)

But in the inter-war period this is what they were increasingly told, not only by writers like Marie Stopes, but by a growing number of their wives. Women were demanding more from their marital partners – both in and out of bed – in a period when marriage began to be seen as a partnership. As we can see in the fiction of the period, the same values were found in extramarital relationships. Increased personal freedom and mobility not only allowed the young and unmarried to meet more easily, but this was equally true for the married. With a stronger emphasis on love in marriage, that same apparently uncontrollable emotion could occur outside it. It is in the inter-war period that we find the origin of the modern companionate affair, the kind of affair celebrated in the cinema in films like *Brief Encounter*. But in this film the couple do not consummate their relationship. Instead the wife returns, perhaps wiser, but certainly sadder, determined to make a go of her marriage. *Brief Encounter* illustrates the fundamental threat of the companionate affair: an affair, which unlike its Victorian predecessor, can all too easily become a companionate marriage.

The Post-war Era

The Second World War, like the First, had a profound and lasting effect on marriage and family life. One of the clearest indications of this is the large peak in divorces that occurred as the war ended. Significantly, during this peak, the earlier (and later) pattern that the majority of divorces are instigated by women, was reversed. At the end of the war it was men who most often took the legal initiative. A common story was of a soldier returning home after several years abroad to find that his wife had formed a new attachment. In many cases these marriages had been hastily entered into by partners who barely knew each other, who had met during a brief spell of leave. The marital problems of returning servicemen were so frequent that the government was forced to make special legal aid provisions for them.

But the upheavals of the war had more profound effects than simply causing ill-considered marriages and the separation of partners. War brings rapid social change because it disrupts old patterns of employment and social relationships. During the Second World War new job opportunities arose, not least for women. People moved into the forces, factories and offices and were thrown together into new and unexpected social relationships. In both the services and civilian life old class barriers were broken down to some extent as people fought, worked and spent their leisure time side by side. Men and women found themselves in quite new social circles. Young people moved out of the control of parents. All of this led not only to the formation of relationships which cut across old patterns and expectations but to a much wider questioning of social values. Many women gained economic independence and could support themselves by their own work. The new and changing wartime social life gave them social independence too. So while the war brought a rise in births outside marriage, divorce and venereal disease, it also led to a change in social values so that, increasingly, both men and women were demanding more from each other and marriage.

In the immediate aftermath of war, there was a return to settled family life as part of the general post-war reconstruction, as epitomised in such family events as the 1951 Festival of Britain. The post-war divorce peak passed and demographers confidently predicted a return to the low pre-war rates. But this phase was short-lived. Within a decade divorce rates began to rise again and soon had far outstripped the peak at the end of the war. From a low of 23,000 in 1958, divorces rose to 144,000 in 1978 when they reached a new high plateau. The reasons for this enormous rise are complex but an important element was a much higher expectation of what marriage had to offer women which, in part, was encouraged by the freer social life that the Second World War had produced.

Attitudes to sex, especially sex before marriage, were changing too. While accurate figures do not exist, a reasonable estimate for Britain in the 1950s is that about a quarter of all men and two-thirds of women were virgins at their weddings. A quarter of men and women began to sleep with their partner before marriage but otherwise had no sexual relationships. So, looking at it the other way round, only half of all men and one-twelfth of women entered marriage having had a sexual relationship with someone other than their spouse. The attitude of the majority at this time was generally against sex before marriage. By the 1970s we see a completely different picture. Most men and women not only began a sexual relationship with their spouse before their wedding day, but most also had other sexual relationships. In fact, the earlier term, 'premarital sex', had now lost its meaning. For the majority sexual intercourse was not something that signalled a step on the road to a wedding as it had earlier, but now it was accepted as part of any 'serious' relationship whether or not marriage was part of the possible future.

This change has several causes. Some of the arguments against sexual relationships outside marriage now ceased to carry the force they once had. Contraception, especially after the pill became available in the 1960s, was now effective and relatively easily obtainable. If it failed, the Abortion Act of 1967 provided what is essentially abortion on request. Fears of venereal disease, which formed a prominent part in campaigns against sex before marriage in the pre-war era, lost their force after the coming of antibiotics (and AIDS was, of course, in an unimagined future). Sanctions against sexual relationships among people were slowly lifted, especially for the middle classes. Colleges and other places where young people might spend time together ended their curfews and installed vending machines for condoms. Friends of the opposite sex became acceptable breakfast guests. Joint holidays or taking your friend home to stay with your parents – and sharing a bedroom – became unremarkable. But perhaps the most significant change was in the way sexuality was regarded. It became not simply an acceptable part of a loving relationship, but also an essential and 'natural' part of such a relationship, whether or not either partner was thinking of marriage. To some extent it could be said that the ideal of the companionate marriage – to which we will return in a moment – was extended to all love relationships.

It also extended across old social-class divides. There are indications that in recent decades relationships within and outside marriage have become much more similar across social-class groups. Much of the formality and the separated roles of working-class marriage which could still be found in the 1950s were declining by the 1970s, although Paul Willis's study of working-class youth culture in the mid-1970s, *Learning to Labour* (1977), still contains echoes of a much earlier period. The 'lads' he describes were using sexually explicit slang and crude labels like 'slag' and 'easy lay' for some of their female companions to put down their sexuality and to disguise their own insecurity and inexperience.

The 1960s and Beyond

The 1960s are often regarded as a period of revolution in sexual conduct. But in terms of sexual behaviour among young people, the as yet unmarried, there is little sign of any sudden change in behaviour. Throughout the century there has been a steady increase in the proportion of couples who started their sexual relationship before their wedding day and in those who decided to sleep together whether or not they had any thoughts of marriage. Cohabitation as a prelude to marriage certainly became much commoner after the 1960s but this, like the other changes, was more in the nature of a steady shift than any overnight revolution.

The one change in the 1960s that might be termed revolutionary was in the way people talked about sex. It became a subject that could be freely discussed among friends. And there was a distinct shift in what was seen as acceptable in the cinema, or on radio and in magazines. The unsuccessful attempt to prosecute the publishers of D. H. Lawrence's novel, *Lady Chatterley's Lover* in 1960 may be seen as an event that symbolised the turning point.

Nowhere was this revolution more striking than in the marriage and sex manuals. From the 1920s, or earlier, until the 1960s their style and content hardly changed at all. Their approach to sex was physiological, their language latinate and their supposed audiences married couples. They provided diagrams, usually cutaway sections of the human body and a mechanistic discussion of positions. They assumed that the husband would always initiate sexual activity but advised him to proceed slowly, to extend 'foreplay' to allow time for their more slowly aroused wives to reach their 'climax'. Intercourse was presented as an activity, like most others, that should be indulged in with moderation. The longevity of these volumes is a testament to unchanging attitudes. One of the best sellers, Dr Van de Velde's *Ideal Marriage: Its Physiology and Technique*, which was first published in Britain in 1920, was still being recommended by marriage-guidance counsellors in the early 1960s.

Those oft-quoted visitors from another planet might be forgiven if they decided that the post-1960s sex manuals described a different activity altogether. Gone were the diagrams, instead there were soft focus photographs of entwined bodies. No longer was there reference to husbands and wives: all became 'partners', who on occasion were not even of different sexes. But, above all, these books no longer presented sex in mechanical or physiological terms but as pleasure for hearts and minds. And there was no tone of restraint at all. Most followed Alex Comfort's line in *The Joy of Sex* (1972) in suggesting that, provided that none of those involved were coerced, anything goes in the pursuit of pleasure. Some books now ignored the body completely and dealt only with sexual fantasy: just twenty years earlier a third of the women interviewed by Kinsey denied that they ever had sexual fantasies.

A parallel change can be seen in sex education in schools, although this came a little later. In the 1960s, British surveys found that many children still received no sex education. For those who did it was biological. By the late 1970s it was quite different. Not only was teaching about sex more or less universal, but the emphasis had shifted to a concern with relationships and emotions. The approach to sexual intercourse and contraception had become much more explicit.

The revolution in sex manuals and sex education can also be followed in women's magazines. In 1955, questions about sex were not infrequent on the problem pages of magazines like *Woman's Own*. But the word 'sex' was avoided and a whole list of euphemisms was used instead, such as 'the intimate side of marriage', 'married in name only', 'physical love' and 'an important side of marriage'. A decade later saw free use of terms such as intercourse, petting and orgasm. There was also quite a different attitude to the sexual relationship of husband and wife. In 1955, a wife had written to say that, after fourteen years of marriage, 'The intimate side of marriage does not appeal to me at all and I rarely allow him to make love to me.' Mary Grant, the agony aunt, was not sympathetic. 'Your husband has a legitimate grievance. However good you are in other ways you are failing in part of your duty towards him.'

In 1980, a woman wrote saying that after twelve years of marriage she had been unable to relax enough to have sexual intercourse and was considering artificial insemination. The

Mary Grant of this era took a very different line from that of her predecessor. 'It would be a tragedy if you chased after these methods of conception . . . you and your husband need sexual intercourse as an expression of your whole selves and of your love for each other.'

This last sentence encapsulates much of the current ideal of the companionate marriage: that the love relationship, including sexual love, should be central to the lives of husband and wife and that the world of each should revolve round the other. Such marriages are a very long way from those of some Victorians, with husbands making occasional trips to their wives' bedrooms. They have also come far from those in the modern homes of the inter-war era with winged chairs each side of the fire, the wireless, and the *News Chronicle* and *Home and Garden* on the table.

But present-day marriage is not an institution without its difficulties. Indeed, a central argument of this book is that marriage has come to embody a series of inherent contradictions which account for its instability. And unstable it is, if we regard the divorce rate as an indicator. In Britain, over a third of current marriages are likely to end in divorce rather than at the death of a spouse, although these figures are relatively modest compared with other parts of the Western world, such as the USA, where only a minority of marriages survive until death.

Historically there is a broad association between the rise of the companionate marriage and the increase in divorce. At its simplest, we could say that as expectations of marriage rise, some are bound to fall short and, assuming that the law allows for a way out, some couples will try again with new partners. Certainly remarriage or marriage-like cohabitation have risen hand in hand with divorce so, whatever divorce represents, it cannot be explained as a flight from marriage or coupledom. Rather it marks a disenchantment with a particular partner and a move to try again elsewhere. But we want to take this idea further and argue that it is not simply rising expectations, but that our very ideal of marriage contains the seeds of its own destruction. There are conflicts on several fronts and, unless a couple are able to negotiate their own way through these, their marriage will be at risk.

One conflict a couple has to resolve is between, on one hand, the ideal of the companionate marriage as a relationship within which all is shared and, on the other, an autonomous life as an individual. Of course, this conflict is an old one and is well known to those who counsel others about their marriages, but it has become much more acute with the rise of the post-war ideal of the loving intimate marriage. If you love someone, how can you want to spend time with anyone else? Should not couples always go out together or, indeed, should they go out at all? It is time together that is at a premium. Of course, as a marriage proceeds, the relationship is expected to change but it is interesting to note the extent to which spouses, and perhaps particularly women, often resent the changes that dilute the intensity of the early 'honeymoon' years of a relationship. Here we have to be a little careful about terminology. About half of all British couples now cohabit before their wedding, so those honeymoon years are likely to precede rather than follow a wedding. Most couples are clear enough about when their relationship began. Typically, it is when they became committed to one another which is often when the decision to live together was taken.

One of the commonest events to disturb the intensity of this early phase of a relationship is the arrival of children. Research has consistently shown that husbands, and especially wives, report a sharp decline in their satisfaction with their marriage with the arrival of children. Although children remain very much part of the ideology of marriage, they do make it very hard for a couple to have time for each other. Children also conflict with the companionate ideal in another way. The ideal of the shared life with common activities is relatively easy to sustain for a couple without children. Both are probably working but leisure time can be spent together and all aspects of domestic life, including the washing-up, can be shared. As the sociologists would put it, role segregation is minimal, as both take a more or less equal part in work inside and outside the home.

These values are well illustrated by a survey of British marriages carried out by Geoffrey Gorer in 1971 (*Sex and Marriage in England Today*) which showed that 'comradeship, doing things together', were held to be the most important things the respondents thought made for a happy marriage, followed by 'give and take, consideration, discussing things and understanding', while 'neglect, bad communication, spouse going out' were the things most commonly held likely to wreck a marriage. Comradeship and doing things together were seen to be much less important in a previous survey in the early 1950s.

All that changes with children. Wives, not husbands, give up jobs or spend less time in the ones they have, to remain at home; domestic work becomes *her* province. The priority given to a husband's career overrides any idea of equality in marriage and previous sharing of domestic roles goes by the board. And the ideal of the companionate love relationship sits very uneasily with the husband out at work and the wife focused on child care and housework. Indeed, one could suggest that wives are double losers in the autonomy stakes. Not only are they responsible for the housekeeping and the child care but their role as emotional housekeepers means that they are more submerged in the marriage relationship. So, while the husband retains and often increases his status in the world of work, and in his space outside home and marriage, his wife, especially if she leaves work or changes to part-time work while rearing children, is likely to lose some, if not all, of the autonomy and social contacts that work may bring, as well as the intimacy of the love relationship that children shatter.

Another conflict concerns sex inside and outside marriage. In view of the trends we have discussed in sexual behaviour before marriage, it might be thought that attitudes towards extramarital sex have become more tolerant. Quite the reverse is true. Throughout the post-war period (and indeed for some time before that) ideals of marriage have become more exclusive and attitudes towards fidelity have become much stronger. The shift is apparent, for example, in the problem pages of women's magazines. In the mid-fifties when husbands strayed, wives were often advised to ignore it. A woman in her fifties wrote to ask an agony aunt what to do as she had discovered her husband had been unfaithful for some time. Should she confront him? She was advised not to because 'men of this age feel a compulsion to have a fling before age finally engulfs them' and the affair would die a natural death. In this same era a woman whose husband had said he was in love with his secretary, was told by Mary Grant, 'I think your husband is under the spell of an infatuation which will pass in time and all you can do is wait patiently until it does.' Another woman said that, although she had forgiven her husband after an affair, 'I just can't forget the hurt of those few weeks.' She was told to 'pull [her] socks up; just as your husband pulled himself together for the sake of your marriage, it's your turn to do the same'. By the 1970s, the tone of advice in these kinds of situations had changed. It was not assumed any more that erring husbands should be forgiven. Rather, the response was that wives should try to understand why their husbands should have started other relationships and try to rebuild their marriage – if possible – through a new understanding. Intimacy and communication were now emphasised. Certainly there is no question of just ignoring it and hoping it will go away.

This shift in attitude is confirmed by opinion surveys which have asked people about their attitudes towards extramarital relationships. All but a very small minority of married people condemn any sexual relationship outside marriage and the important point is that these attitudes have tended to get stronger, rather than weaker, through recent decades. Such a trend surprises some people who point to a general liberalisation about sexual matters and the apparent growth of 'open marriage'. But our point is that attitudes towards sex inside and outside marriage are very different and have moved in opposite directions. Certainly there has been discussion of open marriage and accounts of such marriage often figure in the women's and 'lifestyle' magazines, but such discussions are out of proportion to what by any account is an extremely rare phenomenon. Researchers who have hunted out open-marriage couples for studies have usually had to be content with a handful of respondents.

Pushing in the other direction, there have been increasingly loud voices (often associated with the 'newer' Christian Churches), calling for a return to 'traditional' Victorian values. Given what we have said earlier about Victorian marriage, this is perhaps not exactly what these advocates of Christian values have in mind but, whatever the accuracy of the historical reference, these arguments for monogamy within marriage seem to be accepted by the great majority of the population, at least in terms of what they say should happen.

We suggest that it is the changed view of marriage that leads to the greater emphasis on fidelity. As love and sharing become the central themes of marriage, it becomes more exclusive. If a marriage can provide everything, what can the attraction be of other relationships? Indeed, any other relationship becomes a threat. The commitment to marriage is expressed in love, the shared social life and leisure time and the promise of sexual exclusiveness. Part of this new focus on the sexual exclusivity of marriage arises from the need to demonstrate its special quality in a world where sexual relationships among the unmarried are commonplace. With the development of companionate marriage has come the rise in the importance of the wedding; weddings which are the public notice of the uniquely committed relationship. Rising rates of cohabitation before marriage have done nothing to diminish the importance of weddings; indeed, quite the reverse is true. Not only do most couples marry but most have a 'proper' wedding. Even in our secular society, about a half of all weddings take place in a church. The figures are far in excess of those who regularly attend church services. Indeed, there must be a significant number of people for whom their wedding is the only church service they have ever attended. Even when a marriage is not marked by a church wedding, it is usually a very important social occasion for friends and family. Spending on wedding receptions and associated celebrations is growing and has produced a whole industry to provide the necessary goods and services. Weddings must be seen to be done. This was neatly illustrated by a recent account in a local paper of a couple whose wedding video was ruined by a faulty camera. They took the practical solution and invited everyone back a week later to film it all over again!! Very rare today are brides who are virgins at their wedding, but the white wedding dress is certainly not a thing of the past. Indeed, the new emphasis on the symbolic and public aspects of weddings may be seen as an assertion that, whatever relationships either bride or groom may have had before, this one is quite different and at least is entered into with a symbolic virginity. At a wedding where past lovers of both spouses may be part of the crowd that waves the couple off for their honeymoon, the symbolism of the white dress, the veil and the cutting of the cake take on a new importance.

Despite the strongly held attitude supporting monogamy and the commitment of the newlyweds, our evidence, such as it is, suggests that perhaps a majority of spouses will have sexual relationships outside their marriages. So, there is another contradiction here: as attitudes against affairs have hardened, they seem to have become more common. But the contradictions do not end there, because there seems to be one very important exception to the ideal of openness of present-day marriage: most people do not tell their spouses about their affairs. We may be expected to share everything in our marriages but, as the authors of *American Couples* (1983) Philip Blumstein and Pepper Schwartz put it, 'marriage makes couples more deceptive'.

There are many reasons why people may be having more affairs. We will be discussing this further in chapter 5 but here we should note a couple of points. Opportunities have certainly increased. With greater affluence, there is more travel and there are more holidays. A greater proportion of married women are at work and the workplace provides possibilities to meet people. Earlier we noted that close loving relationships are now often sexual and this may apply as much to those of the married as the unmarried. And that provides us with the final conflict in contemporary marriage. While the Victorian husband would often find his extramarital partners outside his own social class, today's affair partners are likely to be husbands and wives within the couples' own social class. Like spouses themselves, affair partners will usually share the same social background. In some cases, the affair will come to have the same companionate features as a marriage. Affairs of this kind can be more threatening to a marriage, not least because they can become one.

2 Men's Love/Women's Love: Emotional Development and the Gender Divide

Woman wants monogamy;
Man delights in novelty.
Love is woman's moon and sun;
Man has other forms of fun.
Woman lives but in her lord;
Count to ten, and man is bored.
With this the gist and sum of it,
What earthly good can come of it?

Dorothy Parker
Not So Deep as a Well, 1937

Most people recognise that men and women differ in how they experience courtship, marriage, friendship and love, as well as in affairs. They behave in different ways, experience different feelings and have different needs and expectations. In this chapter we will look at how these differences begin – when we are small babies and later growing children. Here we are going to look at the development of feelings and emotions in men and women – not at sexuality, which we will examine in chapter 3. Emotions and sexual behaviour *are* separate – although they are usually experienced as inextricably entangled.

The setting for our discussion is, of course, the world of the West – of an industrialised, advanced society. Men, women and affairs would look quite different in the context, say, of tribal Africa, or communist China. But we are looking specifically at British and American couples who are affected by the expectations of the society they live in. But even within British and American society there will, of course, be an enormous range of behaviour.

For example, in our society women are in general the chief carers of children. But if a man takes on this role, particularly from the beginning, the children under his care are likely to grow up into rather different emotional beings from children cared for by women. As we will show, boys brought up by a nurturing, caregiving man should be more able to be intimately emotionally connected to others than boys brought up by women. Another example of variation is in what a family considers to be sexual. Some families are prudish about sex, others relaxed about it, and still others depart completely from what society defines as normal and permissible sexual behaviour.

Bob, a thirty-one-old married lorry-driver, with two young sons, was revealed to be a molester of little girls. When he went into therapy, it came out that, when he was growing up, all the children in his family had been sexually molested by their parents, as well as by their grandparents. When he reached puberty Bob's parents separated and he soon became his mother's main sexual partner. Meanwhile his two older sisters – who had remained in their father's custody – continued to be sexually abused by the father. Bob's notion of whom he could feel sexual towards was formed quite differently from most other people's. This is a rather extreme example but it serves to illustrate the point that each family varies in its approach to sex and, in addition, that the family we grow up in plays a critical role in shaping our ideas about sexuality and how relationships are formed.

Different cultures or subcultures also have varying definitions about what is sexually stimulating, or what signals 'sex'. Olivia, a twenty-year-old English woman who had gone on a camping expedition with a mixed group from Britain and a Muslim country, was raped by one of the Muslim boys. Exhausted after a day's climbing, she stretched herself out on a camp-bed while alone in a room with him. He responded to a woman reclining on a bed in a room alone with a man as a sexual invitation. But Olivia had interpreted the group camaraderie as friendship in which the act of reclining on a bed carried no sexual overtones.

Developing as Girls or Boys

In order to form a close relationship we need to have a sense of ourselves as individuals; we need a sense of self. Newborns do not have this. They respond to what is done to them. They may smile, for example, in response to a soft, familiar voice. But they do not have a sense of themselves as distinct entities. This only comes through exchanges with those around them, usually parents and perhaps brothers and sisters. For the great majority of infants in our society the most important person who interacts with the infant is the mother. A sense of self is developed in social interaction with people throughout life. Whoever looks after us when we are babies – the primary caregiver – is crucial for our developing sense of ourselves. In our society it is usually a mother, and more to the point, it is usually a female. The fact that the caregiver is female has an effect on both the child's sense of self and on the way he or she relates to others. This stems from the fact that mothers – or the female caregivers – treat boy babies differently from the way they treat girls. After a while, babies also begin to respond differently to female, rather than male, caregivers. The most significant contributor to this difference, as other writers have also argued, is that a mother identifies with a girl baby and, of course, feels separate from a boy. This is inevitable since gender is perhaps the most important single definer of how we experience and view the world. From the very beginning, our gender plays a major role in how we relate to our mothers – whether we (as daughter) identify ourselves with her or (as son) feel different. Gender is also at the root of male/female differences in relationships in another way. It is, as we have said, a basic feature of all our experience. Because of gender a person responds to the world (including a parent or caregiver) in particular ways. In a sense we can say that there are two worlds, that seen from the perspective of a girl and that from the perspective of a boy. We become socialised *as* girls or boys. We then behave as boys *or* girls, and the world (including our parents and caregivers) responds to us accordingly. Thus we live as one or the other gender in a world which itself is split by this same divide.

Research observations made of newborn babies and their parents' handling of them reinforce the point that a mother will and can normally identify with a girl baby in a way she will not and cannot with a boy. Studies have shown that both parents seem to handle newborn boy babies more roughly than they do newborn girls. They also talk more to girls than to boys. But what is interesting about these findings is not only the fact that they indicate the strength of society's expectations of boys and girls, but that they also illustrate the handing down from women to women and men to men of the way they think about themselves. That is, we think about ourselves in terms of our gender – we are, before we are anything else, men or women – and gender, in turn, is defined for us by our society. Our gender informs our experience of the world, and the world's experience of us. That is in part what is being seen in these parents' treatment of their newborn children.

The effect of this gender-related caregiving is profound in creating male/female differences in both relationships and people's experience of themselves. As long as women retain primary responsibility for caregiving with children, girls, having the same gender as their caregivers, will from the beginning experience themselves in relationships as merged, while boys will experience themselves in relationships as separate, just as they were from their caregivers. For us, in considering male/female differences in affairs and marriages, the important point here is that these then become propensities which differentiate the way the sexes behave in adult relationships. As we shall describe later when we examine the experience of affairs for men and women, this tendency to merge or to be separate is central to how men and women think about and report their affairs.

Female Connectedness/Male Separateness

When a baby is born it is dependent and unaware. In any way we can define a 'self', the baby has no sense of it. It feels no distinctions between what is itself and what is other. As it begins to get a sense of differentiation of itself, other people, and the world around, the 'other' is usually a mother. At first the baby does not know what it is to be apart. It is as if there is no bonding between baby and mother; each merges into the other. As the baby matures, increasing the range of things it does, it begins to be aware that there is something which is itself – 'baby' – and something which is mother, father, sister. The baby can see that what he or she does produces a response in the mother or father. Gradually the secure knowledge that the mother is there allows the baby to explore – first his or her body, then the world – all of which contribute to the baby's growing sense of self. Babies who lack love and care have problems developing a sense of self. Some of these babies give up developing altogether: the low survival rates of neglected babies may be explained in part by these babies ceasing to demand. The self has never succeeded in being felt and fades slowly away.

Part of the sense the baby develops that he or she is something separate comes from the fact that the baby's mother is not always immediately available. She cannot always be there and is not able to meet every need the baby has. The baby may feel hungry but has to wait for a feed. He or she may be made uncomfortable by a wet nappy but is not immediately changed. The mother inevitably frustrates the baby because she is separate. Her separateness, expressed in her being unable to meet each need perfectly, actually helps to stimulate her baby's sense of its separateness and hence its self-development. As the baby gets some sense of self he or she also develops something like love for the mother. Until then the baby cannot feel love, just as he cannot feel a sense of self.

Why do we spend so much time talking about a baby's self-development when in this book we are concerned with adult relationships, and how they develop? Because, as we have already noted, there cannot be adult relationships without a sense of self. It might also be said that the reverse is true: our sense of self develops always within a relationship, from birth onwards. In order to love someone else, we must feel a sense of self as someone who is separate.

This sense of separation, central to developing a sense of self, however, is what is most keenly different between boys and girls and between men and women. As we have argued, the typical child-care arrangements of our society tend to produce a mother-daughter bond of empathy or identification, and a mother-son division or separation from the outset.

When Beth was thirteen she and her mother, Dierdre, began to have serious rows. Up until that time they had had a warm and close relationship. At twelve Beth discovered boys. Her mother deeply disapproved. The previous harmony between them gave way to acrimonious arguments. 'You're going to end up just like the rest of them. Ordinary. Boy-crazy. When was the last time you read a book?' Dierdre would shout at Beth. Dierdre hated the fact that Beth, with whom she had so identified as a younger child was both becoming interested in boys at an earlier age than Dierdre had done and was also demonstrating behaviour which both embarrassed and appalled her. Dierdre had been a late developer and a good student. Much of her own self-esteem had come from her success first as a student and then in the career which she gave up when she had children. Hers was a traditional marriage; her husband worked and she looked after their two children. Her little girl, Beth, was also a bright and inventive child who shone in school. The identification between them was thereby strengthened, since they were also alike in interests and temperament. It gave Dierdre a lovely feeling that she understood her daughter and also that she was a good mother. But Beth was much prettier than her mother had been as an adolescent. She also began to mature earlier. So at adolescence Beth began to emerge as different from Dierdre. Gradually Dierdre started to feel that their close and intuitive bond was weakening as she saw Beth becoming very different from her. She cringed when she saw Beth lose her independence, spirit and forthrightness and turn into a flirty little thing, which she now became when around boys. Remembering her own loss of dignity and integrity as she tried to gain boys' attention made it impossible for Dierdre to let her own daughter be, to learn her own lessons and to make her own mistakes. Increasingly, she felt a failure as a mother as she felt she could not identify with her daughter. But identification for this pair had meant that one had merged too fully into the other. Dierdre could not see her daughter for herself.

The same does not happen for mothers and sons. Dierdre had a son, Michael, as well. Although she had difficulty with him when he became adolescent and wanted more freedom than she wished him to have, she gave him far greater latitude. She also did not feel betrayed by him when his interests and tastes developed in, for her, foreign directions. For he had, in a sense, been foreign to her from the outset. When, at aged eight, Michael had desperately wanted to be good at football, she identified with his wanting to be good at something his friends respected, and with his pain at not being quite good enough. But because the world of boys, their interests and responses is so different from the world of girls, she could accept that her experience was not exactly the same. This gave Michael a lot of freedom from her anxiety. Indeed, she let him work out much of this problem for himself. In the end, when Michael and Beth were adolescent, she felt she was a better mother to Michael than to Beth, even though she had felt identified with Beth in a more immediate way.

Beth's and Michael's experience of the same mother was different in large part because of their gender. Beth had loved basking in the warmth of Dierdre's appreciation and empathy. Michael had always felt slightly uncomfortable when Dierdre had become what he had felt to be over-anxious for him. He felt it an intrusion. Beth was a cuddly child, Michael one who averted his face when his mother kissed him. At adolescence Beth felt rudely rejected. But so merged with Dierdre was Beth that she also bought Dierdre's values – and judgement on her – almost completely. The fact that she chose a date rather than a novel seemed to confirm that she was going to be 'ordinary' and that she would lose her mother's respect and approval forever. So merged was she with her mother that her differences and independence felt terrible to her. But Michael's was a different experience. When his mother over-empathised he cut off, even as a young boy. Averting his face was a clear message to his mother: 'Enough. Don't get too close. Let me be.' And she did because he already was something different from her.

Even in less traditional, more egalitarian marriages, mothers spend far more time than fathers in child care, provide more of the nurturance within the family, and more often accept the ultimate responsibility for tasks and responsibilities attached to children, apart perhaps from financial provision. And if the mother works outside the home, whether full or part time, the care of children is then usually taken on not by the father or some other male but by another woman, whether nanny, childminder, babysitter, grandmother, or other female relative. When the children go off to school, especially in the early school years, they go off to the care of other women. Teachers in nursery and primary schools are usually women. So it is not overstating things to say that the child-care arrangements of our society are still overwhelmingly the province of women. Babies and young children spend most of their time in female company.

Since we experience everything by and through the fact of our gender, the gender of the person who forges our first relationship with us, when our sense of our self and its relationship to others is in its infancy, will make a crucial difference. The activities, skills and attitudes which are thought appropriate for men and women are not the same in every society. But in every society the fact of gender organises the way things are done, and the way people behave. In some cultures, for instance, a woman is expected to be soft and lenient; in others to be hard-headed and strong-willed. But in either case the mother's life will parallel the expectations and experience of her daughter in profound ways in which it will not and cannot parallel those of her son. In unspoken, intimate ways the mother and daughter will be bound together. This will happen no matter what else follows. The girl may turn out to be a classical pianist, while the mother is tone deaf; the boy may love photography, while the mother is a film-maker. The mother may prefer her son – but the parallel will still be with her female children.

Lynn, a forty-year-old, twice-married psychologist, mother of three, who has had a very difficult and distant relationship with her mother, speaks of resenting her far less gifted, much more ordinary brother because of his easy relationship with their mother: 'I actually had her standing there in front of me,' the psychologist said recently in an interview, 'looking at me and saying, "I don't know where you came from!" And that's just how I feel. I went into psychology, I'm sure, to find out how it could happen that I could be so different from her. Meanwhile, she and my brother are just the same – they'd be happy sitting at home watching the same TV shows together for the rest of their lives. They don't know what I'm on about; I don't understand them.' There is little sympathy between these two women, and their experiences are extremely different: the daughter a high achiever, very ambitious, very well educated, the mother an immigrant, with little schooling and simple in her tastes and needs. However, none of these are characteristics which will vitiate the fact that on the basis of what is perhaps the single most important category of organising our experience – gender – mother and daughter are bound together. Mother and son are not. Mothers 'know' what their girl babies are like, or will be like, although they may often get it wrong. They have learned what they think their boy babies are like or will be like. And they treat each, from the first, differently. Fathers do this too. But since it will be the mothers who will have more to do with children's attainment of a sense of self and their expectations and behaviours in relationships, we concentrate on them. We should note here that fathers' influence is not trivial, and they indeed act as reinforcers. We will have more to say about this further on in this chapter.

Occasionally, the process proceeds differently. Gender is discounted. The mother is able to identify with the boy baby as if he is she. Rupert, now aged eighteen, and his mother were a case in point. After a number of incidents of self-abuse, which included cutting himself – interestingly a pattern that is much more common among girls and women – and also of severe depression, Rupert became a patient in a short-stay unit in a large US metropolitan state hospital when he was fourteen. The other adolescents on the ward felt a deep aversion to him, largely stemming from their confusion when they were around him. Although Rupert dressed as a male he appeared in all other respects to be female. He developed passionate crushes on male staff, just as he did on male pop stars. He pined for affection openly, and in a way which made him that much more pathetic, because both boys and girls recoiled, not being able to 'place' him appropriately in their scheme of things. The family were sporadically involved in his therapy while he was in hospital. There was no father; Rupert was the youngest of four children, and the only boy, of a very disorganised, uneducated, poor and very strong-willed mother. The older two, who were girls, had quarrelled with her repeatedly and, showing some of that same strong will, had left home, each by the time she was sixteen. Two children were left at home. The older one was a girl of fifteen who was very involved with her church, her godmother, and her godmother's family. While she helped out at home, she seemed largely peripheral to the main, passionate bond which remained – that between Rupert and his mother. His mother spoke of him as her baby, and on a number of occasions recalled romantically what it had been like to carry him in herself, to give birth to him. It was still, fourteen years later, vivid for her when she gazed at him, still one of the primary ways in which she experienced him. Mothers of newborns bring that lens to their babies, but soon it begins to be exchanged for new ones: those through which you view your child as a unique individual developing new skills, new interests, new activities. Rupert's mother seemed genuinely not to see how disturbed and disturbing he was; she seemed impervious to his gender confusion. Instead, she endowed him with particular powers of sensitivity and something bordering on telepathy: he 'understood' her – and she him – better than any two people could ever hope to be bound by common understanding and love. On saying goodbye after her visit to the hospital, Rupert indeed behaved as a two-year-old might on being separated from his mother: he screamed, clung and sobbed. She, too, clung and then finally, after the staff persuaded her to let go, kissed him intensely. (Rupert again screamed, became hysterical, and slid into an even more extreme depression shortly thereafter.) The point about Rupert is that his mother seemed to discount his gender in identifying with him: the identification was complete. This over-identification also prevented his 'self', his own identity, from growing. It grew – that is, he was a male despite himself – into an image he loathed: the hate-inspired self-cutting began around puberty, when Rupert's maleness and sexual urges asserted themselves, and when he could no longer ignore the world's definition of him as male.

Fathers also play a most important role in the way we develop our sense of self, although their influence is different on girls than on boys. Children do indeed have to learn to share their mothers with another grown-up – usually the father in most family arrangements. Even in single-parent families, children have to learn the lesson of the inevitability of sharing. At the same time they must confront the notion of their limited power compared to the grown-up challenger in this sharing battle. The father is a powerful person, both in relation to that child and also in comparison with the mother. Most children will perceive, at a quite young age, that there is a real power difference between men and women. Or, as one three-year-old put it, 'Daddy's the boss of the money. Mummy's the boss of the dirt.' This father also often adores his little girl or boy, so there is indeed immediately something 'in it' for these children to accommodate this powerful other in the triangle. In other words, most children, partly because they have to and partly because they want to, make the accommodation. This is the process that Freud was the first to describe, the one he called the resolution of the Oedipal 'crisis'. But it is a different process, with different results, for boys and girls.

For girls, this first important relationship with someone of a different sex has sexual overtones. Again, this is something specific to our Western culture. The popular icon of a sexually desirable woman is a woman with girlish – even infantile – characteristics. This indicates that we find there is something sexual about little girls. Marilyn Monroe's breathy voice and baby talk in the bedroom mimics a little girl's manner of speech. This is not true of our feelings about little boys. Icons of male sexuality resolutely banish any infantilism of this kind. John Wayne's broad shoulders can bear any responsibility. A manly voice is not a childish one. This is not to imply that there is an overt sexuality in father–daughter relationships. But there is an unconcious sexualising of male-to-female relationships from the beginning. On the other hand, since little boys – with piping voices and narrow shoulders – bear no resemblance to the adult male as sexual objects of their mothers, that element is not present from the outset in boys' first female-to-male relationship. Because little girls learn to take a submissive role in their first relationship with a man, the father–daughter relationship, but not the mother–son one, has the quality of providing a model for later heterosexual relationships.

In the relationship between little girls and their fathers there is a patterning of later heterosexual relationships. Part of this stems from the sexual overtones of their relationship. Little girls act in ways which we would define as 'flirty' – cuddly, looking up at grown-ups with big, round, appealing eyes. The same actions in small boys, whether to mothers or fathers, do not look 'flirty'. The same actions from girls to mothers do not seem at all sexual. But to their fathers they do. Daughters, merged more as they are with mothers, have relationships, and this includes the one with their fathers, based more on emotional connectedness than on shared activities and interests. Fathers and daughters do not often have relationships based primarily on shared interests. Even when they do, there is certainly not the sense of merger that mothers and daughters have. Justin shares a passion for classical music with his daughter, Julia. They play string quartets together with two others. Yet he does not claim to be exactly like her or to understand how she experiences the world. His son, Oliver, is temperamentally much more like Davina, his ex-wife. Yet Oliver and Davina, while enjoying a warm and close relationship, also have never been confused about where the one ends and the other begins. Davina, like Dierdre, has always accepted her son's difference, and Oliver, like Michael, Dierdre's son, has always been clear to keep a wide berth, cutting out a strongly independent role for himself within the family.

The patterning of later heterosexual relationships on those of fathers and daughters which begins so early is very strikingly emphasised by findings in studies of the effects of divorce on children. When divorce results in daughters losing their relationship with their fathers, these girls do very poorly in their later relationships with men. They are much more likely to have very negative views of them, and also to fail to make lasting and trusting heterosexual relationships.

Another piece of evidence for the sexualising of father–daughter relationships is that many warm and affectionate father–daughter relationships go cold and cut off at adolescence, when girls become sexual beings. This is not usually conscious or deliberate. It stems partly from awkwardness: how does a cuddle not now seem sexual? This is a dilemma, in contrast, not present for mothers and sons. Instead, for them the problem is how does a cuddle not seem childish? It also can stem from sexual jealousy, often unconcious, on the part of fathers. When Alan went on a school trip with his fourteen-year-old daughter, he returned home cross and critical of her. He confessed to his wife that he thought that their daughter was probably unhappy with him during the trip as he had been temperamental and critical. The evidence that she was unhappy with him came from his observation that she had spent most of her time on the trip with Brian, 'an obnoxious boy'. Unaware of the conversation between her parents, their daughter also confided in her mother. But her report was all about Brian, the 'gorgeous boy' who had paid a lot of attention to her on the trip.

The emotional merging between mother and daughter is not threatened by the formation of a strong bond between father and daughter. Their relationship – the rehearsal for a later boy–girl relationship – is so different from the mother–daughter bond that both comfortably co-exist. In contrast, fathers help effect a further separation, beyond the one given by their difference in gender, between mothers and sons. Sons identify with fathers; fathers are able to attract these identifications largely because they are seen as more powerful than mothers. In this stage of development, in early childhood – which marks something of a separation, for both sexes, from the mother – girls in fact stay more connected to their mothers than boys, who begin to separate more.

Connectedness and Girls' Early Development

Empathy is a quality often used to describe good mothering. It entails close identification. A responsive mother is an empathic one: she can 'read' her baby – identify with it. For example, it is often said that every mother knows her baby's cry. To someone who isn't listening for his or her own baby's cry, any baby's cry sounds like any other's. But to a mother hers is unique. Moreover, she can usually tell what *kind* of cry it is – tiredness, pain, hunger, the need for contact. Mothers can *feel* these cries, in a way, in order to read them and to respond to them.

This kind of empathic identification, which has an intuitive base, clearly is something that will be fostered in little girls because of the very closeness of their relationship with the mother. It will be reinforced daily within the mother–child relationship. Girls thus have more advantageous conditions for developing this capacity for close and intimate relationships from the outset. The mother–daughter bond promotes both an expectation that there will be connections between people, and a way of defining oneself in relation to the others: watching for their response to you, appraising their effect on you and vice-versa. This propensity to assess and experience the world in this way is both a gift and a liability for women, as we shall see.

For a mother to identify too closely with her infant daughter can become a problem. Identification with a girl baby can easily tip over into *over*-identification, actually *denying* the baby daughter's separateness or her sense of self.

Jackie, a very young mother from a deprived background where she experienced successive abandonments by her own mother, brought her six-month-old daughter in for an appointment with a health visitor. The baby cried on and off for the half-hour Jackie had to sit in the waiting area. Jackie neither held her, nor rocked her, nor tried to feed her. She left her in the buggy to cry, only occasionally pushing the buggy a bit to give it a soothing, rocking motion. When the health visitor finally arrived, she picked up the baby, and her cries eased off. 'She's only trying to get attention,' Jackie said offhandedly, as the trio entered the nurse's office. 'My mum says I was just the same. She says it just spoils kids to pick them up.'

Over-protection can be born of the same thing. The opening scene of the film *Terms of Endearment* shows Shirley MacLaine tiptoeing into her infant daughter's bedroom, ostensibly to check on her. More important than making a check on her daughter's well-being, the real point of her visit to the room is to get something for herself, that is, reassurance that her child is still breathing. Her visit also reassures her that she is a needed mother – she comforts her now awake baby's cries. This mother thinks, presumably, that she is responding only to her daughter, but is 'reading' her daughter's needs as if they were exactly her own.

These two examples are clearly cases of lack of empathy: the mother's over-identification obscures the baby's actual needs with the mother's misread ones: she reads instead what hers would be or have been said to be (or what hers were or still are, as the mother relives and perhaps rewrites her own childhood history). Thus, because of over-connectedness, there is actually a lack of real empathy.

This connectedness, merging, or identification breeds in

girls both the virtues of ordinarily being able to empathise with others more easily, and the problems of fuzzier boundaries. Girls and women are less clear about where the 'me' starts and ends. They consequently have more difficulty in knowing what might clearly be good for them as opposed to others (not to mention in asking for what would be good for them). The difference in how women and men conduct their relationships can thus be seen to emanate from these earliest times.

Simon and Susie were married for nine years when Simon had a secret affair. Susie began her career training under Simon. They fell in love, moved in together and eventually married. For eight years they lived and worked together every day, day in, day out. Their relationship, although intense, was also rocky: Susie often initiated arguments. Always they would be about Susie's perception that she was being neglected, left out, or undervalued. About one year into their relationship Simon began to work long, hard hours, sometimes returning to their shared office after dinner and not returning until after Susie was asleep. Susie wanted more of Simon, more attention. Simon wanted less. For Susie the merging she experienced, the looseness of their boundaries, even down to the working space they shared, comforted her and felt natural. But their too-close, too-merged style of relating made Simon want to break away. Run he did, eventually, into an affair which almost ended their marriage.

Separateness and Boys' Early Development

If boys tend towards difficulty in relationships it is in the other direction – stemming from too much separation, or an *under-*identification. For boys the task of defining a separate self is helped by the mother's perception of herself as a separate person. These firmer boundaries between them help to explain the basis of boy's and men's evolution of a greater single-mindedness in a variety of things, from pursuit of career, to the division made more by men than women between love and sex, and to greater ease in asking for what they may want or need in relationships. A mundane example of this comes from accounts given by mothers of very young babies when interviewed in a study of their first year of adjustment to the maternal role. Many mothers found it baffling that their husbands could come home from a hard day at work and sit down and read the newspaper, often while the baby was crying. These women would be exhausted by hours of being on call for their families, with little sleep. Their most commonly voiced complaint was, 'I don't have time for myself.' And this was on the most basic levels – they were perplexed by how to have time 'to have a pee'. They complained of dirty hair from not finding a space in the day in which to wash it – again, because they were responding to the needs of others first. They were often amazed and baffled by their husband's ability to tune out others and to sit down and relax with the paper. The more accepting of these mothers saw this as the husband's need to unwind, to do something for himself. The less accepting saw it as selfish. However, many also felt envious. They could see that there was a healthy component to their husband's behaviour: the men knew what *they* needed; they had clearer boundaries around the 'me'. It is our argument that this quality stems from that first, baby–mother relationship. The fuzzier boundaries girls are brought up with help to make them people who consider how others feel, who react to and think about others each time they act. They act, as the developmental psychologist Carol Gilligan has described it, within a 'web of relationships'. That is what defines them as much as their actions themselves. 'Self' – if self is in part defined by how someone characteristically acts – for women is in this way tied to others. 'Self' for men is not.

The empathic identification between mother and child can promote a sense of connectedness. The issue of girl babies, we have seen, usually stems from what is *un*-empathic, *over*-identification. The boundaries between the baby's self and mother are more blurred than between self and mother for the boy baby. The problem for boy babies may be the reverse. An *under*-identification, also *un*-empathic, is more likely here. From the beginning the mother knows that there is something fundamentally different about how her boy baby experiences the world. This must affect the mother's sense of knowing what that baby is experiencing. Thus, the sense of being connected, or as some writers have characterised it, merged, with one's child is likely to be less between boy babies and mothers than between girls and their mothers. Boys have the advantage of clearer boundaries and self-definition. But they also have the disadvantage of not having received enough empathic identification – they may be too cut off.

Sam married a woman who is quite timid and undemanding, unintrusive and thrilled by her husband. She lacks the passion and nervous energy which marked Ellen, his lover. Sam does not feel his wife can understand much of his often murky emotional life. His mother was an intrusive, controlling woman and he both loved and ran from her, while he adored his sweet father but was contemptuous of him for being ineffectual. Ellen understood him in all his complexity. But, in the end, he ran from Ellen. They might get too merged, felt Sam, and he nipped the relationship off before it could become anything like his relationship with his mother. At bottom, Sam is sad and lonely at home now with his low-key but adoring wife, but he could not risk what he saw would become a smothering marriage to Ellen.

In the final section of this chapter we will explore the different approaches this different kind of early development creates for men and women – and the different vulnerabilities for each – in pursuing adult romantic relationships. First we turn to further divergent pathways they take during adolescence.

Adolescence and the Widening of the Gender Gap

It is in adolescence that boys and girls are both expected and seem inclined to sexualise or make romantic relationships with members of the opposite sex. Thus it is in adolescence that differences in expectations, beliefs and behaviours in these relationships begin to emerge most clearly.

All recent indicators show that while girls may be more interested in pursuing higher education and professional training and planning for careers than a generation ago, they still put a higher premium on being in a relationship. And they are more likely to want to marry and to marry earlier than boys. While it has become the norm for both sexes to have sexual intercourse before they marry, girls are more worried abut their reputation than boys. In other words, within the arena of greater sexual freedom for both sexes, boys still have more freedom; there is still a double standard. This is not surprising, in the light of what we have just been saying. Girls want to be connected. They will feel more secure not only in their position, but also in how they define themselves, if they are in a stable relationship.

In adolescence, as boys and girls begin to look like men and women, there comes an acceleration of demands that each begin to act like men and women as well. Adolescence can be seen to be a time of apprenticeship in adult gender roles. It is a time when the masculine and feminine are exaggerated. Adolescent girls and boys, like recent transsexuals – that is, people new to being acknowledged as men or women – need to exaggerate those facets of the role which tend to differentiate one from the other: they both need to 'try on' the role and also to gain acknowledgement that they have 'got it right', as men or women respectively.

Because of this, the sexual differences between girls and boys tend to be greatly exaggerated at adolescence as we will show in the next chapter. Later, men and women may begin to converge again. It is when girls grow up, past their teenage years, that they begin to have freer sexual fantasies, for instance. In Nancy Friday's (and others') work on women's sexual fantasies, there is a great range of fantasies – whereas the typical adolescent girl's fantasy does not run much beyond the pop songs: to find one person to love, kiss, cuddle, and even perhaps to make love to, is what is erotic. 'Love' is the aphrodisiac of the fantasy. Older women may believe in love, but for them fantasies do often accommodate other kinds of sexual turn-on. However, as the American social commentator Barbara Ehrenreich and her co-authors Elizabeth Hess and Gloria Jacobs point out in their book, *Re-making Love: the Feminization of Sex* (1986), older women can now be more sexually active without getting a bad reputation. Indeed, sometimes they are seen by men as sophisticated, experienced, confident and even threatening: their sexual experience is greater, and, therefore, perhaps more powerful than the man's. In fact, in adolescence this emphasis for adolescent girls on being 'good' and sexy only if one is in love and loved is crucial for achieving their identities as women. For the teenage girl, it marks her as clearly feminine – in her sexual fantasies, self-image and behaviour. Boys don't have to have love to be sexual. Girls do. Such clarity is helpful at the beginning stages of identity development. With greater confidence as a woman may come experimentation, the attempt to stretch the boundaries of how 'woman' is defined. For similar reasons for boys, if there is to be a period of 'sex without love', it may well occur sometime during adolescence.

During adolescence, as we shall see in the next chapter, the emphasis on heterosexual relationships burgeons. Differences between girls and boys in sexual behaviour, imagery and attitudes widen. It is as if by separating the sexes in this way at this time, when their bodies make it possible and inevitable that they will sooner or later become sexual, we help to tantalise adolescents by accentuating foreignness; by creating a divide we reinforce the forbiddenness of heterosexual sex.

Similarly at this point the emotional differences deepen as well. The main psychological task at adolescence is to discover 'Who am I?', especially apart from the 'who' the adolescent has been, as a child, in his or her family. A large part of the answer to this question lies in defining both one's sexuality and one's gender role. How are you going to be a woman or man? What will it look or feel like? Will you be much like Mother or Father or a bit more like Madonna or Schwarzenegger? Adolescents take first, often faltering steps along the road towards forging their identities. As they do this, the paths of emotional development along gender lines widen. Girls pine for love; boys for sex. Girls congregate in tight, one-to-one pairs, boys play in groups. Girls pick apart feelings, developing a highly sophisticated language for them. Boys finely hone skills, set goals and pursue them. They let lapse any language for emotions which their mothers may have begun to inculcate in them, for their peers and fathers, with whom they now identify as men, are unlikely to be much good at talking about feelings.

Adolescents are expected to transfer their intense affections, developed as children, from Mummy and Daddy to someone else. But they also expect, in doing so, that that same intensity and exclusiveness which Mummy, in particular, delivered, especially at the beginning, will be part of the deal. Indeed, the first intense days, weeks and even months of falling in love do mimic the first years of the intense, exclusive preoccupation of mother and child. So both the expectations and demands for exclusiveness, which we see later in marriage and monogamy, are fixed in our earliest love relationship (mother and child) and then reinforced in our next one, in adolescence.

One very central problem in all this is, of course, that mother–child love is not the same as either adult–adult or adolescent–adolescent love. Transposing expectations from one to the other can be dangerous. The consistent, predictable, intense preoccupation and concentration from mother to child is not possible, and probably not desirable, to expect from one adult to another. And yet it is often just what is expected. When we discuss the models our society has for marriage, in chapter 4, we will return to this thorny issue. For the dilemma of monogamy versus affairs in marriage stems in large part from the transposition of the exclusivity of our very first love to our expectations of all the rest of our loves. Our next love, of course, most commonly develops during adolescence. The moon-June-honeymoon falling-in-love style of this first romantic, adolescent love serves to reinforce just those patterns set in infancy.

Different Expectations: Men and Women in Love

Both men and women want to fall in love, and to be in love. But women say it more often. Until recently a girl's upbringing has been focused on finding a man to marry and thereafter having his children. Nowadays this is less dominant. Nevertheless, even women with satisfying lives apart from families – women with rewarding work and friendships – still characteristically complain of feeling incomplete without an intimate romantic relationship. It is socially acceptable for a woman to be conscious of, concerned with, and to articulate these feelings. Although a man may also crave an intimate connection, it is less likely to be an overt and conscious craving; it is less socially acceptable for him to appear to be bereft without a relationship. It is certainly all right for a man to be bereft without a *particular* woman – for example, in grieving for a dead wife or a broken love affair. But it is less dignified: he is less a 'real' man if that grieving turns into longing for 'a woman' to make him feel finished or complete. It is still part of our idea of a 'real' woman that she be intimately connected with another and so she is, in a sense, unfinished and ill-defined in herself until she is in a relationship. Recently, in an issue of an American women's magazine aimed at the successful career woman, there was an article by a divorced career woman. In it she stated that despite the value of being self-reliant and 'doing things for yourself', a development which the women's movement has helped to promote, she still feels less of a person when not in a relationship with a man. It would be hard to conceive of a man writing this. He may write that he is lonely, that he misses companionship, someone to talk to and a sexual relationship. Saying, however, that he was not complete or not his full self would not sound quite comfortable to our ears. Men talk of their relationships as an extra part of themselves, something desirable that is added. For women it is part of their being.

So while both men and women may want to be in love, and in relationships, they seem to be after different things. Men look for women who can be separate beings who bring them qualities which they enjoy and to whom they can contribute the same. Women look for this and more – a completing of themselves through the relationship. This difference comes out even when women do more of what men have traditionally been able to do, and segment or set boundaries to their sexual involvements (see chapter 4). Even in such situations women are thinking about the other people involved and what the relationship with that particular person might mean about them. They are continuing to define themselves through their attachments to others. Men are not. In keeping with their clearer boundaries, they speak of things done together, or what each person does for the other in the affair, or, for that matter, in the marriage. Their language in describing love is much more practical.

However, the story of what men and women may be seeking in love may be more complicated than this. If we look back at the ways in which that early connectedness or separateness can go wrong for girls and boys respectively, we might see different needs developing – indeed, when extreme, in pathological ways – for men and women in romantic relationships. Clearly, both can have problems with intimacy, and can react defensively either with denial of the need to be intimate or with too much need for closeness. It could be argued that a certain kind of emotional, if not sexual, promiscuity could easily develop in a woman. There can be too *much* of a tendency to connect, stemming from too-fuzzy boundaries.

Men, for their part, may be too cut off from others and so less able to be intimate than women. Empathy is less easy for them. Or a different scenario can emerge as a result of not enough connection in the earliest years. Boys when they grow up may have unfinished business, wanting more intimate connections. As men in love, they may yield to a yearning for an enormous, greater-than-life love. That is, they may be particularly prone to searching for the one great love which will provide the one great, never-obtained intimate connection not quite ever forged with their mothers.

Adult romantic love can be experienced in this way by men (the 'unfinished business' of an under-empathic 'merger' with a mother). Indeed, in some men this connection may be defended against because it is imagined as potentially smothering. As Stuart, a graduate student in his late twenties who has recently ended a three-year marriage after his wife began an affair with her boss, has said: 'I don't think I'm really made for love, even though I want it.' Stuart's wife had fallen in love with her boss after Stuart had spent months at a time away on fieldwork. He had preferred their relationship to be distant in this way, punctuated by reunions. Previous relationships were also characterised by distance – with both physical separations and emotional withdrawals. Stuart's mother, a frail and unhappy woman, had been over-involved with him until the birth of her second child, when it felt to him that she had 'dropped' him. He experienced her as really never quite understanding him, yet coming closer to it certainly than his brutish, alcoholic father had. He hated his younger brother (who as a grown-up now lived at home with his mother). He felt contempt for him. He also was quite certain that his brother was homosexual, and explained this as a result of his being so identified with their mother. Over the years a myth grew in the family that Stuart, his brother and his mother were really very much alike at bottom: sensitive, literary, cultivated. The myth also included the allegation that Stuart had rejected his poor mother, and his younger brother was the one who rescued her from their uncaring and loutish father. Stuart, indeed, developed a remote and independent style. He had not made the connection that this remoteness was an attempt to save himself – whatever was unique to him in comparison to his mother, including his masculinity – from being sacrificed to his mother, as, indeed, he felt his brother had been. Isolation characterised his emotional life, and made him very seductive to many women. He was seen as very 'masculine' – independent, self-reliant and also 'hard-to-get'.

The yearning, the unfinished business left by under-identification, may help to explain why men have a deep need for women, in ways women do not seem to need men. This is evidenced by the fact that, of all people studied, single men do worst on measures of mental and physical health, and men who do not remarry soon after a divorce show a comparatively high incidence of mental and physical breakdown. Men, indeed, do remarry at faster rates than women, and this may in part be explained by men's deep need for a secure and predictable union, complemented, of course, by women's greater ability to offer the empathy which men seem to seek. This may be part of the phenomenon of living in a web of relationships.

Stuart's story illustrates the point that, in men, the need for intimate connection is often a denied one: men do not slaver after romantic love the way women do. It is not all right for boys to pine away for love the way it is for girls. An anorexic-looking, lovelorn male offends our sensibilities yet we often do not take a lot of notice when it is a girl in such a state. It is not macho to be girl-crazy. Yet we may smile fondly at the gaggle of teenage girls who go three times in one week to see a film with their favourite (male) film-star in it. This is not to say that women may not also show pathology in the same way – running from too-intimate relationships, in particular because their mothers, and sometimes their fathers (especially true in some cases of women running from too-powerful men) have been smothering. But for women not to have connections is more pathological, because these connections are both how they define themselves and how they are defined. Instead of isolation, women may indeed show fear of intimacy through their involvements in *more* relationships.

Women may also suffer because they depend too much for their identity on this intimate connection. Margaret, a well-put-together, upper-middle-class woman of fifty-five, wife of a successful business executive, came into psychotherapy because she had made a suicide attempt. Her husband had walked out of the marriage after thirty-three years, two children, and one recent grandchild. Margaret's mother had died when Margaret was sixteen. She had been close to her mother, identifying strongly with her. She had known her somewhat older future husband, a friend of the family, all her life. Soon after her mother's death, they fell in love and became engaged, marrying when Margaret was eighteen. She had been the 'perfect wife'. So perfect in fact, that she felt herself to be nothing else. They had shared everything – but on closer analysis this meant that Margaret had gone along with everything her husband had wanted. His peripatetic business life had meant she had literally dragged all over the world after him. She was serenely happy doing this. She loved dressing up as the business executive's wife, being introduced as 'Mrs Watson', loved the power which she saw emanating from him – it filled her with a sense of her own power and pride. She loved the hotels, the golf club, the dances and the restaurants, and she loved giving him his two children and beautiful home. His pride in her job made her day. She looked forward to his approaching retirement now so they could do even more things together. In contrast, with this prospect ahead of him, he fled. The story is not unusual, but it is a story which could only be a woman's without being considered unusual.

Before we move on to our discussion of different sexual development in men and women we want to return to one point. Women and men are different, but in one critical way they are the same. They both want love, and they both think exclusivity and love go together, since they are both reared in similarly intense mother-and-child pairs. The similarity stops there; the differences in how the emotional needs and patterns unfold have been sketched in this chapter.

The different pathways along emotional development find their counterpart in men's and women's sexual development. For not only are men and women primed to want, think about, and experience emotional relationships differently, their sexuality is forged in markedly different ways as well. The different formation of their sexual needs, experiences, attitudes and imagery is another feature of the gender divide which in turn divides men and women in their experience of affairs.

3 Becoming Sexual

Sexual intercourse began
In 1963
(which was rather late for me)
Between the end of the Chatterley ban
And the Beatles' first L.P.

Up till then there'd only been
A sort of bargaining,
A wrangle for a ring,
A shame that started at sixteen
And spread to everything.

Then all at once the quarrel sank;
Everyone felt the same,
And every life became
A brilliant breaking of the bank,
A quite unloseable game.

So life was never better than
In 1963
(though too late for me) –
Between the end of the Chatterley ban
And the Beatles' first L.P.

Philip Larkin, 'Annus Mirabilis'

In our account of the development of relationships, we stressed how girls and boys define their identities in relation to their mothers. So, while maleness develops as what is separate and different from a mother, a girl continues to share a common identity with her primary caregiver. These separate developmental paths result in different desires and needs for relationships. What excites women is the world of emotion and intimacy. They want to love and be loved. But love turns out to be a good deal more elusive than sex. Conversely, men find love is on offer but find it less desirable than sex. Both genders use fantasy to bridge this gap between desires and realities. While men fantasise about erotic women, women create images of strong but tender men who are loving and faithful, yet sexually skilled. To understand how these differing desires form and shape our heterosexual relationships, we must turn our attention to the patterns of sexual development in boys and girls.

It is fundamental to our argument in this book that sexuality develops through quite different pathways in women and men. In outline, our claim is that, while for men the developmental process is one of bringing sexuality into their intimate relationships and so making sex a social activity, for women it is the reverse. They develop their sexuality from and within their love relationships. This may seem an odd claim. Some may insist it is at variance with what is obvious and apparent all around us; that boy meets girl and they begin to spend time together and build a relationship. If this persists, sooner or later it may become sexual. Kissing and hugging leads to an exploration of more intimate parts of each others' bodies and so to sexual intercourse. For most, therefore, sexual activity begins within the context of an established relationship. Indeed, the usual convention is that it is the growing 'seriousness' of the relationship, like Philip Larkin's wrangle for a ring, that permits and justifies the increasing sexual activity. From this it would seem to follow that sexuality begins to be expressed within a social relationship. But to take that view is to ignore the different pathways which have brought boy and girl to their first mutual sexual explorations, as well as the ways their sexualities develop from that point on.

We believe that people have to learn to be sexual. Our sexuality is not biologically given, but a highly complex part of our social being that each of us creates within the social world in which we grow up. Of course, our biology is part of the process but it does not determine what we become or what we do. It is the same biology that is involved in the creation of adults who are homosexual or heterosexual, those who marry and have a single sexual partner for life and others who make a profession out of their sexuality and have several dozen partners each week. Our sexual lives are very varied and different. We vary in what we do, who we do it with, how we do it, how often we do it, what we feel about it and what gives us pleasure.

As well as individual variation, each culture has its characteristic patterns which permeate all aspects of sexuality. For
instance, while in much of Europe and North America female
breasts are very much the focus of what most men desire in
women and are central in the public imagery of sex, in other
cultures they figure little in sexuality. In Latin America, rather
than breasts, it is female buttocks that are accentuated in
fashion and in images of women. In some societies a phase of
homosexual relationship may be an expected pattern for young
men before marriage, while elsewhere any such activity is highly
stigmatised and frowned on. There is a similar variation in the
extent to which young women are or are not expected to enter
into sexual relationships before marriage. Or indeed in the
ways in which they are encouraged to regard their sexuality –
as something passive which will be aroused by the love of a
good man, as a source of pleasure for themselves and their
partners which they can control or something they can use to
obtain and maintain relationships with men. The attempts to
explain this great variety of human action and experience in
terms of biology or physiology have been a dismal failure.
Instead we need to turn to the social development of individuals
and the beliefs and rules which members of each culture hold
about sexuality to understand how this variation may arise. It is
during childhood, and especially at adolescence, that we learn
to become sexual. It is not simply that we must come to know
the conventions of sexual behaviour to respond appropriately in
each situation, but our feelings and desires are shaped and
channelled as part of our social being. Much of this learning is
not explicitly sexual but is part of the growth of a general
understanding about social relationships and about our bodies,
modesty, what is private or public and so on.

Childhood and Sexual Development

Since Freud first began writing about childhood sexuality it has
become conventional to regard children, even from birth, as
sexual beings. But it is a very adult perspective to see all

childhood activities that involve genitals as sexual in the same way as they would be if adults did similar things. Their meaning to a child may be quite different. So, for example, if parents notice the periodic erections of the penis of their new-born son, it is quite likely that they misunderstand what they see. Although babies and children indulge in behaviour which we often label as sexual, its meaning for the child may not be sexual at all. In middle childhood when children play doctors and nurses and undress and examine each other, it is misleading to regard this as the beginnings of sexual experimentation. More accurately, they are satisfying an understandable curiosity about how bodies are made. While such knowledge will undoubtedly come in useful in their first sexual encounters after adolescence, their mutual explorations have a quite different meaning and purpose from similar actions for adults.

Childhood games of nurse and doctor carry other important lessons for children. They come to understand that adults are likely to disapprove of such activities and may call them 'dirty'. In our society, children learn to do these things in private and hide their activities from others, especially adults. They learn what it is to feel guilty and associate guilt with games involving their genitals. Indeed, they learn that special rules apply to their genitals: that they should not be talked about in public, they should be hidden in most situations and that similar conventions apply to excretion. This learning builds an association that dominates much of what children come to understand about their genitals – that excretion and the genitals are closely linked, that both are to be hidden and that they are the subject of shame and guilt. But such learning does not apply to all members of our society in equal measure. In a study of mothers of one-year-olds in Nottingham, John and Elizabeth Newson, psychologists who carried out a classic study of child development, found that working-class mothers were much more likely to smack their children for touching their genitals than those in the middle class, a point that is likely to be associated with some of the class differences in adult sexuality which we discussed in chapter 1. Although the Newsons did not report on this, had they explored attitudes in some of the ethnic communities they are likely to have uncovered widely varying responses ranging from those who believe that genital play is natural and healthy, to other groups who take a much more restrictive and punitive position than the Nottingham working-class mothers.

Cutting through such cultural variation is the even more important divide of gender. Mothers do not treat their sons and daughters in the same way. Sanctions for girls touching themselves are generally very much stronger than those for boys. There is another important gender difference. There is one situation when boys routinely handle their own genitals, when they urinate, which does not occur for girls. These processes create a great gulf between the ways in which girls and boys come to regard their genitals. Gender is also important in the ways in which children come to talk about their anatomy. From a young age boys usually have a number of words that they use for the penis, and adults use these words in conversation with them. Girls' vocabulary is often much more restricted and it may be quite late in childhood before they have any name for their vagina or clitoris. Commonly parents will use a single word like 'bottom' for all parts of the female genitals.

As boys and girls approach puberty they have a wide knowledge of the family and wider social conventions that govern attitudes to their bodies. They will have a clear idea of what is permitted in public and what they are better advised to keep private. Adult disapproval of genital play and a wide range of matters to do with excretion and reproduction provide obvious topics which children can share with each other. Indeed, the exchange of information among the peer group before puberty is *a*, if not *the*, primary source of the understanding of sexual matters that children acquire. That knowledge is built up in the context of membership of one or other gender, a context which will have already taught children a good deal about the power relations of men and women and the expected role each will take in adult society. Girls who are closer to their mothers in a physical as well as an emotional sense, learn about the domestic world of women, while boys are likely to spend more time outside in the public world with their fathers. For each there is ample opportunity to observe and learn how men and women regard and treat each other and these are matters of great interest to children.

Girls at Adolescence

Adolescence is a time of redefinition when what children have learnt about their own and other bodies becomes specifically sexual knowledge. The rules of personal modesty and behaviour that have been assimilated during childhood begin to be transformed into the rules of sexual conduct. The knowledge that has been built up during childhood begins to be put together with the feelings and experiences of adolescence. As the adult body form develops, it is not only the adolescents' own view of themselves that changes, but others begin to see and behave towards them as sexual beings. Adolescents have love and sex on their minds and begin to acquire knowledge of the sexual culture of their society. Having sex becomes part of their imaginings.

Children find it very hard to see their parents as sexual beings and discussion across the generation about sexual matters tends to be very limited. Most adolescents come to feel that what they are experiencing is something not possible to share with the parents, and this gives a very special sense to their discovery of the sexual world as being a unique journey being undertaken for the first time. This further forces their learning of sexuality into the private sphere where it is much less easily shared than other aspects of social relations.

At adolescence the focus for boys and girls is very different. Girls' primary interest is in relationships, intimacy and love. All their experiences of the intense friendships of childhood, the feelings of closeness and rejection, are now brought to bear in the first tentative contacts with boys and their imaginings about them. Ample models for romantic relationships are available in their culture, in books and magazines, in films and on television

and in the conversations of their female friends. What most are
seeking at this stage is love, not sex. Love and intimacy are
more easily talked about, even across generations, than sex, so
that the major concerns of girls remain in the sphere of open
discussion. Boys, as we shall see, are primarily preoccupied
with sex and that largely remains hidden and part of their
private imaginings.

The feelings which a girl experiences in these early love
relationships may not be labelled as sexual at all. Only with the
beginning of kissing and petting, because these are understood
to be sexual activities, may a girl begin to identify her more
diffuse and indefinite feelings as sexual and she may start to
experience what she comes to call sexual arousal. Orgasm may
be first experienced as part of petting before a girl has ever
experienced intercourse, or it may first happen long after that.
For a substantial minority, or perhaps even the majority of
women, a first orgasm is experienced only after a good deal of
experience of sexual intercourse. Women's experience tends to
be a long drawn out process of learning to be sexual. Sexual
arousal increases with sexual experience.

As women have more sexual experience they tend to use a
wider range of techniques and fantasy tends to play a more
important part in their sexual arousal. According to Kinsey's
classic study, most women start to masturbate only after they
have had intercourse for some time, again indicating that as
they explore and learn to be sexual they widen their range of
sexual activities. Kinsey's research was done in the 1940s.
Changing attitudes since then have brought forward the usual
age at which girls reach their sexual milestones. But more
recent work suggests that the basic patterns of the development
of female sexual activities has remained the same. Most women
develop the capacity to experience orgasm at some time after
adolescence. Frequently, though not universally, orgasms are
first experienced with someone else rather than alone through
masturbation. As we shall see this stands in great contrast to
the pattern for boys.

A study which details these patterns, *The Sexual Behaviour of*

Young People (1965), was undertaken in Britain by Michael Schofield in the early 1960s. A representative sample of nearly two thousand young people between the ages of fifteen and nineteen were questioned in depth about their sexual behaviour. Most of the adolescents passed through a progression of activities in a regular sequence, although the timing showed great individual variation. At thirteen, a third of the girls in the study had dated and kissed a boyfriend. By fifteen, half of them had tried deep kissing and had their breasts stimulated through their clothes. Another year would pass before the same proportion had experienced fondling of their breasts under their clothes. From then they moved on to heavy petting and, by the age of eighteen, 12 per cent had had sexual intercourse; a figure, incidentally, that is a good deal lower than surveys in subsequent decades.

Most girls (82 per cent) described their first partner in sexual intercourse as a 'steady' boyfriend while only a minority of boys (45 per cent) used the same description for their first partner. Girls also tended to have a longer continuing relationship with their first partner. Reflecting the values of our culture, the author of the study comments, 'while girls seek security, boys seek adventure'. Although in the longer term the great majority of the young women and men wanted to marry, the men tended to give later ages for this than the women. When asked for their main reason for intercourse at the time it first happened, the most common reason given by girls was love, while boys said sexual desire. For a fifth of girls but a third of boys their first partner was also thought to be having intercourse for the first time. Not surprisingly given the conventions of our society, girls more often chose partners much older than themselves. For nearly 40 per cent of them their first partner was an adult (i.e., over twenty-one) compared with 2 per cent of the boys. First experiences were not always particularly pleasurable. Only a minority (30 per cent of girls and 48 per cent of boys) said they liked it first time. But interestingly enough, boys were more likely to say they were disappointed than girls – a point we can relate to girls' relatively unformed notion of sexual pleasure at this stage in their development. Only 28 per cent of girls as compared with 81 per cent of boys reached an orgasm during their first experience of intercourse. An important concern and source of anxiety in these first encounters is the issue of contraception. While most teenagers are well informed about the theory of contraception, practice may be another matter. Unless the couple are able to communicate easily about sexual matters, both may find it difficult to raise the question of contraception.

An important point about these early encounters is the extent to which girls really want sex at all at this stage. Early learning, whether in schools or through conversations with parents or among the peer groups, seldom emphasises that sex can be a source of pleasure. Adolescent girls often regard sex as something that boys will want and will push for. And so it becomes a price that is paid for love and intimacy, something to be granted to a boy as a token that they are going steady. Its price may be high for a girl, not only because of the obvious risks of pregnancy, but because her reputation may be at stake. To give away sex too easily could jeopardise the chances of finding a steady partner. Despite all the changes in attitudes to sex and marriage which we discussed in chapter 1, commitment to marriage, or at least 'serious' relationships, and to the idea that love should precede sex, still remains very strong in Britain.

Boys at Adolescence

In complete contrast to the situation for girls, the great majority of boys have a considerable sexual experience before they enter any romantic and potentially sexual relationship with a woman, or indeed have any kind of a sexual relationship. Men begin to learn to be sexual on their own, not with a partner. Masturbation is almost universal among adolescent boys. Through masturbation boys not only learn how to channel and focus their sexual feelings, but with the accompanying sexual fantasies they learn and organise patterns and definitions of what is sexually arousing for them. Although most boys develop techniques and fantasies for masturbation in private, the images and models that fill their head are, of course, taken from the world around them. Most frequently they will use pictures in pornographic magazines which, by their style and the poses they portray, show the adolescent how his society defines a sexually arousing female body. With these images and other imaginings drawn from the society around him, the adolescent furnishes his own world of erotic arousal. It is that head full of erotic images he brings to his first romantic (or unromantic) encounter with a woman.

This may not be his first sexual experience with another person because adolescent boys may masturbate with a friend or with a group of companions. Such situations are often portrayed as essentially competitive where boys try to impress their friends with their performance. But perhaps more importantly they are a time when boys can define male sexual arousal more closely by observing other boys. They can also provide a first experience in offering sexual pleasure to another and so the need to recognise the feelings and desires of a partner. And they can indicate individual differences – not everyone likes the same things. The need to communicate desires helps to develop a sexual vocabulary and a language for speaking about sexuality. But, for many, the vocabulary learnt with other boys is not one that they feel can be used with girlfriends.

These early male sexual encounters are not homosexual, indeed at this stage in sexual learning this category is only likely to apply to sexual activities with adults of the same sex, not boys of a similar age. The accompanying imagery and fantasy of the activities of these boys is of female, not male, bodies. Involving, as they often do, pictures of women's bodies, and discussions of how these may be arousing, male–male sexual encounters may also serve to develop a shared male heterosexual view of female sexuality.

When boy finally gets to meet girl he is likely to bring to these first encounters a rather contradictory set of desires and anxieties. Impelled by the values he has learnt through childhood which are likely to be strongly reinforced by his male companions, his interest will be in making sexual conquests, achieving intercourse and getting a girl to do what he thinks she ought to do. But he may feel ambivalent about what will give him most sexual pleasure. While the cultural conventions lead him through the steps of increasing intimacy, fondling his partner's breasts, moving below her waist to seek hand–genital contact and finally intercourse, his own experience of sexual pleasure at that point is likely to be a very different one based on his experience of masturbation. A further difficulty is that in masturbation a boy is completely in control of what happens and he structures his technique around his own pleasure, while early experience of intercourse is likely to be with a partner who expects him to take the lead and with whom he has neither the confidence nor indeed the language and vocabulary to ask for what he wants. And even if it is something to which he has given any thought at all, he probably does not have the faintest idea of how to help his partner towards what she wants. As we have mentioned already, first partners for boys are likely to be younger and as inexperienced as themselves. Not surprisingly then, on first occasions the earth seldom moves for men, most do not enjoy it and a significant minority fail to reach an orgasm.

Much will depend on how much guilt and shame associated with masturbation is brought to these first experiences and, of course, on the role of the female partner. Where a young couple can communicate their mutual needs and experiment, they are likely to find mutual pleasure fairly quickly. But the couple may find communication very difficult because they have not yet learnt a language for sex. Also it may be hard for them to find suitable places where they are not likely to be interrupted where they can pursue their mutual sexual education. Snatched moments in semi-public places are not best suited to the sensitive and subtle process of mutual learning. For those who delay this education until the honeymoon, privacy may not be a problem, but for them the long wait and increased expectation may mean that honeymoon sex is a great disappointment.

As we have discussed earlier, boys come to define their male self-identity by separation and by what is not associated with their mothers. They learn to crush their needs for closeness, dependency and emotional expressiveness. So they grow up with a strong message to avoid closeness and getting close to a female partner may arouse great feelings of anxiety. Closeness may be the price they have to pay for sex and they may strive to maintain a distance as far as possible. One way to do this is not to become too involved with any partner. A striking finding in the Schofield survey that supports this idea is that only about half of all teenage boys had sex more than once with their first sexual partner (as compared with over three-quarters of girls).

Another way to avoid closeness is to limit sexual contact to the main event, reducing foreplay and afterplay to a minimum. Of course, here there is likely to be tension between the boy and his female partner: the girl pushing for more involvement and intimacy and extending the range of shared activities, the boy trying to limit involvement. Class differences may be very significant, with middle-class patterns of socialisation encouraging boys to be more mindful of their partner's needs and pleasure, so that they may find it easier to learn the language of love and closeness, while for working-class boys the pull of the male group may conspire with the low expectations of the girls for intimacy to limit the extent of sexual encounters. Early sexual experience may be seen much more in terms of 'scoring' than the beginnings of a loving relationship.

Experiences of masturbation and the fantasies that go with it have to be reconciled with the experience of having sex with a real woman. The shame, guilt and association of sex with dirt can produce not only ambivalence, but quite angry negative feelings. So a teenage boy may be caught between the attraction of a woman who can offer sexual pleasure and a confirmation of his role as a successful male who is wanted by a woman, and repulsion towards a person who arouses his guilt and shame and needs to be punished for this. These ambivalent feelings may be lived out by having a series of very brief relationships, leaving each girl as soon as the relationship shows signs of becoming 'serious'. That seriousness is usually marked by growing expressions of affection and love which may serve to increase the boy's guilt, a guilt which is then assuaged by breaking off the relationship at just the point where the girl is expressing her needs, punishing her for having these guilt-provoking needs. In middle-class couples there is often a longer period in which sexual activity is kept at the level of petting before moving on to intercourse which may allow the boy a greater opportunity to begin to cope with his ambivalent feelings. As the petting relationship proceeds it is more likely to become mutual. So not only does boy touch girl, but girl touches boy. Girl may touch boy and bring him to orgasm, so making a direct link with his own masturbatory experience and provide a bridge between this and heterosexual experience. We suggest that this bridge may form an important learning situation for males and helps to bring their sexual experience into the social context of a relationship.

Women and Men Together

What each generation needs to discover anew is that having sex involves pleasure and learning a whole set of sexual rules and conventions. At least a minimal degree of communication is required to let a partner know what you want them to do and to understand their own needs and desires. A new vocabulary may be needed as the words used to refer to the genitals and other parts of the body in the single-sex peer group may not be thought to be appropriate to be used with a sexual partner of the other sex. New conventions of behaviour need to be developed for what previously has only been done in private. Undressing and dressing must be managed in a social situation. What do you do afterwards? How do you manage the return to the conventional world? What do you say?: 'Did the earth move for you?', or do you just roll over and light a cigarette as they do in the films?

How are the differing needs of girl and boy to be met? To perpetuate the romantic ideal she must convince herself that he is not like all the others and that he really does want more than one thing. He must learn to accept intimacy and to talk the language of love. Boundaries of the relationship must be constructed; how do you move from the shared world of the peer group and friends to the more exclusive one of the couple? How much time will you spend together as a couple? How will the relationship be presented to family and friends? What are the limits for other heterosexual relationships? One of the most important conventions of a serious relationship is that it becomes exclusive – a point we will need to return to at length when we come to consider relationships outside marriage. Among teenagers, starting sexual intercourse is strongly associated with the educational achievement of the girls. Those who left school earliest were most likely to have started sexual intercourse before the age of nineteen, according to the British survey of adolescents by Schofield. Not surprisingly, the age at which sexual intercourse starts is strongly related to the age of marriage; those who begin earliest are likely to marry at the youngest ages.

As we would expect for any aspects of social behaviour, teenage sexuality shows some clear social-class differences. Working-class girls and boys are predominant among those who were earliest in beginning sexual intercourse. The finding that middle-class adolescents spent longer at the petting stage before moving on to intercourse may be linked to the class differences in parental prohibition of genital play that we noted earlier and it also fits with the picture found by Kinsey and many other researchers that middle-class couples tend to use much more and varied foreplay (and afterplay) throughout their adult sexual lives.

Positive experiences that enhance the process of sexual learning are more likely for middle-class women. Some of these are related to their male partners. It is important to remember that most sexual partners are from the same social background as each other. Male attitudes towards their female partners vary with social class. In one American study of a group of working-class men who were questioned about their sexual attitudes, less than 15 per cent thought it was their responsibility to bring their female partners to orgasm. For a middle-class group of university graduates, over 80 per cent felt this should be part of their concern. While we may well wish to reject the very passive view of female sexuality that this study embodies, it does suggest that men in different social classes take a very different attitude towards their partners' sexual pleasure. It seems reasonable to assume that this is likely to have a critical influence on their partners' developing sexuality. Part of the middle-class male's identity is built around the idea that he is able to please and satisfy his female partners. He comes to see his own pleasure partly as a reflection of what his partner feels. Working-class attitudes may be more typically macho, his pleasure comes from women who say they need and want him and give in to his advances. Female attitudes may complement these male ones. While middle-class women may feel more confident about their sexuality and more able to express their needs, working-class women may have much lower expectations and a more passive attitude towards their own feelings.

Studies of marriage point to closer communication about emotional matters and more concern for intimacy and sexual feelings in middle-class couples. They are likely to talk more about sex and find out more about each other's needs and desires. Their shared erotic world is more likely to be one in which they both recognise that sexuality is centred in the mind rather than the body. Associated with this are the much wider and more varied range of sexual activities which middle-class couples employ. They do more experimenting and value novelty in love-making. As we discussed in chapter 1, the pattern of working-class marriage and sexuality with its sharp division of roles between men and women can be traced back to origins in the late nineteenth century when marriage patterns became more formalised but also more female-centred because of the uncertainties of male employment.

Studies of the sexual behaviour of married couples show that frequency of sexual intercourse is highest at the beginning of the sexual relationship and declines thereafter. A study of American couples, for example, found that almost a half of all

couples were having sex at least three times a week in the first
two years of marriage but that less than a fifth of couples
married for ten years achieved this frequency.

Frequency of sexual intercourse for married couples

Years together	% having intercourse less than once a week	% having intercourse three times a week or more
0–2	17	45
2–10	27	27
10+	37	18

Source: Blumstein and Schwartz, *American Couples* (1983)

Of course, figures such as these are rather an imperfect way of
representing a very wide variation in behaviour – patterns vary
enormously from couple to couple and each couple changes
over time. Some relationships may go through bad patches
when sexual activity may be minimal and then pick up again as
the relationship improves. Other couples may maintain a much
more regular pattern of sexual activity. A very common, if not
universal, experience is that sex becomes a lot rarer when there
are young children around. Couples may maintain a high rate
up to their first pregnancy but then activity falls off and may
not show much sign of recovery until their youngest child
reaches at least toddlerhood. Second honeymoons are not
uncommon when a couple reaches a point when they begin to
emerge from the broken nights and high level of demands of
all kinds that young children impose – a period for women, at
least, when sex may have become the last chore of the day.
While frequency of sex may not return to the level of their first
months together, it may be a great deal more frequent than it
was when they were more completely absorbed in children. But
thereafter a slow decline sets in once again. Many reasons may
combine to create a decline in a couple's sexual activity. Either

or both may feel bored or too tired to bother. Sexual interest may decline or a spouse may simply find it more difficult to become sexually aroused. Intercourse is likely to have a rather different meaning for men and women. There is evidence to suggest that, at least after the initial phases of a relationship, women may come to value intercourse more than men. The reason may not be because they have an increased desire for sex itself but because making love may provide an opportunity for emotional closeness and sharing with their partner which they may find hard to find in other situations.

Of course, it takes two to tango, and declining rates may be the result of changing behaviour of one or both partners. Male declining sexual interest in a habitual partner seems to play a major part in the fall-off in frequency of intercourse in marriage, 'the charms of novelty, gradually slipping away like a garment, laid bare the eternal monotony of passion, whose forms and phrases are forever the same' as it is put in *Madame Bovary*. What is significant here and of obvious relevance for any consideration of extramarital relationships, is that the decline is not usually a falling interest in sex as such but a lack of interest in sex with a particular partner. A similar kind of effect has been found in studies of many animal species and among those who study animal behaviour it has come to be called the 'Coolidge Effect' after the American President. The story goes that President Coolidge and his wife were visiting a government farm. They were taken on separate tours. Looking at a cockerel Mrs Coolidge enquired if it could mate more than once a day. When she was told it could, she asked that the information be passed to the President. When the President reached the cockerel's enclosure and was told about its sexual performance, he asked whether the same hen was involved each time. When he was told that it was a different hen each time he paused and looked thoughtful, and then said, 'please tell that to Mrs Coolidge'.

In our own species the Coolidge Effect is not simply a matter of doing the same thing with different partners, but, as many couples discover, may be a matter of doing somewhat different things with the same partner. Indeed, couples who create a varied and developing sexual relationship are likely to maintain an interest in sex and a high frequency of intercourse. It is exactly this point which has been discovered by the authors of the modern sex manuals that offer a wide range of possibilities and suggestions and which makes their books so popular with couples. What is involved here is not simply what couples do with each other, but also what they talk about and the extent to which they can acknowledge and recognise each other's sexual needs and fantasies. Those who bring a wider range of experience to their relationship and can share this with their partner, including at least some of their private world of fantasy, are most likely to maintain an active sexual relationship. Conversely, sexual relationships which are confined to intercourse with little by the way of foreplay or afterplay or discussion of sexual matters are likely to show the most rapid decline. As might be expected in view of what we have said earlier about social-class differences in the styles of sexual relationships, the decline in marital sexuality tends to be rather more rapid for working-class couples.

So far in this discussion we have been concerned with marital sexual intercourse. If we broaden it to include other kinds of sexual activity, we find an even more striking example of a male–female difference. Kinsey's classic study of sexual activity was centred on what he inelegantly called 'sexual outlets'. Based on the hydraulic-plumbing analogy of sexuality which was dominant in the 1940s and 1950s when his studies were carried out, his concept of outlet included all sexual activities which led to orgasm. Expressed in this way, he found that male 'total outlet' declined steadily from a high point at adolescence, while that for females was more or less steady.

Men become sexual at adolescence with a very high frequency – at least by female standards – of masturbation. Later, assuming they are heterosexual, they begin petting and intercourse with women. By their mid-twenties most men are experiencing most of their orgasms in heterosexual intercourse with masturbation continuing to provide some 'outlets'. Rates of intercourse, which initially made up for much of the drop in frequency of masturbation, decline with age. Masturbation declines too but at a somewhat slower rate so that by middle age it has become relatively more important once again.

Once again we should make our caveat that these are overall average patterns which conceal individual variations. Hetero-sexual relationships may begin and end. Initial phases of new ones are likely to have high rates of intercourse while gaps between relationships may involve low rates of casual inter-course and a lot of masturbation.

The female pattern has a very different shape, reflecting the increasing importance of masturbation for many women as they have more sexual experience with other people. So as frequency of intercourse declines as relationships mature, masturbation often increases, giving an overall steady rate of 'outlets'.

The decline in satisfaction with marriage and the drop in sexual activities which goes with it, which seem characteristic of Western marriage, may not be a universal pattern. It has been suggested that while Western marriages begin hot and become cooler, the opposite might be more typical of couples whose marriages are arranged and have no sexual or social relationship before marriage. It is often said that these couples grow to love one another. No systematic research on marital sexuality, such as we have for Western marriage, exist for cultures where marriages are arranged – itself a comment on different attitudes to sexuality. However, there are a number of studies of marital satisfaction. In Western marriages it is typical for the levels of satisfaction for both husbands and wives to show a similar and parallel decline and this follows the decrease in sexual activity. In studies of societies where arranged mar-riages are common, similar patterns are found in both arranged and 'love' marriages. So it seems that, regardless of the feelings of a couple towards one another at the start of a marriage and the extent to which they may know each other at this point, satisfaction, and probably sexual activity, declines as a marriage proceeds.

Sexual Difficulties

There are some who miss their steps on the path through
adolescence to adult sexuality. Some men, for instance, never
manage to bring their private solitary world of sexuality into an
intimate relationship with a woman. A common adult male
sexual pattern is to engage in sexual activities which have a
small or non-existent intimate or, indeed, social component –
sex for sex's sake – a pattern that is much rarer for women. An
obvious example of this is a common pattern of cruising for
male homosexuals which involves sex with a large number of
partners in the most impersonal way possible. Such activities,
like masturbation, hardly involve a social relationship at all. Of
course, not all homosexual relationships have this character.
Many involve long-term loving and intimate relationships. But,
very significantly, cruising is not a characteristic feature of
female lesbian activity.

There are a number of patterns of male heterosexual
relationships which share features with the cruising patterns of
homosexual men. Perhaps the most similar is 'the heavy
breather'. Probably thousands of what are usually called
nuisance phone calls are made each day in Britain by men to
women who are generally unknown to them. What the heavy
breather tries to do is to engage a woman in conversation on
the phone long enough to masturbate. Not surprisingly, there
have not been systematic studies of men who engage in this
behaviour, but there are some clinical case histories. As one
might expect, these suggest that men who make nuisance calls
tend to have rather unsatisfactory sexual relationships with
women. These are men who may have a great deal of guilt and
shame associated with sex and are very ambivalent in their
relationships with women. They both want women sexually but
are also repelled by them. They are not content to masturbate
on their own but like to engage women in their activities,
though in the most distant and anonymous way possible.
Generally these activities are explained in terms of power. Of
course, women who are the recipients of these phone calls may

feel very vulnerable and persecuted by them. However, it may not be the power that this behaviour gives to the man that he is seeking. Indeed, it seems much more likely that it is the ambivalence and powerlessness in heterosexual encounters that lead men into making nuisance phone calls. The powerlessness they feel is protected by the anonymity of the telephone.

Massage parlours provide a similar kind of sexual experience without intimacy but with a little more direct social contact with a woman. Here men are buying the services of a woman to masturbate them. While the woman may be partially or fully undressed, she does not in most circumstances have sexual intercourse with clients. Sexual intercourse would be too threatening to these clients who wish to get their sexual gratification but at a safe social distance from a woman and in a way that repeats their earlier adolescent pattern of masturbation.

A significant minority of men who buy the services of a prostitute do not seek sexual intercourse, even in this situation where it is potentially available to them. Instead, they either get the prostitute to masturbate them or masturbate in front of the prostitute. In the world of commercial sex there are many other situations that provide opportunities for men to masturbate while watching women, or films or pictures of women. While it may be true that it is cheaper for men to buy these opportunities for masturbation than it would be to pay for sexual intercourse, it is hard to believe that such services would exist on such a wide scale if these were not what some men preferred. So why then do so many men opt for masturbation in front of women rather than sexual intercourse? The obvious answer is that there are men who have not been able to move on from their adolescent experience of masturbation to satisfactory intimate sexual relationships. Many women find these forms of male behaviour degrading and suggest that this is what the men intend and what gives men their sexual pleasure. As with the example of the heavy breather, it seems unlikely that this is the usual male intention. These men are probably very little concerned with the feelings of the women whose services they buy. Indeed, it is probably just for this very reason that they buy sex, because it absolves them from any pressure to enter into an intimate relationship. It is uninvolved sex at a distance which allows the adolescent fantasies to live on as the primary object of desire.

There are many reasons why some men cannot develop their solitary adolescent sexuality into an intimate sexual relationship. Some may never overcome the shame and anxiety they associate with masturbation, while others may have too many fears of loss of autonomy to allow themselves to get close to a woman and so find sexual intercourse threatening. Relatively anonymous sex with many different partners – whether prostitutes or willing amateurs – is another way to avoid the possibility of close relationships that may be too threatening.

A related pattern is the compulsive Don Juan – the man who can never resist making a pass at any or every woman he meets. Sometimes such men are described as being addicted to sex. But the description is misleading as it is the conquest rather than the sex that they are seeking. These are men who have come to depend on sexual conquest as a way of maintaining their own self-image. Most women turn them down but the odd one who says yes makes them feel good. They have become fixed at the adolescent stage of scoring. For them sex has lost its meaning. They move on too quickly to gain intimacy through their sexual encounters, or, indeed, to find much pleasure in intercourse. All that matters to them is that a woman has been persuaded by them to say yes. Freely offered sex is of little interest to them.

Very many fewer women than men seem to find multiple partners and one-night stands very satisfactory. As Shere Hite found in the sexual histories she collected from what were probably the most sexually 'liberated' section of the American female population in the late 1970s, some women had tried relatively anonymous sex with multiple partners but, unlike men, very few persisted with such patterns for very long. Equally, there are no female equivalents of the male masturbating patterns seen in nuisance calls or in the world of commercial sex. Again, this underlines the basic divide between male and female sexuality.

The only situation where women may commonly seek forms of heterosexual contact other than intercourse is where the prohibitions against intercourse are strong, as, for example, before marriage when heavy petting avoids crossing that all-important line that preserves virginity. The other rather similar situation is in some extramarital relationships. Here, too, a line may be drawn which permits sexual activity with partners outside the marriage, providing they stop short of intercourse.

The point these examples of sexual difficulties illustrate is that men especially are all too capable of uncoupling sex and love relationships. Indeed, for some men they may never become fused. They develop patterns of social and sexual relations which permit them to find sexual pleasure in situations that avoid any close intimate relationship.

Women's most frequent problem lies in other directions, in difficulties in achieving full sexual satisfaction within intimate relationships. As women get older they are more likely to experience regular orgasms. But what is important here does not seem to be their age or the duration of their sexual relationship(s) but the amount of positive sexual experience they have had with or without a partner. Women who had one or more satisfactory sexual relationship before marriage, and particularly those who began to masturbate before or early in marriage, are the most likely to experience regular orgasms with their marital partner. Frequent changes in partners do not seem helpful to women in developing their sexuality, indicating they need time to get to know each lover. These female patterns strongly suggest that women need positive experience to learn to have regular orgasms. They need the opportunities to learn to become sexual.

Given the importance of mothers as carers of children, it might be thought that the quality of a daughter's relationship with her mother might be associated with her sexual development, but such an influence has not been found. Instead, it seems that it is the father who plays a more crucial role here.

Women who report a poor relationship with their father, or had a relationship that was interrupted during childhood by the father being away for long periods because of work or a divorce, are more likely to be among those who may find it difficult to reach orgasm regularly with an established partner. A good relationship with a father contributes to the daughter's developing sexuality in a number of ways. Daughters who have happy childhood memories of the father may feel more comfortable and less anxious in the company of other men than those whose early relationships were interrupted or fraught. A good childhood relationship may help to build a girl's self-esteem and confidence and make it easier for her to feel good about herself and her body.

The general atmosphere in the home during childhood seems also to play a role. Women who report that their parents had a good marriage, and that sex was not a taboo subject of conversation in the home, are more likely to have good sexual relationships. Not surprisingly, those who were made to feel that sex is dirty, unpleasant or simply a duty, are less likely to be sexually happy in their marriages.

Some kinds of relationships with fathers and other men in childhood may have specifically detrimental effects on a woman's sexual development. Women who have experienced sexual abuse may feel very guilty to have been the object of adult sexual attention, especially if some of the feelings they had at the time were pleasant. This guilt may then colour adult relationships in ways which are likely to impede the development of their sexuality. Turned inward, guilt may lead to feelings of shame and unworthiness, or it may be projected outward to make their feelings towards male partners particularly ambivalent. But there are many forms of sexual abuse and, depending on the child's age at the time, what happened, who the abuser was and how the experience was assimilated, the effects on later adult sexuality are quite variable. Some forms of abuse may not be experienced as sexual events at all and may leave relatively minor consequences, while others create a premature and inappropriate sexuality which then may cast a shadow over all adult relationships. This point reiterates the principle described earlier that the impact of childhood experiences depends on how they are perceived at the time. Their meaning may not be the same as it would be to an adult. Adults and children do not see sexuality in the same way, hence the need to protect children from involvement in adult sexuality.

The first relationship of mother and infant is often spoken of as the first love relationship, and may be seen as a prototype for subsequent relationships in youth and adulthood. But we have already noted that the quality of mother–child relationships does not seem to be a major determinant of female sexuality. This makes the point that the factors that shape female sexuality may be rather different than those which are important for other aspects of intimate love and relationships.

Another discontinuity that is observed in development is between attitudes towards body contact and later sexuality. Families vary widely in the extent to which their members touch each other. Some are very physical with lots of hugging and touching, in others there is little physical contact between parent and child after early childhood, if then. It is often believed that children growing up in families where there is a lot of warm physical contact are more likely to develop into adults who value and enjoy sex. However, the evidence does not support such an idea. Sexuality seems much more dependent on family attitudes to specifically sexual matters, emphasising the fact that adult sexuality is rooted in the mind. This point is linked to the one we have made earlier. Becoming sexual after adolescence involves developing a sexual identity and the means of communication about sex with a partner. While these developments are based on a whole range of childhood notions and experience, there is a break at adolescence so that sexual development does not consist simply of using childhood skills to form relationships in a new sexual mode. It is more a case of the new sexual development taking off from the base of attitudes and relationship skills that are present at adolescence. Developmental continuities through adolescence are not strong. Childhood experiences do not determine what happens in adulthood, they simply make outcomes somewhat more or less likely. Good, or bad, post-adolescent experience can completely overshadow what has happened in childhood. Very negative attitudes towards sex can be overtaken by reassuring and enjoyable sexual experiences after adolescence and – the reverse may happen – positive childhood learning can be set aside if early sexual experiences are bad. Experiences after adolescence are perhaps particularly important for women, given the relatively long period of adult life over which sexuality may develop. Among these experiences may be extramarital affairs.

4 His Affair – Her Affair: Affairs, Marriage and Gender

> I have never met a woman who experiences sexuality in this depth within a marriage of ten years or more, no matter how much passion she may feel for her husband, no matter with what empathy and precision they have come to know each other's physical needs. It was simply a different order of experience ... I have no idea how to integrate this insight with the demand for loyalty, the need for abiding relationships that must often be based on exclusivity when sexuality is involved, the destructiveness of lying to a person whom you love and live with and to whom you are unalterably committed in friendship; and yet the equally intense destruction of allowing him to live with the knowledge that you are involved passionately with someone else.
>
> Jane Lazarre, *On Loving Men*, 1981

Affairs cover a wide range. We define them as a relationship which is sexual (although not necessarily involving full intercourse) between two people, at least one of whom is married. That one or both is married is crucial. While we do not take the view that all affairs are barometers of flaws in a marriage, we do see them in relation to marriage. Consequently, in order to understand the varied phenomena we call affairs we need first to look at how people define their marriages. For the purposes of this discussion marriage includes long-term co-habitations, as the rules for these seem very much the same as for formal marriages.

While our society may not have a clear definition of what an affair means, we do have a well-defined view of the ideal marriage. It is companionate and romantic, and it stresses intimacy and togetherness. While there is a nod towards the needs of the individual, the criteria for intimacy are much better spelled out than those for autonomy. This means that there is much room for individual judgement and manœuvring when determining the boundaries between the marriage and the individual. This manœuvring includes sexual conduct. Sometimes marriages have an articulated code of sexual marital conduct but often, apart from the original marriage vows which call for monogamy, they do not. Sometimes what happens is that over time each individual in the marriage evolves his or her own code of conduct. This may change as the marriage changes, without discussion between the spouses. These codes may remain individual and private. Undisclosed and undiscovered, an affair can remain a private matter and, in theory, may never challenge a marriage. But once an affair becomes known, that private, individual process of what is permissible within marriage becomes the domain of both spouses. It poses clear questions and choices about the boundaries between autonomy and sharing for that marriage. Marriage and how it is defined is the central component in dissecting affairs. What is the experience of an affair and how does it relate to marriage?

In research, in novels, and in personal accounts of affairs we often encounter attempts to classify what is being told, and what has happened. We need this because we are confronting something shocking. Affairs fly in the face of stated convention, if not of statistically common practice. What sort of affair are we hearing about or having? Is it a one-night stand, a serious love, a deeply sexual alliance? Does it threaten the marriage? Has it been going on for a long time? How often do the lovers meet? How much of their time does it take up? Is it secret? If anyone knows, who knows? Is it in retaliation for a past affair? Does or would the spouse mind?

Each of these questions represents an attempt to classify some dimension of the situation and suggests that the answer will determine how we should think about it and how we should react to it. However, underneath these attempts to manage or understand affairs lie some very basic assumptions which do not get articulated, and which we think are perhaps the most important ones. These assumptions are ones which may help in large measure to explain the why, the how, and indeed the why not of any affair. In addition, they may help to account for the different impacts affairs may have on marriages. These are assumptions about marriage and its functions and thus about the relationship between affairs and marriage. These run deep in our thinking. They underlie all work, both clinical and research, on affairs, as well as the attempts people in affairs make to understand their individual experience. We think that in order to understand the phenomenon of affairs and marriage it is vital to unearth these basic assumptions which exist within the framework of the present-day companionate marriage which we described in chapter 1.

Although there have been attempts to classify affairs, there have been no attempts to classify the models, or views of, or expectations about marriage which precede the affairs. Nevertheless, much of what has been written or reported about affairs and marriage either explicitly or implicitly takes one of the following three views:

1 The affair is a symptom of something wrong with the marriage. This view holds that an affair is essentially indicative: if the marriage was good then there would be no need for the affair. Often the meaning of the affair is taken to indicate exactly what was wrong with the marriage. For example, if the affair is sexually satisfying, this may point to a sexual weakness in the marriage. If the affair is deeply intimate this indicates that the marriage was not intimate enough. If the affair is exciting this points to the need for the marriage to become more exciting. Most clinical work, such as marital therapy, begins with this assumption. (In chapter 6 we will look further at some of the issues raised in therapy with marriages in which there has been an affair.)

2 The affair is an enhancer to a satisfactory marriage and can even make it better; an affair does not necessarily harm marriage. This view is usually espoused by proponents of open marriage, and is often accompanied by more or less explicit

contracts. Spouses are explicitly permitted to have extramarital relationships because such relationships are assumed to be enhancing. What is enhancing for one partner in the marriage is assumed to improve the whole of the marriage. Often this position is stated in a different form: if extramarital relationships are not permitted, this would mean the marriage would be entrapping or suffocating, denying the partners' individual personal growth, thus stifling the joint enterprise of marriage since the individual would feel stifled within it.

These two views are sometimes explicitly, but usually implicitly, held by marital therapists and other clinicians, and by those doing research on extramarital relationships, and are very often present in people's own reports of their own affairs. The first is the view most prevalent in our culture.

3 There is a third view which we find surfacing in reports people give of their own extramarital relationships which is that the affair seems to have little direct relationship to the marriage itself. For many people, when they are generally assessing their lives, everything is interrelated. But some, in terms of how they define and demarcate their marital relationships and their affairs, do not experience any significant overlap, any more than they see their work lives overlapping into their marriages or friendships, or their platonic friendships into their marriages. They feel comfortable with the separation between the two and they find this separation clarifies their marriage.

Each of these views depends on an idealised notion of marriage. In the first, marriage should be for everything. Any interactions which are romantic, sexual, or overlap with marriage compete for interest, energy and time with the spouse and so encroach on what is rightfully in the marital domain.

In the second, marriage is seen as being essentially for the growth of the individual and consequently not sexually sacred or exclusive. This is the so-called 'open marriage'. Usually, however, other things are defined as exclusive. These are preserved in the implicit or explicit contract. For example, intimacy may be exclusive, so that one is not allowed to get too close with the partner in the affair. Or place may be special, so that there are injunctions about where an affair may be carried on: 'Never in our bed/house/town/in front of the neighbours'. Often, but not always, the emphasis in these marriages is on shared honesty, which is held to increase intimacy and confirms it as the central facet of what makes the marital relationship special. 'We let each other grow. We are tough enough to take our spouses having affairs because our love for the other and consequently our respect for his/her personal growth is so great.' These other aspects define the marriage and what is special about it, not sexual monogamy.

Things are not so clearly laid out in the third view. This is the situation in which at least one of the spouses has begun a process of redefining the functions of his or her marriage and the affair may help to clarify what is usefully or rightfully in the marital domain. It is a view which accepts a segmentation of marriage. It does not push marriage to be for everything. But, unlike an open marriage, the retreat from the original marital ideal is not explicit. One, or both, spouses privately adopts the segmented marriage model. The model acknowledges auto-nomy more fully than the model in which marriage is for everything. It provides a basis from which to pursue an affair. Often these are the affairs which remain undisclosed or undiscovered. If the marriage does benefit from an affair of this kind it is because the segments of the marriage which function best have been clarified.

'My husband cannot give me intimacy or intensity,' says Laura, a thirty-nine-year-old art restorer, married for nineteen years. 'My affairs do.' Laura has had three affairs, one long-term, the others brief. They have all been secret. Once she decided that it would help her to accept her husband if she sought romance and sexual excitement from other men in affairs, her marriage became markedly more stable. Benefits to a marriage such as this may accrue but they clearly depend on secrecy, an issue central to the conduct and effect of affairs.

Christina began an affair with a colleague when she had

begun a series of changes in her life: her children had both gone off to school, she had recovered from an incapacitating physical condition, and had begun to commute to London part time to re-establish herself in her old career. She began to feel free and alive again. Part of that feeling came from contact with an attractive and sympathetic colleague, with whom she eventually began an affair, who knew her in the context of her career rather than her former all-embracing context of mother and wife. She had no desire to impose her new work concerns on her husband since these had never been interests which had drawn them together. Instead, the demarcation between her career and home life evident in the geographical and daily separation between the two also existed in her emotionally. Marriage could be divided off from work. Emotions could be divided off from marriage. This revised view of her marriage evolved in silence. She did not know, nor did she risk finding out, if her husband shared her conclusions. Secrecy was her chosen strategy.

This third view arises with some frequency in the stories which appear in this book. We are not surprised, for it is our view that the double pressure that marriage be for everything, on the one hand, and that people be together for a lifetime, on the other, means that over time a large proportion of married people will feel that marriage has let them down in one respect or another. Dividing a marriage into segments – some of which work and some of which don't – is an understandable response to this experience. What is surprising is the fact that some people make the leap from the realisation that if other facets of their lives can be segmented off from their marriages so can their sexual conduct, even though this goes against marital covenant, while others who also divide their marriages into segments do not. The segmented model refers particularly to segmentation in marriage: cutting off what happens sexually outside the marriage and what happens within; affairs are not to do with the marriage.

Most marriages begin in the marriage-is-for-everything model. Unavoidably, though, they become segmented, although not, of course, necessarily in sexual matters. In every marriage couples grapple with more or less difficult negotiation points. We are referring to something more than differences in taste and whim. At various points in life something critical occurs for one member of the couple which either runs counter to the other's wishes and values or takes one spouse into a different direction, away from the other. This could be a job, or job change, a development of a new but important interest, or the addition of a member of the family through birth or a child's marriage, for instance. Changes within the members of the couple and events outside the marriage both conspire to ring changes over time in a marriage. These often result in one member of the couple spending more time and energy apart from the other. The intimacy with which the marriage begins changes. It often shifts to an intimacy which exists in certain areas, but not others. It can be a deeply satisfying one, but it is rarely, if ever, over time in a marriage, an all-encompassing one.

At each 'negotiation point' for the couple there is an increased chance that autonomy will win out over intimacy. If the marriage survives, people adapt to this process by expecting certain, rather than all, things from their spouses. There is an inevitable shift towards more autonomy as the marriage unfolds, particularly when children arrive.

In this naturally evolving fashion every marriage moves away from the marriage-is-for-everything ideal from which it starts. Ideals being ideals and not real, however, this formula still remains the one people continue to espouse, despite their reality. And just because there is increased autonomy in other areas does not mean that there is therefore permission for sexual autonomy. For when sex is involved the stakes and issues shift into a different gear.

If marriage is, in reality, over time not for everything or, at least, does not have to be fulfilling in every domain, what *are* its functions? If people are able to segment their marriages, into what segments are these falling? The answers to these questions, as we shall see, begin to suggest some categories of affairs.

Segmenting Marriage: the Four Dimensions of Marriage

It seems reasonable to divide the experience of marriage into four dimensions. These are the public, the practical, the emotional and the sexual. By these we mean the following:

1 The public dimension refers to the roles the spouses act in their joint social life and the ease and enjoyment with which the couple and family participate in the social world. For example, Tessa and Craig are very involved both with their children's school and in politics. They are seen, and experience themselves, as a couple who work well and in sympathy with each other in the organisational and social functions these two activities demand. The social dimension of a marriage may be a most fulfilling and important one for a couple or it can be very empty. Or it may not be very important to a couple to share an intense and full social life.

Laura, the art restorer, came to expect, especially in the days when her children were small, that most of her social life would be lived in the company of women and children. As the children grew up and she returned to work, her social life began to be consumed by colleagues. Her husband, a solitary man in contrast to Laura's gregariousness, shied away from this world. He participates little in her social life but she is not troubled by this. Indeed, she relishes the freedom his withdrawal brings.

2 The practical dimension encompasses domestic and daily activities which demand the couple's co-operation. For instance, Craig and Tessa comfortably apportion childcare, cleaning, cooking, and bill-paying. Unlike many couples, each feels deeply supported by the other in the running of family life. Again, the organisational aspects of a shared domestic life can be supportive or obstructive in a couple's life together. Or it can be a non-issue. Some women, for instance, may take over

domestic organisation, while their husbands assume financial responsibilities, with neither ructions, nor resentment.

3 The emotional dimension embraces empathy, friendship, support, shared interests and values as well as understanding and ease of communication, especially of feelings, values and deep interests and the degree of intellectual rapport and stimulation a couple experiences together. Tessa, for example, feels like she is, 'Talking Greek to Craig when I mention things which interest me. He just doesn't get it. Sometimes he doesn't even understand the words I use.' But in contrast, Michael, a middle-aged father of three tells 'everything to Jennie [his wife]'. She is his 'best friend'. And Jennie concurs: 'There is nothing I keep from him. His perspective is always useful and interesting.' They share many, if not all, interests, including gardening, walking, swimming, novels, the same films and food. Indeed, this couple feels, at this point in their lives, very fortunate in feeling satisfied not only on this dimension of marriage, but also the other three. This has not always been the case, for a few years ago Jennie felt almost abandoned by Michael, left out of his life in favour of his work, and diminished by his relative lack of interest in their three children's development. Their marriage demonstrates the point about the evolution of any given marriage. The quality of their relationship has improved in every dimension as their children have grown and as Michael has become less anxious about his career. There is now both more overlap of interest and time together to develop their capacity for deeper friendship.

4 The sexual dimension refers to sexual satisfaction, to the pleasure, excitement, freedom and interest which a couple experiences together sexually. Tessa, for instance, would rate her happiness with this as low, while rating her happiness with the public and practical dimensions very highly. As we shall see, the sexual dimension, and the emotional one, are particularly subject to changes and fluctuations over time in a marriage. But, in contrast, Nicholas and Debbie had an embattled, fourteen-year marriage which ended in divorce. Yet for them

sex was always fulfilling, interesting and pleasurable. Again there is a wide range in both satisfaction with and the importance of the sexual dimension in marriage.

One member of a couple may feel more or less happy with each of these dimensions, while the other may not. In addition, the satisfaction and comfort levels with each may fluctuate over the life cycle of the marriage. Craig is reasonably happy with both sex and the level of intimacy in his marriage, while Tessa is not. Yet earlier in the marriage she was happier with sex and also was more tolerant of the gaps in their mutual understanding.

For many, not being content with one aspect of a marriage does not mean that they will look for satisfaction from an affair. But for others discontent is either the motivation for beginning an affair or the glue which ensures its continuation. Yet these people may feel very devoted to their marriages, because they are happy in its other dimensions. Tessa has always got emotional sustenance primarily from her friends and colleagues. Sex has fluctuated in importance for her and, in any case, she and Craig have been at least moderately compatible with each other. But recently she started an affair with a colleague. Despite her passion for her lover she remains attached to Craig and deeply sustained by the smooth and supportive public and practical functioning of their marriage.

Segmenting Affairs: the Four Dimensions of Affairs

If marriages can be segmented in this way, so can affairs. While, potentially, any affair may be important on these same four dimensions, some dimension may not be present in the affair or else might not be very salient. Most people, for instance, put boundaries around their affairs to ensure that there is no public dimension at all. This is critical in a secret affair but, even in open marriages, most people try to conduct their affairs with more than a little discretion, hiding them at least partly from the public eye. Clearly, in an affair there is a

sexual dimension, but this may not be its most crucial characteristic (at least for the people in the affair). Similarly, the
emotional dimension of an affair may be more or less important
or satisfactory. For Tessa, both of these dimensions were
extremely important and satisfying. In contrast, Annie's first
affair was very sexual but emotionally cool, while David's affair
on a business trip was sexually satisfying and emotionally hot
only during the affair's duration.

Within the boundaries of secrecy, if an affair endures it must
develop a satisfactory practical dimension. Sometimes affairs
also develop public ones. Any affair of some length has its own
rules, customs and habits which are like oil to its engine, and
are more or less satisfying to the participants. In the context of
these rules, the affair develops a practical side. For instance, it
became customary for Annie to cook a simple meal for her first
lover; she also occasionally washed some of his socks. Such
customs, and other habits, both in bed and out, such as a light,
jokey style of communicating, and rules over what could be
mentioned and not, evolved. These both sustained and defined
their affair. These rules, habits and customs enhanced the
practical ease with which the affair could be conducted; indeed,
it endured for a number of years. The public aspect of an
affair, even when secret, can also help to maintain it. Jessica
and Daniel, because they are in the same academic field, were
often together as colleagues, arguing over fine points, contributing to each other's seminars and lectures and responding to
each other's papers. This public face, that of stimulating
colleagues, was enriching, contributing to their passion. Indeed,
the secret lent an additional frisson: their affair was the
forbidden, being played out almost, but not quite, publicly.

In unusual cases, however, affairs have both public and
practical dimensions. Cathy and Bruce are a case in point.
Affairs conducted between colleagues and workmates can more
easily encompass these other dimensions and still remain
secret, as theirs did. Cathy was Bill's administrative assistant,
hence the line between lending professional and personal
administrative assistance blurred easily. Along with Bruce's

professional appointments Cathy also made his and his children's social, medical and dental ones. While she dropped off work for him, she also ferried his children around town. When they went on professional conferences they also took vacations. Along with her professional salary, Bruce also helped her out with her mortgage as well as other occasional personal expenses. Their public lives and the practical logistics of running these lives easily meshed and crossed the boundaries between the professional and private. They were a good team on all four dimensions.

His Affair and Her Affair

In addition to the underlying assumptions about marriage which lie behind our thinking and conduct in affairs, there is another fundamental aspect: the gender of the person having the affair. We all make assumptions about ways in which being a man or woman inform both our experience and our expectations of sex, as we saw in chapters 2 and 3. Broadly these assumptions may be thought of in these ways:

1 One view says that men and women have different sexual needs. The assumption here is that women are more likely to be faithful, and are, because for them love and sex are inextricably bound. An example of this is the case of Ron and Norma. Ron was consumed by jealousy of an affair Norma had had in the distant past. He presumed Norma had been in love with the other man; his jealousy of her love for him was all-consuming. Yet if Norma had denied loving him (which, in private she had done), she would have been even more damned. For as they were both Irish-Catholic, working-class people, Norma's having a sexual relationship with a man she did not love was too unseemly and terrible: good Catholic women, especially if they are mothers, simply do not have sex for the pleasure of the experience.

2 Another claim is that women are becoming more like men, or that sex for women has become masculinised. This idea tries

to explain the results of recent surveys which show that women now are having almost as many affairs as men and, unlike in the recent past, are reporting that love and sex are not, in fact, inextricably linked for them.

3 As we have argued, there are male/female differences from the beginning. These differences emerge in men's and women's different expectations in relationships. Men and women also behave differently. Just because women may be having more affairs than before does not mean they are behaving more like men. Just because they tend to become emotionally involved does not mean they equate sex with love. In affairs as in other relationships women and men are different, but these differences are more subtle than the first view, above, would have it.

It is this third view which we adopt in this book. It is one of our aims to make the case that men and women are acting differently in affairs, even if they are beginning to have affairs with comparable frequency. We do not believe that women's experience of sex has been masculinised. Women still show different attitudes and behaviour in many areas connected to their marital affairs.

The difference between David, the husband of Ursula (whom we met in the introduction), and Annie, in the way they thought about the effect of their behaviour on their marriages and their affair partners, tells much about differences between men and women. David was surprised when one of his affair partners showed that she felt angry and rejected after their two-week affair during a business trip was ended by him on their return. She had expected some follow-up, some word from him, some indication from him that he still thought about her. 'She knew I was married,' he countered, surprised by the ferocity of her reaction. He had thought that she had understood what he had understood about the implicit boundaries to their affair. In contrast, Annie made everything as clear as possible to her first lover before they began their affair: she was married, would not leave her husband, had a child, could not spend much time with him, and was that all right with him? Both these people talk of these affairs as bounded, not about love, but more about pleasure, sensuality, and self-exploration. The gender-role differences are consistent. Men and women do not operate according to the same principles: they construct the situation differently with different strategies to maintain the marriage and the affair; and they act and judge themselves along different dimensions in their attempts to maintain their own views of themselves. This clearly emerges when men and women give accounts of how they have conducted their marital affairs, and underscores once more the basic differences between the sexes. Annie felt she had done the honourable thing as a woman by being completely open about what she could give and what she could not. She was taking care of her lover, as well as herself and the others potentially involved, as a good woman should. David, in contrast, assumed a grown-up, smart, and mature woman would be able to take care of herself and read the signs for herself just as he would have done. From their respective points of view, each behaved responsibly, using mature judgement.

Men and women use different moral reasoning, and different criteria are attached to what they report themselves doing. There are male and female filters through which each makes sense of their experience. These views of themselves reflect moral thinking processes which Carol Gilligan has described as coming as if from a 'different voice'. The voices emerging in these accounts are indeed distinctly either male or female.

In the next chapter we will take up the questions of who is likely to have an affair, the when and why, and what sorts of affairs people have. First we turn to a consideration of some additional issues which illuminate the experience of affairs: the place in them of sexuality, of intimacy, of risk-taking, and of jealousy, possessiveness and guilt. Secrecy is central. In this chapter we want to consider its significance in the affair itself, while in subsequent chapters we will look at its impact on marriages.

Affairs and Sex

For most people marriage is still the crucible in which they learn most about sex. Marriage is the supposedly sacred vessel in which to have it. Mostly within it, though increasingly before it, boys grow into men who learn to link their intimate feelings to their sexual ones and girls into women with sensual appetites in addition to their need to be close to and loved by somebody. But obviously sex occurs outside marriages, for there are many affairs. Sex is a pivotal aspect of affairs and is central to our definition of them. For most married couples, if sex is not involved in outside relationships, however intense, with the opposite sex, they do not feel threatened. Such relationships are usually permitted, while sexual ones are not.

In the sixteen-year marriage of Bruce and Kay, Bruce's five-year affair with Cathy, who was his administrative assistant, was tolerated because Kay believed that their relationship was platonic. She went further – she appreciated it, because Cathy also helped her out, ferrying her children to and from school, making appointments for them, and helping her with typing. She welcomed Cathy's connection with her family, despite the fact that Bruce spent more time with Cathy than with her; and that her children seemed as much at ease and as affectionate with Cathy as with herself. She accepted that Bruce went away with Cathy on ski holidays and that they spent many hours during weekends playing tennis or swimming together. In other words, the other woman was as, if not more, intimate in most ways than she was with her own husband. Yet as long as Kay was assured by Bruce that 'There is nothing sexual to my relationship with Cathy,' she allowed Bruce and Cathy all the time together they wanted.

The revelation of outside sexual relationships has profound effects on all marriages except the few open ones. This can be so even if the sex is perfunctory, unsatisfactory and short-lived, although the briefness or dissatisfaction with it are often offered by the spouse as mitigating factors for the affair. The sexual element of the affair can be more or less important. But whatever the importance or delight in the sexual aspect of the affair, if there is sex its revelation is a wound to the marriage.

Why should this be so? More, why should it be the sexual, more often than any of the other three dimensions of marriage, which seems to be the point of betrayal? In chapter 1 we discussed some of the historically based reasons for this: how the patriarchal roles of the Victorian marriage have been replaced by a marriage founded on intimate friendship and companionship, for which other intimacies have become more threatening. And how many more close relationships, including those before marriage, have become sexual, so that there is a greater need to assert that a marriage is unlike any other relationship. The result is a marriage contract which, initially at least, places more emphasis on the sexual fidelity of the spouses than was perhaps true a generation ago. You can be friendly with, spend time with, harbour and even display special feelings towards, share money with and even live under the same roof with others. But you cannot have sex with them, or so says the modern marriage contract. Therefore, to have sex outside marriage is to break that covenant and to call into question the very basis of present-day marriage.

All marriages evolve implicit additional rules for their basis. These begin, as Annette Lawson has shown in her research, with the ideal that 'marriage is for everything'. What is supposed to be special to the marriage is everything within all the four domains, the public, practical, emotional and sexual. But, of course, other people cross into these domains over the years of marriage, encroaching on that specialness. Cathy took over all of Kay's domains in Bruce's life, sharing them with Kay. In Tessa's marriage, there have always been others, both men and women, who have been more emotionally satisfying, closer to her in understanding, than her husband Craig. In Laura's life, her husband has never had a special place in either the public or practical dimensions of their marriage. Instead, various friends and lovers have taken what she at first expected would be his place. People apparently make adjustments in their view of what is special about their marriage. For Tessa, the public

and practical dimensions of her marriage are what are sacro-
sanct. If another woman took over her role in family outings,
upset the smooth functioning of their domestic partnership, or
took her place in their social circle she would feel hurt and
jealous. Craig, it must be said, does not share her marital
assessment, and for him, knowledge of her affair would be
extremely painful because, for him, marital sex is still sacred.

The redefinitions these people have made of what is sacred
to their marriages are not, though, the common currency of
what defines marriage. The common definition of the boundaries of marriage, in which sex with another is forbidden, is the
one on which we tend to fall back – especially if we are the one
whose spouse has had the affair. Redefining that boundary of
marriage is uncharted territory, apart from the few who tried to
do so in the wave of open marriages in the late 1960s and early
1970s. But in these redefinitions questions persist: if one
redefines marriage as most special in its public or practical or
emotional functions, how does one describe what, in particular,
sets it apart from other relationships which are also public,
emotional and practical? Degree? Amount? Types of shared
activities? Or simply sharing the same household? How do you
present this specialness to the world if you publicly remove the
exclusive sexual bond the world supposes? In other words,
marriage covenants which forbid affairs have a special hold
because they are clear. In an unequivocal way they state exactly
how one is special to one's spouse. Insecurity, possessiveness
and a sense of betrayal almost always accompany the revelation
or discovery of an affair. That insecurity arises in large measure
because someone else has usurped the supposedly unique
sexual role. The sense of betrayal is also about the secrecy and
accompanying concealment and dishonesty which often are
necessary for the conduct of affairs, but it is at root appreciated
as the betrayal of the marital vow of monogamy. The possessiveness also stems from the indignation over someone else taking
what is clearly stated to be one's own rightful place, in one's
very own bed.

Moreover, men's sexuality, as we have seen, may predispose

them to seeking variety through sex rather than intimacy. As we have seen, both sexual satisfaction and intimacy fluctuate over the course of a marriage. So there may be points when men may be vulnerable to having affairs. They have a natural capacity to segment, or cut off. They may believe it is perfectly possible to conduct an affair which does not get in the way of other aspects, which are special to their marriages, apart from sex.

Women may be drawn to affairs, thinking that affairs would not necessarily destroy marriage because, in the sexual learning they have acquired, they have learned about the separate worlds of the sensual and the emotional. Paradoxically, they have learned about this split in those marriages which might be the very windows through which they can adopt the view that a marriage can be segmented. Again, given the fluctuations over time in satisfaction in marriage, they may also think that they can get something from an affair which is different from what they are getting in their marriages, and that this can be obtained without destroying their marriages. Tessa is a case in point: she claims that she has a strong marriage, even though she is having an affair.

However, given the fundamental expectations that marriage will be monogamous, intimate and honest, secret affairs, if discovered, will result in insecurity, guilt, betrayal and jealousy. Sex is central to affairs, in part because it is central to the potential reaction of one's spouse on discovery. To expect otherwise is naive.

The Tie That Binds: Secrecy, the Forbidden and Excitement

Most affairs are, and remain, secret. This is because there are very few open marriages, while the segmented and marriage-is-for-everything models promote clandestine affairs. The prevailing view of affairs as detrimental to marriage, even morally abhorrent, dictates that most people do not reveal them. Secrecy is at the centre of most affairs, yet honesty is supposed to be at the centre of most marriages. In chapter 6 we will indicate some of the ways in which secrecy about affairs can be damaging to marriages, particularly when secret affairs are revealed. When they are revealed, if not already over, affairs will often end. (In chapter 7 we will return to this theme.) This is in addition to the ending of some marriages. Yet the secrecy itself might be part of the sustaining power of affairs. Ironically, it seems that secrecy can be central to both an affair's life and its death.

The risk of exposure can be central to an affair's excitement. Doing something illicit or forbidden is part of what sex is supposed to be about, or at least that message often lurks behind our sexual development. Behind closed doors, in the back seats of cars, after dark, and in husky whispers, these all speak to the forbiddenness of sex. Even marital sex is hidden from children, grandparents and the neighbours.

The forbidden is frustrating but it is also exciting. In adolescence, when we endure countless constraints from society and our families on our having sex, foreplay, petting and the lead-up to penetration can be among life's most exciting sexual experiences, even while intercourse itself may be unsatisfactory. Memories of groping in back seats or in bedrooms while keeping an ear out for parental footsteps are memories of often frustrating but exciting times. There is none of that in marriage. Sex in marriage may be emotional and intimate and become technically satisfying. But it is familiar and it is not forbidden. As we argued in chapter 3, familiarity can in time breed sexual stagnation. Affairs introduce once again the frisson of adolescent, forbidden sex, sex done behind someone's back. It is no longer a parent's back which must be watched but that of a spouse. It can in this sense be revitalizing and extremely exciting.

In addition, the risk of exposure can fill assignations with both urgency and shared complicity which heighten sexuality. Sharing secrets can be binding. The thrill of the secret and the sharing of it can itself lift an affair in importance. In discussing an affair she had with one of the contractors who was working with her on a house she was decorating, Susannah, a successful interior designer, talked about how she and her affair partner conducted themselves with perfect professional aplomb in front of their work colleagues. This enhanced the sexiness of their affair: they had a shared secret put over on everyone else. Moreover, they had to 'wait until the coast was clear' to show their feelings for each other, and the waiting heightened the excitement. Feeling 'naughty' about this also made sex more playful. Feeling complicit in something which was hidden both from spouses and also co-workers bound this couple even more tightly.

Illicit affairs can also be dramatic, especially if there are signs that exposure might be near. The threat of exposure, or a brush with it, might begin the end of an affair, or at least lead it into a more anguished phase in which partners consider whether or not to end it. In this same affair Susannah came close to exposure. Her husband suspected that someone else had been in his house while he had been away on business. He began to badger her, scrutinising her for signs to confirm or dispel his suspicions. At the risk of exposure Susannah hastened to cool her affair, but this only made her lover more persistent. The affair went through a phase of dramatic endings and reunions. Finally, in desperation, her lover sent a supposedly anonymous note to her, pretending that it was from a third party, threatening to tell her husband about the affair if she did not consent to another assignation with him. Up until then, in this ending phase, their reunions had been bittersweet, tinged by an urgency that this might be their last meeting. When she received the letter Susannah felt as if she had been thrown into a cold shower. The affair was over for her, the thrill of the game gone as she realised how deadly serious it had become.

If in marriage everything is to be shared, this one thing which must never be can assume a particular sweetness: it is mine, not yours. This was a subtle attraction of Christina's first affair. Cooped up in her house for far too long, while her husband streaked ahead professionally and, in general, seemed far more competent than she, Christina was desperate to create something of her own. In addition to her newly formed small toehold in the dance world, she had her affair. Its secrecy was imperative not just for her marital survival but also for her own self-importance: it was hers, nothing to do with her husband.

The very secrecy which itself breeds guilt, then, can be the very thing which keeps an affair exciting, important and which binds its partners together. In that sense, in secret affairs, the secrecy itself may be the very heart of them.

The Other Side of Secrecy: Guilt

There are gender differences in secrecy. The pressure to keep silent is great for both men and women, but women find it more difficult to split off or segment their feelings. The pressure in them to tell comes in part because they have a harder time putting thoughts and feelings about their affairs away than men do.

There are also gender differences in guilt. Both men and women feel guilty about affairs. But again, men, more able to segment their emotional life, are more able to cut off from this guilt. Women increasingly try to control their guilt by bounding their affairs. But just as men have learned to cut off more easily, because of their development women have difficulty splitting off their emotions. Another source of the gender difference is, as we have noted, the double standard which still operates, if somewhat modified from a generation ago. Sexual women are still wanton, while sexual men are potent. As a result men are less likely to forgive their wives when affairs are revealed than women their husbands. Women's advice columns cry out for patience, advising women to go along to the local Relate office to discover why their husbands have had affairs and to use the experience to heal their marriages. The different responses of men and women are of course consistent with the developmental differences to which we have referred through-out this book. A man acts; his wife's lover, as competitor, must be eliminated. Action must be taken to eliminate the competition. If the competition has usurped his role too completely the wife herself has to go. A woman, in contrast, nurses, picks apart and embraces her own, as well as others', feelings. She considers the common good, the feelings and fortunes of the family and of her spouse. She does not act precipitately. She still follows the advice of the columns and stays. Partly because of this, women are the ones more likely to be divorced if their affairs are discovered, while men are more likely to remain in their marriages. In addition, women may also feel more guilty than men if affairs are revealed, because of the pain and emotional mess they have caused. While no one is supposed to cause distress, women are supposed to be emotional protectors, not purveyors of pain.

Open marriages circumvent guilt if affairs stick within the marital contract. In segmented marriages guilt may be reduced: people often feel justified in pursuing something which they think they are not getting from their marriages, especially if they feel they have tried but failed to do so. The problem with this model, however, is that the decision to limit the marriage is one-sided. It thereby goes against the spirit of openness and intimacy which are prevailing assumptions behind most marriages. Guilt then arises around the fact that there is both secrecy about the affair and the private recasting of the marriage as a limited business. As she says in chapter 6, Susannah's husband would not 'fit into the box' she needed. He could not become more demonstrative or passionate, so Susannah decided that after years of trying to make him fit it was better to accept the limitations of her marriage and to satisfy herself elsewhere. Susannah feels slightly guilty that she reached this decision without consulting her husband. But most of her guilt stems from his imagined pain were she to be discovered. As long as her affairs remain secret she shields herself to a large extent from guilt. Secrecy protects her from guilt as well as her husband from pain. In the marriage-is-for-everything model people feel guilty as they conduct their affairs, as we shall see Simon felt about his, in chapter 6. In this model people are cheating on the marriage as they would like it to be; they have not given up on it. For them marriage is not limited. Therefore they are draining energy, time and attention, and sometimes other shared resources such as money, from it.

Laura, an art restorer, has a segmented marriage. Guilt is not a strong component of her affairs. Yet it is an issue which she faces when contemplating exposure. Exposure or discovery breed guilt. At that point Laura would feel like a 'scarlet woman' who had betrayed her marriage. Richard and Polly are in a marriage-is-for-everything marriage. After exposure of Richard's affair guilt has overwhelmed Polly and Richard's marriage. Richard is repentant, Polly accusatory, her children her accomplices. Richard is an outcast and the marriage continues to be drained by the affair.

Guilt may also surface when other matters, apart from the marriage, suffer as a result of either a preoccupation with or a diversion of energy to the affair. Children or work are the chief areas which can provoke guilt of this sort. Christina began to be afraid that she was not giving enough time to her children, partly because she kept adjusting her schedule to accommodate her affair. Nick, an academic and father of young sons, began to feel that his work was being neglected when his lover, with whom he had had a child, began to make unpredictable and increasing demands on him. Guilt about how his work was suffering, among other things, helped him to end the affair.

Guilt operates for both men and women as a pressure to disclose and to keep silent. Guilt seeks relief; it is a terrifically uncomfortable burden to bear. And quite mistakenly many think that confession to the spouse will bring about this relief. When there is a secret affair guilt is always around, consciously or not, in all but open marriages. The pressure to tell is from the imagined relief of confession, the pressure to remain silent from the imagined consequences. In chapter 6 we will focus on the various consequences for marriage of confessing a secret affair, keeping silent about it, or having a secret affair discovered.

Affairs: Putting the Marriage at Risk?

Clearly there are risks to a marriage in having affairs. When we interviewed people in the course of preparing this book we had an idea that people in affairs were risk-takers, compared to people who did not have affairs. Risk-taking could be pathological, non-pathological, a conscious impulse or an unconscious one. It seemed a possible framework into which we could fit people who had affairs. However, while it is true that affairs do represent risk-taking, we have found that a lot of people in affairs do not, at the time at least, see themselves as taking great risks. They often deny risk-taking, while also acknowledging that they are not playing entirely safely with their marriages (otherwise they would not be so secretive). They tend to acknowledge the full extent of the dangers before they begin affairs, and afterwards when they look back on them. As Annie, who had affairs when both her children reached eight months old, respectively, and whose marriage finally ended with a third one, said, 'I didn't really think about all the risks, the effects on my husband, all of that. No. I don't think I could have carried on if I had. *Now* I think back [on the affairs] and I just can't *believe* what I did, the chances I took.' She is in her second marriage now. 'Now I would never do that. Never. I am fully aware of the risks and I would never take the chance and do that to Jonathan [her present husband].' Melissa, whose affair with a mutual friend of both hers and her husband's made her 'cheerful', and consequently a 'better mother' said that, although her husband eventually knew about the affair, she was not aware at the time of the emotional risks she was taking. Indeed, despite herself, she did become preoccupied with the affair and she feels, looking back, that she made her husband suffer even though he appeared stoic throughout. To have subjected him to that pain was risky. In retrospect, she questions her wisdom in having the affair.

Similarly, before they have affairs, in the stage of contemplating them, people are often aware of risks. It is like contemplating going off the high diving board, being acutely aware that to take the plunge involves a number of near escapes, potential disasters, so perhaps one should just climb down safely and not take the plunge. Rita, a thirty-five-year-old mother of two, a doctor and writer, described her near-plunge: 'I was in

Boston, visiting relatives, when the nephew of one of their friends also came into town, and was staying with them too. It was amazing – we were so alike, as soon as we began to talk, we found an immediate connection – an immediacy I have never felt with Donald (her husband of ten years). We even looked alike! On our last night there together we went out for a drink and ended up telling each other what we both felt. We kissed but then stopped. Then I had to really pull back – I just couldn't do it. Threatening my marriage, the stability of my life, my kids' lives – and I do love Donald – I just couldn't.' She went back to Birmingham the next day. She still thinks about this other man, especially when she and Donald have their difficult and distant times. But she did not take the plunge. Instead she saw the dangers and 'climbed back down again'.

This notion of risk-taking, to distinguish those who have affairs from those who do not, is also complicated by the fact that although people do see themselves, after the event, as having taken risks with their marriages by having affairs, others who did not have affairs, looking back over crisis periods in marriage, saw staying in their difficult marriages as having been risky. Theirs is the risk of staying in what could and sometimes does become a dead and often painful marriage. However, those who have secret affairs are, undeniably, taking a kind of risk with the survival of their marriages, especially should the secret emerge, which those who stay, even in troubled marriages, are not. It is a different kind of risk, that of having rocked the boat, actively doing something to change the status quo, the risk associated with any change. Because the affair is secret, it also puts at risk the implicit trust that the marriage is monogamous, and hence trust in the marriage itself.

One folk notion is that this risk-taking is akin to dare-devil stunts; the risk itself gives meaning and staying power to the affair. There may be something in this idea. During the height of the affair the negative accompaniments to risk-taking, such as anxiety, guilt, insecurity and loss of predictability, do seem to become submerged. Positive aspects of risk, excitement, thrill, the headiness of unpredictability, are paramount. These are often decisive for continuing what is indeed risky. When these are paramount, the affair has a life and energy of its own.

Sam talked about the thrill of breaking through constraints to phone Ellen, his old high-school girlfriend. It is like the thrill of safely completing an obstacle course. Moreover, the anticipation of meeting, the plotting to arrange contact, gave the affair an extra shared dimension. The sheer time and thought devoted to the execution and operation of an affair adds to its impact, as does the thrill of successfully negotiating risky courses and solving tricky puzzles. The person having a secret affair has to be thinking about it an inordinate amount since its logistics require so much time and energy – how to meet, when to do so, how to conceal the meetings or contact. Such expenditure of effort, coupled with anxiety, means there is an attention to the affair often out of proportion to the feelings it inspires. Such time and attention themselves can lead to an exaggeration of a person's feelings about the affair: 'If I am prepared to spend this much time and energy then I must feel a lot or it must be important.' Or, alternatively, it can lead to an affirmation of the affair, following such inevitable questions as, 'Do I really want to spend all this time and energy arranging, concealing, worrying? Perhaps I should give this up.' And should there be an affirmation of the affair's importance, the commitment to it becomes strengthened.

But when an affair begins to end, the negative feelings attached to the risk begin to dominate. In this period a person feels the endangerment to the marriage, the acknowledgment that secrecy from the spouse is a betrayal, and the accompanying guilt and shame. This is the time when a person often most feels guilt or shame, for earlier the thrill has acted like a shield against them. When Christina's second affair began to end, because her affair partner was threatening to tell his wife and so to end its secrecy, she had to question whether she could continue 'bending her life out of shape' to carry on seeing him. Its threatened publicity forced her to face the effect on her husband and children of her affair. The confrontation yielded

enormous guilt and shame. Instead of affirming her commitment to the affair, she committed herself anew to her husband
and to family life. The thrill, lost, felt like danger now.
Confronting her marriage's endangerment helped her to end
her affair.

The risks stem from several sources. If the affair is secret,
the stability of the marriage usually depends on that secrecy
being maintained. However, since an affair always involves two
people, the secrecy is not under any one person's control. It
could be revealed through the affair partner, or through his or
her network, either wittingly or unwittingly. It could be revealed
through discovery by a third party. Linda, for instance, found
herself quickly having to invent an elaborate and scarcely
believable story to cover up a lie. She had told her husband,
John, that she had been with college friends on a day she had
spent with her lover, Jim. However, their neighbour subsequently made a casual reference to having seen Linda and
Jim together on the day in question. Stories of this sort are
legion. Often the attempts to salvage things through invention
such as Linda's do not succeed. Partners have to meet to
conduct their affair, so all affairs have a public aspect which
means that secrecy is never complete. Similarly, any evidence,
for example credit cards, diary entries, letters, phone bills with
records of individual calls, can lead to the discovery of the
secret. In Nora Ephron's *Heartburn*, is discovery of this sort
(evidence through credit card and phone bills, and diary entries
among other revelations) which confirms the wife's suspicion
that her husband is having an affair, and this leads to the end
of their marriage.

But there are other sources of risk: the change in attitudes
and goals through the transforming emotional and sexual
experience an affair can provide. Even when both people feel
they know what they want from the affair, and are determined
to bound and control the experience so that it does not interact
with their marriage(s), sometimes the experience overwhelms
them. It goes out of control, leading to outcomes neither
wanted in the beginning. This is plain in the case of Jessica and

Daniel. They had been lovers in graduate school; Daniel was at that time married, but in the process of leaving his wife. They had an intense, romantic and deeply satisfying sexual relationship, which ended abruptly when Daniel got cold feet and left, with Jessica devastated. Both went on to marry, in Daniel's case for a second time, and to have two children each. Fifteen years later they met again, since Daniel now had a job in Jessica's field, and had moved to a nearby town. Professionally, they now had frequent legitimate reasons to meet. Both marriages were relatively stable, although Jessica's sexual relationship was unsatisfactory and she and her husband were rather distant with each other. Daniel and Jessica began to see each other with no thought of leaving their marriages. Their occasional professional contacts led to more frequent social ones. Jessica's conscious agenda was to heal old wounds; Daniel's was to absolve himself of guilt. Jessica's unconscious agenda was to reclaim her lost love and this, with the wisdom of retrospect, seems to describe Daniel's as well. In a few months they became lovers, as excitingly as before. Each tried to contain the relationship by labelling it as something special and extra to their marriages. Within a few months, however, Jessica's marriage was over (her husband had also recently begun an affair and wanted to end their marriage) and Daniel's was faltering. Neither wanted to keep to the boundaries of something extra; both had come to resent the intrusions to their relationship which their spouses represented.

Sometimes the risk of discovery comes from the spouse's reactions to the changes in the person having the affair. When Richard and Polly had been married twelve years, Richard began an affair with a co-worker. Richard and Polly had had two children, born eighteen months apart shortly after getting married. When the children were born Richard was pursuing his dental studies. The children became Polly's sphere, while Richard increasingly lived on the fringe of family life: he provided economic security, while spending very little time with his family. Nevertheless, his presence was expected and regular at particular times. He was, for instance, around on weekends, and he did not leave for work before the children went off to school. Polly tolerated his minimal involvement, as long as he stuck to familiar routines – helping out in the mornings and being there for weekend activities. However, when Richard began his affair, he also began to break these routines. Occasionally, he would leave earlier than usual. Sometimes he would not be home for portions of the weekends; once he missed a weekend altogether. Sometimes he would work later than he had before, and sometimes he would be away for work. During his affair, he stretched the already tightly constructed limits of his family participation so that Polly could not tolerate his stretching them any further. These changes stemming from his affair provoked Polly to challenge him to be more involved with his family, even to a greater involvement than that before his affair. In fact, her challenge precipitated Richard's confession of the affair, and a crisis in their marriage. Even now, four years after the affair ended, they have still not recovered from their marital crisis; it is not clear whether they will, indeed, remain married, even though the affair is now long over.

Sometimes the risk to a marriage comes from the fact that the experiences in the affair lead to a different expectation of marriage, and changed demands on the spouse. The difficulty is that these changes come about unilaterally; the other spouse has not undergone the same redefinition of the marriage. Since marriages have many aspects, any given marriage can be redefined as needing strengthening in any number of areas.

When Linda got so much talking, understanding, readily demonstrated desire and appreciation from her affair partner Jim, she no longer felt she could tolerate her husband John's taciturnity, his infrequent praising of her or the fact that he almost never told her that he desired her. However, when Linda began to ask for more – more talking, more praising, more telling her that he wanted her – he responded with, 'What we have is normal. Men aren't like that.' Linda could not counter with, 'Yes, they are. I know one who is,' much as she wished she could. This couple was able to renegotiate their marriage, with the help of a marital therapist, and without John ever discovering Linda's affair. However, there are many couples whose marriages have ended. A fuller discussion of this will appear in chapters 6 and 7 when we talk about the effects affairs can have. The point here is that affairs can provoke changes in people – in the way they feel about themselves, in the way they conduct themselves in their marriages, in the way they feel about marriage and in the way they feel about their spouses. These changes may pose risks to their marriages.

Affairs and Intimacy

Clearly, many people derive a good deal of intimacy and emotional sustenance from their affairs. The case of Linda and Jim is a case in point. Linda had become distant from her husband, especially after she became a mother. John, her husband, is a person comfortable on his own; whole days could pass without more than a few words exchanged between them, and John would not have noticed. But Linda did, and felt increasingly unhappy and lonely. When she began her affair with Jim she felt a deep empathy, appreciation, vitality and mutual desire to be in each other's company. Jim was warm, funny and compassionate. Linda spent most of her free time with Jim, losing touch with many of her friends in the process. She had never felt so deeply in love, emotionally safe and happy as when she was with Jim. Clearly this affair, despite its intensely painful aftermath, as we shall relate later, brought with it for Linda huge emotional rewards. However, it is not only when there is a felt deficit in marital intimacy that affairs can have such emotional impact. Christina's first affair gave her a new type of appreciation, friendship and shared interests. She acknowledges that this coexisted with another set of activities, interests and common values shared with her husband.

As we have already noted, those people who operate with segmented models of marriages are those for whom marriage has some limits. We do not want to convey the feeling that an affair for them is without losses or difficulty apart from the obvious one of risks to the survival of the marriage. Sam perhaps encapsulated some of this when he stated that each time that he has had to conceal something about his affairs from his wife he feels sad. This is especially so in the beginning of an affair, with the first concealments, and when one is affected, emotionally, by the affair partner, or by things which happen in the affair, but one cannot, obviously, tell one's spouse. For Sam, who on the surface seems to accept that he is not going to be monogamous in his marriage, this conceal-ment feels sad, for it simultaneously shows and increases the distance between him and his wife. Each letter stuffed into his briefcase, each surreptitious telephone call breeds more dis-tance, and further walls-of-intimacy. When his parents died, he shared his deepest pain with his lover; he never knew whether it might have been better to have done so with his wife. Yet their intimacy was by then already limited, a limit increased by his affair, a process begun and sealed by previous ones. When Linda went through the break-up of her affair with Jim, she could not share any of her intense pain with John, her husband. She suffered physical symptoms, even ending up in hospital, so weakened was she by her suffering. Although she confided in a few safely distant friends, she could not tell her husband, paradoxically the one person with whom she was trying to become more intimate. This made the break-up from her intimate connection with her lover much more painful; during her mourning (which felt, especially in the beginning, very much like an extended 'cold turkey') she often questioned the worth of enduring it, cut off as she was from the very intimacy she sought. There may be rewards from affairs, as we shall see when we discuss their effects in chapter 6. But clearly they do pose risks from their aftermath. We do not want to exaggerate the position either way. Having an affair, or not having one, in a marriage is for most people not a straight-forward proposition. Affairs may appear to some a solution to its many contradictions. For some they are, but for others they simply multiply the problems. Even those who have an overtly open marriage may have great difficulties at times managing the boundaries of their affairs and of that marriage. In the next chapter we look at the question of who is more likely to have an affair, and under what conditions, while the following one examines the issue of both the sometimes ample rewards and the enormous problems which having affairs can bring.

5 The Who, Why and What of Affairs

Be faithful darling, while you're away,
For when its summer a heart can stray . . .
If you go dancing and he holds you tight,
and lips are tempted on a summer night,
your heart beats faster, when the stars start to shine,
Just remember darling, remember you're mine.

Pat Boone,
'Remember You're Mine', 1957

People have affairs for a host of reasons. But there are some factors that make it more likely: the model of their marriage, the point they have reached in their marital life cycle, and particular aspects of their own history and background. These include each partner's script, from their experience in their own family of origin, about affairs and love relationships: and they include the strength or weakness of intimacy of a given marriage, how they have negotiated issues of autonomy in the marriage, and the satisfaction a person is having with sex within the marriage. In addition, the decision to have an affair and its impact will be different for women and men, for each comes to affairs, as they do to marriage, via different sexual and emotional developmental pathways. There are predisposing factors for having affairs. This chapter examines what these factors are.

The open or segmented models of marriage, in effect, promote affairs directly or indirectly while the model which says 'marriage is for everything' puts them way beyond the limits. Although some people will have affairs just because they are forbidden, as we will see in our discussion, many are stopped by this interdict. In effect then, the model of a marriage acts as a mind-set influencing both the likelihood of an affair and the way it may be played out. However, models of marriage are not fixed for all time and one of the effects an affair may have is to lead to a change in the model.

Marriage Over Time: Points of Vulnerability and the Marital Life Cycle

In the life cycle of marriage, affairs are more likely to occur at certain points, all other things remaining equal. There is no empirically based research to support this notion, but there are indicators as well as intuitive reasons for supposing that there are four primary points of vulnerability. The first point is in the early years of marriage, especially before there are children.

When Kate was married to her first husband, feeling unhappy and quite sure she had made a mistake, she felt that to end the marriage, while not simple, was made enormously easier by the fact that she had had no children with this man. She left him for Jonathan, her present husband, with whom she has had two children. 'Thank God, we didn't have children,' she says, glancing towards her two as they played in the next room, and gulping as if to say, 'Yes, that was indeed a close shave.'

Having affairs in the early years of marriage might also be argued in many cases to be a carry-over of sexual behaviour before marriage, especially among those with a number of premarital sexual partners. Linda and John had lived together for five years; both had had a number of sexual partners before they met and believed that to restrict each other sexually was 'not right'. Each had a number of affairs during the time they lived together. After they married John carried on having casual ones, but Linda felt uneasy about this. She refrained from having any affairs until after their first child was born, and when she had hers it was of an entirely different nature from the others she had had, and nearly ended her marriage. Affairs in this early period of marriage might also be argued to be testing one's commitment to the marriage or working out its boundaries.

William and Nicola had been among the first to marry in their social group. They had been lucky enough to find part of an old rambling house to live in, with lots of space. The social life of their unmarried friends very much centred around their house and the parties they all held there. As William explained, 'I think at the time – this was the late 1950s – we saw ourselves as a progressive couple. We joined in with all the social life of our friends. At a party we each would dance with other people and sometimes flirt. Our rules said that kissing and maybe a bit of petting were OK, but not sleeping with other people – at least when we were both around. We did have a sort of understanding that if we were apart for a long time no questions would be asked. Looking back on it, I think we were rather naive, but also idealistic. Much of the time we behaved like our unmarried friends.' After five years, it was perhaps inevitable that one of them should get seriously involved with someone else. Nicola decided she wanted to leave the marriage. 'Separating hurt for a time but was relatively easy. We had no children and little enough property to divide up. I think it was our families and friends who found it as difficult as we did. They saw us as the ideal young couple. We were very young but I certainly don't regret the time we spent together.'

A second vulnerable point is when children arrive. For a woman, becoming a mother often means feeling that she has lost her sex appeal. Another man's sexual interest, confirming that she is more than a wife, mother and general dogsbody, can be enormously seductive. For men, becoming a father can mean becoming marginalised, pushed aside by wives' preoccupations with children, and pushed off the centre of the emotional stage, out to the wings, away from the intense emotional business between mothers and children. Another woman's sexual interest, confirming one as something other than a side-issue in domestic arrangements and, what's more, interesting, even riveting, can be definitely tempting.

It was no accident that Annie began two of her affairs when each of her babies was about seven or eight months old. Each affair confirmed her sexuality. After pregnancy most women find the weight they have gained difficult to shed, and this was true in her case. Nursing often makes one feel that one's breasts are no longer erotic zones but simply feeding vessels. Exhaustion, and post-birth tenderness means sex takes a back seat for many months. This was how Annie felt, and her husband, undemonstrative at the best of times, did nothing to counteract her demoralised state. It was a revelation to Annie that Joe, the man she met in an evening class, found her so sexy. With him she knew that she was sexual again.

When Polly had their two children in quick succession, soon after they had married, Richard felt increasingly unimportant. Polly and he had met and married young, passionate about each other to the wedding day. Polly became pregnant almost immediately. Always a bit overweight, she gained an enormous amount during her pregnancies. Her interest in sex waned with her pregnancies and never returned during their children's early years. Always exhausted, preoccupied with managing two extremely active and demanding children, Polly not only showed little interest in Richard but the interest she did show seemed to focus on when and how he was going to be around to help her. Resentment built up. They never could seem to recapture that early passion, and Richard spent more and more time away from home. In his practice, a young dental assistant began to show an interest in him. She was fun. She enjoyed many of the same interests which he used to share with Polly, but which she never had the time or energy for these days. They went out for long walks, canoe rides, climbed mountains and saw films together. She enjoyed him and admired him, as he was senior to her in the practice. Whereas at home Richard was seen as a nuisance, with his lover he was a king.

A third vulnerable point occurs when the couple enters middle age. For when a couple has reached a time of consolidation of both family life – when it is likely there will be no more children – and of career development, a time of reflection occurs. Questions arise about whether the life you find yourself in is comfortable and now desirable. This phenomenon has been labelled a 'mid-life crisis', which is an overstatement of what occurs, normally, for everyone. There is no reason to believe that, along with career and other identity issues, and along with rethinking and prioritising of values, what also gets reconsidered are such issues as monogamy and the definition of one's marriage.

Nick, the proverbial mild-mannered academic, at the age of thirty-nine met a woman at a community organisation, began an affair with her, and set up a second family, unbeknownst to his first family. The attraction to his affair partner, a woman entirely different from anyone he had known well before, was overwhelming. She was demanding and unstable, but also passionate, in contrast to his dependable, cool and undemonstrative wife.

In addition, if mid-life entails an appraisal of what fits and what does not with a view towards the years left to live, clearly it is a time ripe for beginning affairs. This appraisal in mid-life may focus on aspects of oneself not currently expressed in one's marriage. An affair may well become the pathway through which these goals develop.

A fourth point, and one which often coincides with the third, is when children leave home. Time on one's hands, without the common bond of children, can expose gaps, even chasms, of interests and concerns between the couple and can simultaneously create opportunities to meet others and reveal emotional and sexual holes in the marriage. These together can predispose a person to having an affair. The life cycle of a marriage clearly can provide part of the backdrop to an affair.

Moira married, young, the first boy with whom she ever went out. When the youngest of her three children began primary school, she returned to secretarial work. Fourteen years later, when the last of the three children had moved away from home, she had risen to an administrative post where she was responsible for the day-to-day running of a small family business. She enormously enjoyed the work and the feeling of competence it gave her. But once the children had left home she felt restless. A recently divorced female friend asked her to go with her on a holiday to the Mediterranean. Moira had never been away before without her husband and children, but with a little persuasion she went. On the second night they were away, she had been slightly shocked when her friend picked up a man in the hotel bar and spent the night with him. A couple of evenings later the friend set up a double date with her man and his companion. 'I suppose I knew when I agreed to go out with them what would happen, but it was a revelation to me when we slept together. He seemed excited by me and, to be honest, I was by him . . . We spent the rest of the holiday together but I decided not to see him when I got home. I knew it could not go on and I don't think I really cared that much for him anyhow,' she confessed. The homecoming had only been a couple of months before the interview. When asked about her marriage and whether or not she would have another affair, she looked very thoughtful and said, 'We'll see'.

Particular Problems in an Individual Marriage

Because contemporary marriages are assumed to be both companionate and romantic, they are particularly vulnerable. They are supposed to be fulfilling on too many fronts, in too constant a fashion. If our ideology permitted a lapse in romance at, for instance, the time of having small children, with an expectation of a rekindling when children reached adolescence, perhaps more of us would accept the lapses which do occur in marital harmony. But, instead, many people end up feeling that their marriages have failed them, becoming alarmed rather than patient, losing the perspective that the painful state might end, yielding to another more fulfilling phase later. Over time, even the best friendships and easiest partnerships hit points of difficulty or estrangement. Individuals in marriages in which friendship is the key may well grow apart in some ways, while remaining intimate in others. Christina's marriage exemplifies this. Although in her estimation she and her husband were 'mostly compatible', she felt that he could not share her work as a dancer, a dimension of her life in which she felt herself flowering. In the period of her life in which her first affair began, she felt quite alienated from him because of this. But if a marriage is supposed to be intimate in a consistent, stable, constantly upward trajectory over most (if not all) dimensions of friendship, even the 'friendliest' marriages will be vulnerable. In Christina's case it was the dimension of her self-discovery. If you bring in the expectation of romance, which usually contains the expectation of sexual fulfilment under its mantle, the marriage becomes even more vulnerable. Christina had felt very satisfied with her sexual relationship with her husband. However, hearing him say that she looked beautiful and how much he desired her had lost much of its lustre, while hearing her new lover say it had not. In addition, there are conflicting images of what is sexually stimulating. Sex is assumed to be fulfilling as part of a loving, committed relationship. But it is also exciting when it is new, forbidden and spontaneous. Spontaneity may be hard to sustain as a marriage matures. Familiarity and routine, which are central to the domestic life and love which define most marriages, conflict with this aspect of sex. Again, Christina had satisfactory sex with her husband but exciting sex with her lover.

Romance, of which sexual fantasies may or may not be a part, also feeds on notions of spontaneity and newness. Thus it may also be in part our expectations about marriage which make marriages vulnerable over time, when newness and spontaneity can no longer be the rule. A marriage can get worn away in any of these areas – the sexual, romantic or any number of indicators of intimacy or friendship – and so become vulnerable to an affair. Any marriage will suffer ups and downs in satisfaction with support given, with the ability to discuss things comfortably and with the amount of time and contentment with shared activities. Additionally, the public, practical, emotional and sexual aspects in any marriage are each variously affected by outside events, and over time any marriage will feel more or less deficient in any one or combination of these dimensions. Therefore, it can be argued that any marriage can be vulnerable, at some point at least, to an affair. If you take any marriage, give one of the partners the increased opportunity to meet a compatible person with whom to have an affair, catch that marriage at a point when at least one important dimension of it feels considerably lacking and when it is at a particularly vulnerable point in the marital life cycle, you have a propensity for that partner to have an affair.

Personal Legacies: 'Family Scripts'

'I would never do to my husband what my mother did to my father.' In these words Jane, a thirty-three-year-old researcher, talked about her lack of interest in having an affair. She has been married for twelve years to her former boss. Indeed, her own marriage technically began as an affair, as her husband was still married to his first wife, although they had already agreed to divorce and were living apart when Jane and her future husband met. Her own mother has been married four times and, during the marriage to Jane's father, had had a long affair with her father's best friend. This affair broke up her parents' marriage. In all her marriages her mother had affairs, and in two cases married her affair partners. Jane remembers the children feeling the pain caused by her mother's affairs, both her mother's upset when affairs went go wrong and her father's anguish about the affair which broke up her parents' marriage. She feels an affair would be a bad thing for a marriage, and she is quite sure that her husband feels equally strongly. He began their affair only when he was well and truly out of his marriage and looking for another stable relationship. Her marriage is in part organised around the strength of a belief in monogamy, shaped by the message from her script in the term coined by psychiatrist John Byng-Hall, around affairs: that they break up marriages and cause pain for all.

Others take the same script, that is, that their parents had affairs, and make something very different from it in their own marriages. For Susannah, the experience of her parents' affairs has given her both permission to have affairs in marriage and a model of how a marriage can remain stable and happy despite having affairs in it. The difference from Jane's case is that

Susannah's parents' affairs were benign experiences for her. Others say that the unhappy experience of their parents' monogamy, especially combined with the change in sexual mores in their sexual coming of age which made them able to experience sex as a 'good thing', has shown them the folly of monogamy. Nick, the academic with the second family, points out that his parents' relationship felt arid in the extreme and there was a decided flavour of 'sex is wicked' with which he was raised. Moreover, in his family demonstrativeness was suppressed, with a consequent emotional sterility. When at university in the 1960s he discovered the delights of sex he found a way to feel alive and uninhibited for the first time. Feeling that he could make a woman feel wonderful as well gave him an emotional connection with another which enlivened him. In his marriage he and his wife have now worked out an agreement that he is allowed to have occasional brief affairs. This is because he so fears becoming repressed, and sex is the one area in which he is not inhibited, that he considers that living under the dictate of monogamy, as his parents did, will contribute to a further repression or inhibition of feeling in his life. In his case Nick has affairs to ward off his fear of monogamy while Jane avoids them to contain her fear of a marital break-up.

However, others repeat rather than correct their family scripts of monogamy and affairs. Susannah's case illustrates that, as does Joanna's.

Joanna, a forty-five-year-old mother of three, and a teacher, stays monogamous, despite an often tempestuous marriage and a number of opportunities to have affairs, in part because of the example of her parents' monogamous marriage. 'It is not that I thought they had the ideal marriage. I think it's more subtle than that. I think the example was that part of what allowed them to stay together was that they did not "stray" – and they felt that they could trust that the other was always focused on him or her. A friend who has affairs once described the person in whom he is sexually interested like being in the foreground of the painting, while the other, your spouse, fades into the background. That's what I think my parents always had, even when things might have been rocky between them: they were always in each others' foreground, and knew it. I think that's very important. I expect that in my husband and think he should expect that from me. I don't want anyone taking my foreground.'

While for others what their parents did or did not do in their marriages is not so important, for many people monogamy or affairs was an emotionally important theme in their parents' marriages. In this way it is a script issue: a powerful script around affairs or monogamy from one's past will influence one's sexual and marital boundaries.

The Impact of Cultural Practices

Jaime, of Latin American extraction, but now resident in both the US and UK, has intermittent affairs, which are not emotionally binding, but are 'fun' and built on shared events and interests: women he has met at conferences and who enjoy food and wine, and sex, as well. The boundaries are clear and he feels he never leads them to think otherwise. These boundaries are of time and place, as well as of emotions: they may share sex and evenings out while they are at the conference, for example. When they part, their affair ends. He shares this style with many Latin men, he claims. He does not feel it detracts from his passion for his wife of twenty-five years. As far as he knows she does not know about his affairs, but he is not sure, since she might not mention it if she did. He thinks she might have had one or two herself, but he does not want to know. If he dwelled on it he would get upset. In some ways, he says, his culture permits the having of affairs, but not the knowing about them.

Maria, also of Catholic and Latin American extraction but resident in the UK during her adult life, corroborates this. 'I do not want to know if my husband has affairs. All of my friends in Argentina have had affairs. It is only the ones whose husbands have found out, or who have found out about their husbands' affairs, whose marriages have not survived. We are not shocked by the idea that marriages can accommodate affairs, on an intellectual level. It is dealing with it emotionally that is difficult and which can break up a marriage. But we do not expect not to have affairs. It is curious. In our culture there is a sort of expectation that it will happen. You just need to protect yourself and your spouse from it becoming public and ugly.' She goes on to criticise the notion in her adopted country that marriages ought to be open, that couples should tell each other everything. 'That is not necessarily what marriages are for, and I don't think that this is the sign of health and love in a relationship. I think telling can be a very unhealthy thing for it. Latin men and women do a lot of things separately and there are some good things to be said for that. Their marriages are not so stifling.'

A recent article in *The Family Networker*, a journal aimed at family- and marital-therapists, has made the same point. In some Western European countries, particularly Catholic ones, the attitude towards affairs and marriage espoused by Jaime and Maria seems to prevail, at least in the middle and upper classes. These are countries where the role of husband and wife are more separate than in Britain and there are lower expectations of marriage being for everything.

But when couples change cultures and move to a different country, they can be particularly vulnerable to having an affair because an intense relationship with someone from that new culture may help them to acculturate. This may be particularly the case if one member of the couple gets very involved with the new culture, while the other steadfastly remains rooted in the old. Or it can happen out of loneliness, when one of the couple has a job which takes his or her energy and time away from the spouse who may feel very dislocated and lonely. A relationship with a new man or woman, particularly from the new culture, may help the lonelier spouse to ease into his or her new life, despite the too-absent spouse.

Teresa, a Spanish wife accompanying her husband to the UK when he did his Ph.D., began a social work course after a long period of loneliness, alienation and marital estrangement, stemming from her resentment of her husband's seemingly effortless acclimatisation to the new culture. On her course she began to feel more a part of life in this new country; and she also began to work closely with her supervisor. After a time they began an affair. When she returned to Spain he wanted to carry on the affair but, no longer needing him in the same way, she gradually lost interest.

Gender and the Impulse to have Affairs

Cutting across all these factors and influencing each is the gender divide. The points of vulnerability in the marriage's life cycle will be experienced differently by men and women. The fact that, when there are children, the woman is a mother, affects the motivation for an affair very differently from the fact that the man is a father. Motherhood and sexuality are often at odds with each other: mothers are not only not supposed to be sexy but they are also often too tired to bother with sex. In addition, a woman's experience, privileges and expectations of marriage are different from those of a man's. Thus, the vulnerability in risking marriage or exposure by having an affair will be different for women and men, and so they will have different reasons for and different predispositions towards having affairs. Women have less powerful positions in the world of work and politics and they still do much more at home. Even the most up-to-date surveys about the 'New Man' show that the increase in 'family time' and domestic tasks from him is trivial. Women, whether they work or not, are assuming most family and domestic tasks and responsibilities. This establishes conditions in which they can easily feel both undervalued and resentful over time in their marriages. They then can become vulnerable to another relationship to restore flagging self-esteem. Men, on the other hand, may want to remain central to their wives and families, but too often become peripheral. This establishes conditions in which they can easily feel remote, unnoticed and unappreciated which in turn creates a vulnerability towards women who confirm their attractiveness and importance. In other words, men and women, in general, have different complaints about married life (a point about which we will have more to say in chapter 8) and so are each vulnerable to affairs for different reasons. Men may complain that their wives are not sexy enough. 'Ever since the children things have been different' has been said during interviews, especially by men, time and time again. Men say that 'their wives don't understand them', by which they seem to mean that their wives are no longer as interested in focusing on them and the shared interests they had before children as they once were. On the other hand, women say that their husbands and they 'cannot communicate' and that their husbands do not seem to value them any more. Whether sexually or otherwise, they more often tend to feel exploited. Different patterns in the development of emotional needs, strengths and weaknesses, and in the development of sexual behaviours and attitudes, explain much of these gender differences. So does the divide between them in societal terms: domestic and economic differences mean they face different social and economic risks if their sexual affairs are revealed or if their marriages falter or break.

When an affair is revealed the marriage is more likely to be at risk if it is the wife's affair rather than the husband's. Old-fashioned double standards combine with the gender dynamics of marriage to make the price of affairs higher for women than men (as we shall explore further in chapter 7). It is sufficient to point out for the moment, though, that women are not usually as good as men at splitting off love and sex, so they may force love into their affairs and may feel a more powerful conflict between this and their marriage.

However, if a wife does divide sex and love off from each other, she may be seen to be cheap, wanton or whorish instead of deeply sexual, and may be rejected by her husband in the end, anyway. When Annie had her third affair she told her husband because she had accidentally become pregnant by her affair partner. This affair was a holiday fling, unimportant except that she felt she had been treated in a cavalier fashion

by her casual lover. It is unlikely it would have come to light if
she had not become pregnant or had decided to terminate the
pregnancy. Instead of her husband being relieved that this
time, unlike her second affair, she had not been in love with
her partner, her husband turned this against her. This unimportant, 'just-sex' affair precipitated the breakdown of their
marriage.

Generally, men are more likely to have the opportunity to
have affairs – they have more mobility, more chances to meet
other women and, even if wives are working, in comparison
with them men have more control over their time and fewer
demands on it from home. They can, if they choose, manœuver
their time to be out, and be in a position to meet other women,
more than their wives can. The contrast between men's and
women's opportunities for affairs is often greatest for working-
class women, and especially when they are not working. They
seldom get out to meet other men and they are homebound.
However, especially if there are young children, even middle-
class men are freer both to begin and to carry on affairs than
are their middle-class working wives. During her thirteen-year
marriage to her school sweetheart, Sharon had felt little sexual
desire for her husband. She had had one affair, early in their
marriage, during an enforced separation. It had nearly
destroyed their marriage. They went on to have three children.
Sharon did not work. But, as soon as the youngest went off to
school, Sharon took on a part-time job, found some time and
freedom of her own, and the opportunity to meet men, and
within months had an affair.

There is still a difference in social attitudes about what is
acceptable for men and women even given the existence of an
affair. The range of the kind of people it is all right for a man
to have an affair with is greater than the range for women. Men
have freedom to cut across classes and social groups more
easily than women. Matthew, who worked as a research
scientist for a chemicals company, had a number of affairs. He
had some with friends, and friends of friends, one with a
woman picked up in an airport, and one with his secretary. In

contrast, Sharon had an affair with a member of the clerical staff at the place where she worked but felt very embarrassed because his social status was lower than hers, and ended this affair in part because of that. Men can have affairs with younger partners more easily than women can with younger men. Again, Sharon's clerical lover was also younger and this contributed to her inability to take the affair seriously. On the other hand, when she slept with a friend of her husband's, who was the right age and class, this was serious even though it was much more short-lived. Indeed, this was the affair which made her think that she might have to leave her husband. There are, thus, more constraints of both opportunity and choice of partner for women than for men.

Indeed, a common reaction from a woman on discovering a husband's affair is, after feeling hurt and betrayed, anger and envy: envy that he got there first and anger at the inequality of opportunity that allowed him to have an affair when this had felt closed to her. When Matthew's wife found out about his affairs, apart from her shock, sense of betrayal, jealousy and hurt, she envied him his opportunity. She had, after all, been dutifully running their family life, tuning out all opportunities. She was left feeling unsexy and unappreciated. Perhaps she had been foolish, she admitted, to have been so oblivious to other men's attentions all those years.

Personality: Is there an 'Affair-type' Person?

The question remains: why some people and not others? Plenty of people are in unsatisfying marriages, have the opportunity, are at a vulnerable point in the marital life cycle, yet still do not have affairs.

There have been various attempts to explain differences in terms of personality. Often these classifications of those who will and those who won't involve calling those who will pathological. If one starts with the view that affairs are, by definition, pathological because they are ways of consciously or unconsciously acting out against the marriage, people who have affairs *are* acting pathologically. In this view they are variously deemed 'immature', 'narcissistically disturbed' and 'sick'. From such a perspective such labels may seem to make sense: people are not being direct, responsible, or 'adult'. But this is not only a judgemental view of marriage but also implies a simplistic model of people's motives.

From the perspective of either 'open marriage' or that which regards marriage as something which may need to shift in functions over time, there are other explanations. One of these is that people who have affairs are people who will take risks. But as we have discussed earlier in chapter 4, this notion does not distinguish those who will from those who won't. Nevertheless, the view persists. Seen romantically, this explanation makes people who do have affairs seem creative and avant-garde. Of course, they may also be potentially destructive. Certainly, this would be the view from the standpoint of those who believe that marriage is for everything. Risk-takers would be people who are unable to commit themselves, or people too blinkered to see the potential consequences.

Strength of religious belief or commitment to the ideals of monogamy also does not necessarily differentiate between those who have affairs and those who do not. Survey after survey show the same result, that monogamy is almost everyone's ideal and as an ideal it has grown stronger and more widely held in recent decades. However, more and more people are having affairs. Churchgoers do not seem to have fewer affairs than non-churchgoers. What people say they should do ideally and what they actually do are different things.

There is some evidence that those who have had more sexual relationships before marriage are more likely to have relationships outside marriage. The rise we see in extramarital sex may be in part because there are now more married people who had more partners before marriage. While this may be statistically true, it does not explain why Mary, who had five premarital partners, and is in a rotten marriage, forbids herself to have an affair while Susan, in almost exactly the same circumstances, would draw on her past sexual happiness and confidence to have an affair in order to make herself feel rejuvenated.

Affairs and the Need to Retaliate

Some people have affairs because their spouse has had one. The motive is to pay back, to hurt as you have been hurt, or to gain back a balance of power. Or envy may rear its ugly head and, as we have already noted, one's spouse's affair gives the other spouse permission to have one too. Or it may serve both these ends.

In an open marriage the strategy of evening things up is explicitly permitted, even promoted. Ursula, whose affair with Sean was first discussed in the introduction, began her affair with him in part because David, her husband, had been having affairs. Their marriage called for her to have an affair since, as an open one, it associated the ability to do so with a kind of personal growth, or the lack of affairs with retrogressive processes. David encouraged her affair, while she waited for the right opportunity, person and time in her life. She needed someone who was interested in having a limited affair with her, someone who was not too much like David, who shared with her something David could not and who appeared when her children had become slightly older.

Women get rude awakenings from attempts to equalise or to pay back more often than men. Because it is more difficult for many women to segment their sexual and emotional lives, to cut off one set of emotions for one person from a similar set for another, they have more difficulty in keeping to the purpose of this type of affair. In Linda's case she fell deeply, passionately in love with Jim, although she began the affair because her husband had had a casual affair a few months earlier and she wanted to equalise the sexual power balance in the marriage. She thought that, like John, her husband, she could segment her affair and her marriage and, in doing so, she would strengthen her marital position. What she did not expect was that she would fall as deeply in love with Jim as she did. After it was all over she ruefully accepted that while John might have been capable of segmenting, she could not trust that she could ever cut off again.

Melissa and Lawrence, however, were able to get the marital balance back again through a retaliatory affair. Lawrence had an affair with Barbara, a mutual friend, after discovering Melissa's affair with Max, another friend. At the end of both the balance of marital power was equal and familiar again. Lawrence's retaliatory affair worked to maintain balance in the marriage. Although his affair was not covert, neither was it flaunted nor endlessly discussed. It was noted when it ended, thus reassuring Melissa.

Such rebalancing probably does not often occur, even if that is the intent. Especially when the motivation is primarily an eye for an eye, the effect often completely misfires. When the spouse who had the first affair feels especially guilty, for instance, there is often a sense of relief when he or she finds out that his or her spouse is having an affair. It lets the first spouse off the hook. This may not be what the new affair is intended to do. Another often undesirable outcome is that the new affair is seen as a worse offence because the spouse let it happen knowing, from his or her own experience, how painful its effects could be.

The Pull of 'Unfinished Business': Settling Old Scores

Affairs may begin because of unfinished business. That is, old lovers, even ex-spouses, or old friends or colleagues from an earlier time who have been mutually attracted to each other but who have not acted on it out of extenuating circumstances, or old crushes suddenly declaring an interest – all of these have extraordinary seductive power and can precipitate people into having an affair. The seductive power stems largely from the unfinished character of these relationships. Either there is the need to become the victor, if one has been rejected, or to relieve oneself of guilt if one has been the one who has walked out. Both may pertain in the case of past loves or ex-marriages.

Or there may be a need to see if the power to feel the way one once did is still there, especially in the case of past loves or old crushes and attractions. If this is coupled with other things, that seductiveness grows even stronger. If, for instance, one is going through a stale sexual period in marriage as well as feeling middle aged, with life starting to pass one by, one might be particularly vulnerable to fantasies of getting together again with an old flame. Yet meeting the same person, years earlier, while in the youth of a still new and exciting marriage, might not have exerted the same seductive power. There is also the feeling that, in a way, one is not transgressing marital vows so deeply; the person who had been there first, the college love, the high-school sweetheart, the first spouse, has some prior claim. The case of Daniel and Jessica is one of these. When they met again both were in marriages which had begun to feel distant, even 'dead' in Jessica's case. Both were nearly forty. Jessica's husband commented, 'I'm only an interlude between Daniel "mark 1" and Daniel "mark 2" anyway,' when he was told about the affair, thus confirming that sense of prior claim. In Margaret Atwood's novel *Cat's Eye*, on a visit to Toronto, the heroine, now remarried, sleeps with her first husband, with deep familiarity and affection. Although she is married to someone else it does not feel like 'adultery'. Yet in their relative youth she had begun sleeping with this first husband illicitly before their own marriage, when she was the girlfriend of someone else. During that earlier phase of their sexual relationship she did feel like an adulterer, betraying her boyfriend of the time with the man who was to become her first husband.

There is sometimes a confusion of time and place in affairs of this sort, with the earlier time seeming better, for it was a time of younger, often seemingly less complicated days. 'To me he always looks like a young boy,' says Jessica of Daniel. She feels connected with her old self, the younger girl she feels herself to be at times through being with him.

Sometimes an affair can become a long-term sexual friendship. Gordon described a relationship which had begun some years before his marriage with someone who had been a student with him. They had gone out together for a few months and, although they had got on very well together, it had not been a very intense relationship. They had met up again by chance a few years later. Both were then married but they found a lot to say to each other. Gradually a pattern emerged in which once or twice a year they would spend a couple of days – and nights – together. Sometimes the demands of their separate lives and, in her case, a divorce and remarriage, interrupted but did not end the pattern. Neither, it would seem, had either ever thought seriously of settling down together; but, equally, neither could see any reason for not continuing their relationship.

The Oedipal Affair, a Variant of Unfinished Business

When Wendy's father was dying, after she had been married for five years, she began to spend a lot of time with his business partner. Some of this was necessary, since her father's complicated business matters involved her, and his partner was helping her to sort them out. In addition, they began to meet at hospital visits. Wendy had known him all her life, but latterly she had seen little of him, since in the first few years of her marriage she had lived in a different city. Slowly, during her father's illness, their time together increased. Shortly after he died they began an affair. Wendy's greatest friend and love had been her father; she and her mother had a distant, embattled relationship and the family had always been polarised. Wendy and Dad formed one coalition, while her brother and mother formed another. Wendy had always felt that her father preferred her to her mother, and she knew that *she* had always preferred her father to her mother. In addition, Wendy had known that from adolescence she had been attracted to her father's partner; now to know that he returned it was thrilling. They conducted a clandestine affair for five years, during which time her marriage broke up. The affair ended when Wendy realised finally that she would never be able to be married to this man, who would not leave his wife of thirty years whom she still loved. Wendy was perfectly aware of the Oedipal-like nature of her relationship: she knows that she is, and continues to be, attracted to older men, and especially to older, warm men who remind her of her father. She is also aware of the thrill she got from knowing that she was having an affair with this man behind her mother's back and behind his wife's back. His wife, of course, was a woman old enough to be her mother.

Gene and Ann are eighteen years apart – Ann is forty-eight, Gene is thirty. Ann's elder daughter is two years younger than Gene, her younger daughter, six. Five years ago Ann and Gene became lovers. All of them lived together until recently when Ann's younger daughter left home. Gene's mother is an undemonstrative woman whose husband was rather weak and remote. Ann is emotional and warm, her ex-husband an alcoholic and womaniser, who treated her badly throughout her marriage. Gene is the cool, dependable one in the relationship, on whom Ann can rely. Although Gene is ambivalent about staying with Ann, in part because he may want children at some point, he feels intensely drawn to her and protected emotionally by her; moreover, he gets satisfaction from being the dependable, strong man for her.

Life Traumas: Affairs as a Response to a Re-evaluation of Life

When George was thirty-five, a university professor of sociology at a major university, with two children and a wife he had known from adolescence whom he had married before he finished university, he was diagnosed as having a brain tumour. During the months of hospitalisation, out-treatment and in-activity, which ended, fortunately, in complete recovery, he spent a lot of time musing on the meaning of life in general and of his own life in particular. In this time he crystallised the until then vague notion that he did not love his wife (although he was fond of her); that if he were to live he wanted to study how people thought about the meaning of their lives, rather than what he had been studying until then; and that he wanted to live more passionately, with more feeling than he had been living until then. A few months after his recovery he met a woman who had attended one of his lectures, a woman completely different from his wife – dark where his wife was blond, intense where his wife was cool, confident and assured where his wife was diffident. This woman was confident that she wanted George, pursued him and with little effort won him. She, too, was married. They were lovers for seven years, until she ended the relationship. George did remain married for three more years, until his children left home, but no longer had a sexual relationship with his wife. He searched, those three years, for another passionate woman, finally finding her and then he left his wife.

Following serious illness or trauma, such rethinking of life, its meaning, and what one really wants to have achieved before it ends, especially if this occurs in middle age, can become a catalyst for an affair. Like illness, a life-change can also bring this about. In Matthew's case the significant catalytic life-change was being made redundant at the age of forty-three. Matthew became depressed without a job or job prospects and threatened with loss of his middle-class managerial perks, all of which had boosted his ego and filled him with pride. Depression sapped his zest for family life as well. On a trip to a job interview he met an unconventional woman who hotly pursued him, turning his life around in the process. As a result he left his family, and at least temporarily suspended his life as a middle-class professional, trading it in for that of an un-encumbered world traveller. The loss of his job indirectly changed his life as he traded in one identity for another in the company of the new woman in his life.

The Affair as a Compulsion

Some people seem unable *not* to have affairs. They are unable to relate to others of the opposite sex *without* sex. This is more common among men than women. This should not surprise, in the light of what we have been saying about differences between men and women. Intimacy does not come as easily for men as for women. If men are going to have a problem in forming close relationships it is likely to be because they find it hard to be intimate. In more severe cases they distinctly fear becoming too close to someone. Because men's sexuality develops first in isolation and only later becomes blended with intimate feelings, it is also not surprising that men can have 'just sex'. Splitting sex off in this way, afraid of intimacy, more men than women are likely to seek sex with lots of people. Because having sex is having a kind of relating it gives these men (and sometimes women) the feeling, however fleeting, that they are making some connection with someone. So, briefly, it establishes a sense of independence from one's spouse: 'I have others, not just you.' This acts as an antidote to the fear of being too intimate with one's spouse. The affair partners are not usually emotional competitors to the spouse, since the engagement with each is both transitory and superficial: there is always the next conquest to look for after this one has been made. So in this way intimacy with the affair partner is avoided as well.

For men there is also the fact that through sex masculinity is affirmed. The belief is that the more women who succumb, the more masculine one is. It is a belief based on accepted cultural messages. But having sex with many partners does not confirm a woman's femininity in the same way. And fear of intimacy is not usually a woman's problem. When a woman shows this sort of compulsive sexualising of relationships it is usually a sign of deep pathology, since it goes so clearly against normal developmental patterns.

Some people have labelled this sort of behaviour 'sexual addiction', comparing both the 'fix' which casual sex gives and its compulsive nature to genuine physical addiction. In these ways it *is* analogous. It works: sex in this way does protect against intimacy and it does confirm that someone finds you attractive. It is also for many people intensely exciting and pleasurable, because it is doing something forbidden. It *does* offer a 'fix' in the same way that drugs do. But, of course, it is not an addiction. There is no real physical dependence, and 'withdrawal', although perhaps psychologically as intense as 'cold turkey' or other addiction cures, is not physically painful or dangerous.

It often does *not* work, of course, in the long term. Because of its frequency, it means taking many risks with one's marriage. Because many of the players end up feeling exploited, this type of affair often results in severe distress. Some spouses turn a blind eye, accepting that her, or his, spouse has 'this problem'. But not all do. In the age of AIDS, too, there are new risks as a result of compulsive affairs. In these ways such affairs are riven with dangers, if temporarily palliative to those who have them.

In summary, there are particular vulnerabilities in the course of any marriage because of people's own histories, and these contribute to why some people have affairs. Someone may be at a vulnerable point in the marital life cycle. Another may have a marriage which may have become eroded in an important way. Some women may feel unable to feel close to, be able to communicate with, or feel overworked in comparison to their husband. In the case of a man, he may feel peripheral to, unappreciated or undervalued by his wife and family. Combine these factors with the opportunities to meet people with whom to have an affair and the time in which to have one, and one might well be on the way to having an affair. And if this scenario does not apply in every specific case, it does apply in hundreds and hundreds of others.

6 The Impact of Affairs

Love, oh love, oh careless love,
Love, oh love, oh careless love,
Love, oh love, oh careless love,
See what careless love has done.

American Blues

The impact of an affair can be positive, neutral or disastrous. Or it may be a mixture of these. The nature of impact will depend on whether an affair is secret and never discovered, secret and then discovered, or, finally, whether it was open from the beginning. There can be effects on the marriage, on the people having the affair, on the spouse who is not, and on others indirectly involved.

The question of impact has no straightforward answer. It consists of a number of separate questions. What has been most affected? Are these effects direct or indirect, specific or general? Have there been changes in the expectations of the marriage, the sexual relationship or satisfaction with intimacy and friendship? Has the marriage improved, remained the same, got worse or ended?

All of these potential effects, from the specific to the general, indirect to direct, and on whom, are influenced by whether or not a secret affair remains secret or, in open marriages, whether an affair has remained within specified boundaries. If an affair is secret and then becomes known, the impact of discovery itself will be enormously important. For this reason we will look separately at the impact of a secret affair after its discovery, in a later part of this chapter. First we will discuss the impact of secret affairs which remain secret or affairs in open marriages which remain within contractual boundaries.

As well as the broad range of possible effects, there are two major underlying issues that we need to deal with first: the way the gender of those involved influences the outcome and how this links to the model of their marriages.

Gender and the Effects of Affairs

In view of what we have already said about the development of men and women (and see chapter 7 for a discussion of the different social consequences for each of marital break-up), it is not surprising that men and women report the effects of their affairs differently. The differences are both in degree and kind.

On the whole, women still become more emotionally involved in affairs than men do. This involvement is no longer confined to being in love. For most women, especially as they become more sexually sophisticated, in part through their marital experience, the correlation between sex and love has loosened. Women now do not have to think they are in love to have sex. The issue of affairs can no longer be seen as 'women are monogamous, while men are polygamous'. Women may have affairs which do not involve love but they do usually seem to have affairs which are emotionally involving. Because men can cut off, given their clear boundaries, they can have affairs which have minimal effects on their emotional lives. Even when men have emotionally involving affairs, they can stop thoughts about their affair partners, or their spouses, segmenting their inner life in a way that women seem unable to do. Women carry thoughts around with them, imagining their lover's life, ruminating about whether or not they have offended, or have been careful enough with the other's feelings. They cannot turn these thoughts on and off as easily as men do.

Women are aware, from the beginning, of the possible impact of their having an affair on their family and friends, as well as on their lovers. Thus, early on they may specify as clearly as possible to their lovers the boundaries around their affairs. This also is a step towards ensuring that these men are not misled. Guilt about being the cause of pain cuts at the heart of their self-respect as women. Indeed, they are often disappointed and dismayed by their lovers' failure to be as clear to them about what they can expect. Even when affairs are chiefly about sexual pleasure, women seem to be concentrating on others' feelings and by the same token trying to safeguard themselves from an emotional mess. These worries about the potential mess and their specification of rules are probably defensive strategies: women know that they must protect themselves from getting too enmeshed with their lovers. Their potential difficulty is maintaining the relationship, getting too close or merging with their partner, while for men, the difficulty is to let themselves get close enough without the intimacy becoming threatening.

Women and men talk about different things when they discuss their affairs. Men talk about the effects affairs have on their own feelings or on their plans. Women mention how their affairs have affected their children, friends, affair partners and husbands, as well as themselves. Men do not necessarily mention whether or not someone was hurt. Women are often at pains to tell you that they did all they could to make sure no one was hurt, even if someone was.

Annie's first affair with Joe illustrates these features. Her affair was primarily sexual; its effects were chiefly on her sexual confidence and pleasure. Their affair began when her first child was seven months old.

It was a revelation. My husband had not been interested in me sexually since the pregnancy and, truthfully, I had pretty much gone off the idea of myself as sexual as well. Then along comes this incredibly sexy, younger man from my evening Italian class – I had decided to get out and do something besides changing nappies for a while – and he starts telling me how he's having fantasies about me. Well, anyway, you can guess what happened. It was absolutely fantastic sexually. But he was not a real competitor for my husband's place and he certainly knew it. I made it crystal clear to him before anything began that I loved my husband, and that being a mother and having a stable family life were central to me. He was a hippie – he thought I was terribly boring and strait-laced – but had this incredible sexual energy. I got it clear from him that he was fine about the limits – they suited him, too. I don't think he would have been interested in me for a moment if I hadn't been married. When I was with him – and that would be at his house on certain, specified hours of certain days only – I would cook him something nice. I even sometimes washed his socks for him: he was such a slob I couldn't help it. Sometimes I would think about him alone in his tip of a flat during the week eating tins of beans and feel a little pang, while I was making great dinners of meat and two veg – but I also knew that this was also just what suited him, too. Apart from wanting to be with each other because we had such a great time in bed – and fun, too, out of it – I felt comforted by the fact that the arrangement suited both of us equally.

Annie met this man at clearly appointed times. There were rules and conventions about what could be mentioned and how far feelings could go. Her family remained resolutely separate from this man. As long as this suited them both the affair continued. When Annie became pregnant again it dwindled, as her preoccupation with her family and husband increased.

Or Anna, an Argentinian psychiatrist living in England, who talked of how in each of her six affairs she has been careful to be discreet in large part because she 'did not want Jose [her husband] to find out – not only because he might kill me – and certainly divorce me! – but also because I could not bear the thought of how it would feel to him to find out.' She thinks that Jose also has affairs, but conceals them for fear she would leave if she found out. So his probable affairs are secret too. Anna claims her discretion is driven in part by compassion for Jose's shame should he discover she had slept with other men. But she does not imagine he is motivated by a commensurate desire to protect her.

What both women are reporting is their concern for others in the affair, their affair partners, their families and their husbands. They are acting then as 'good' people, women who think about others. And to ward off the female tendency to merge with others they insist on specifying the boundaries of their affairs.

There is another factor at work here. Because of the still extant double standard, women are quicker to feel guilty about being sexual. They are able to see a greater range of possible consequences of affairs because if their affairs are discovered the dangers are much greater, as we shall see in chapter 7. In contrast, men report how their affairs have, or have not, made them grow psychologically, or change, or whether or not their affairs have made them feel better or worse. They discuss how affairs make them think about their goals – 'Do I want to be married? Do I really want *this* person?' Unlike women, they do not spend much time imagining what their affair partners are really thinking or really wanting, nor how to protect their affair partners from making mistaken assumptions about their affairs. Unlike women, they assume that these affair partners will take it upon themselves to ask for clarification about what the affair means, how far it can go and how each figures in the other's life and plans.

'Wonderful passion', said Sam of his affair with Ellen. 'It made me re-evaluate my marriage. It made me think very seriously about whether or not I could leave my marriage for her.' Or, 'It makes me feel great – tingly. I love being in love,' said David of his affairs in his open marriage to Ursula. And then David, too, talked about his plans: 'I would never leave Ursula, and she [his affair partner] did not really seem to understand this, so I had to get myself out.'

It is probably not that men do not care about the impact on others of their affairs, but they seem to be less aware than women of the web of effects on others. Their socialisation has not prepared them to be so. Similarly, while women certainly talk about the affair's effects on their plans, these are not their first responses. Instead these arise in the context of discussing the web of effects on everyone.

When Linda was struggling to end her two-year-long, intense love affair with Jim, her suffering was compounded by guilt over the fact that her depression was taking valuable energy away from her three-year-old daughter and from her husband. She was already racked with pain over Jim's agony. For Jim was making desperate threats and demanding that she take responsibility for his desperation. This was happening just when she was trying to extricate herself from him. She was in a bind. The effect of the affair in the end was a recommitment to her marriage. But in the course of trying to effect this she also had to look after the very person she was trying to leave.

These differing responses between men and women are, of course, consistent with, and indeed a product of, their social-isation within each gender. To be a woman means to consider one's actions within a network of social relationships and in relation to others' responses to them. To be a man means to consider one's actions in themselves, how they will project into future actions, how one's identity, through one's feelings about those actions, is further shaped or confirmed by them.

One net effect of gender differences is that women are more likely to be emotionally involved in their affairs than are men. While women may be having more affairs than they were in the past, their greater emotional involvement makes them likely to have fewer affairs than men. In general, women's affairs, even when bounded and mainly sexual, demand a greater degree of emotional expenditure than do men's.

Model of Marriage and Effects

The expectations one has about marriage in general and one's own in particular obviously affect both the likelihood of an affair and its effects. The marriage-is-for-everything model assumes painful and negative effects; the segmented marriage model assumes it is possible to have little overlap between affairs and marriage; while in the open model affairs are thought to benefit or else not affect marriages.

In the marriage-is-for-everything model people usually hold that affairs always happen because something is wrong with the marriage. The effects in this kind of marriage are always in some sense bad, even if the couple later acknowledge that an affair has increased their self-esteem, made for better marital relations, or given them valuable knowledge. Affairs are bad because they let a marriage down. In marriages spouses should be able to communicate directly to each other. If either is missing something from the marriage, it is up to the spouse to set things right within it. An affair which is additional or compensatory to a limited marriage is not seen as good. Even if a person in an affair feels replenished or a marriage is pacified by it, guilt for having failed the marital ideal undermines these positive feelings.

A case in point is Simon, a middle-aged chairman of a research institution. He had a brief but intense affair with a much younger woman and briefly did think of leaving his marriage for her. Although he felt revitalised by his affair he feels he unforgivably betrayed Susie, his wife. Guilt erased the rewards from the affair. For instance, while having his affair he concluded that Susie's cloying dependence on him drained his desire for her. Under pressure from him she set up her own research project, moving her office to another building. Previously this couple had been virtually inseparable, even sharing an office. Their marriage was in fact revitalised, as was Susie's career. Simon, having felt far too merged with Susie for his own comfort, now felt much happier about his marriage. Yet Simon thinks his affair was a terrible mistake since it was a betrayal of the intention and spirit of his marriage.

In the segmented model the two domains of experience, marriage and affairs, are separate. Yet even so people concede that there are indirect effects from the affair. For example, Melissa, a thirty-three-year-old mother of two, reported that, although she had felt that her affair and marriage were separate, she had felt 'wonderfully sexual' and that this had so enhanced her spirits and self-esteem that she was a much more cheerful mother and wife. Laura, a thirty-nine-year-old art restorer, reported that her marriage was much easier as a result of her affairs because she could accept her husband's limitations more easily when she was getting more passionate sex and greater intensity from other men.

In the open model, affairs are enhancing as long as they stay within bounds. In this model each member of the couple is seeking actualisation above all else. The model assumes psychological growth and constrains jealousy and possessiveness, which often get out of control and can be destructive. The ugliness of betrayal is avoided because there is often no secrecy and because there is an understanding that this would not constitute betrayal. Ursula's and David's affairs fit this model. David once challenged their contract by getting too attached to his affair partner. From Ursula's point of view he spent too much time with her, and more importantly he wanted to be with her more than with Ursula. The marital contract was questioned, the issue of betrayal arose, possessiveness and jealousy reared their heads, and mutual confidence was shaken. Open marriages do not always avoid pain in affairs, because marital contracts are not always robust and because the temptation may arise to break them. Once that is done, betrayal comes into play, as it did for David and Ursula.

Specific Effects of Affairs

Affairs can bring about self-growth, sexual pleasure, changes in marital expectations and satisfaction, shifts in the quality of friendships, and can also have effects on children.

Both men and women report personal growth, or self-actualisation, through their affairs, in some cases through becoming intimate with someone who has stretched their horizons. Ursula, for instance, reports that Sean, an artist, stretched her artistically. Or sometimes the affair offers people a completely new experience. Laura, the art restorer, learned that she could be sexually abandoned through her affairs. Sometimes the affair provides a context in which to reaffirm something one already knew but had lost in oneself. David relearned his romanticism through his affairs.

Sometimes the self-growth is centred on sexuality. In Annie's first affair this was true. Occasionally sexuality is indirectly important. Ursula was at pains to play down the significance of the sex itself in her affair with Sean. Yet David reports feeling happy for her about her affair because it, 'Does so much for her confidence – and it certainly has made her more uninhibited sexually.' He also reports that he does not feel threatened by Sean since, 'He is so completely unlike me. I know that Ursula would never want him over me. We would never leave each other, as we both have the ultimate qualities each wants in the other.' Ursula comments in a separate interview, 'I am sexually satisfied with David. However, Sean is very sensitive in a way that David cannot be and he understands my art – he's an artist – in a way that David simply could not. More important, though, is the fact that I have something that's only for me. That makes me feel *so* important, affirmed, desired and appreciated – and that feeds back into my sexual relationship with David. Sean just is not as good a lover but he adores being with me. We kiss a lot. In some ways it's very innocent. I just feel romantic and it's exciting being loved by two men in very different ways.' But her confidence is increased and her inhibitions unleashed because, 'Having an affair is illicit. There were not many things forbidden to me about sex while I was growing up. But affairs are forbidden. This makes them exciting.' So while sex with Sean is not wildly exciting, Ursula as an adulteress is.

Affairs have brought people increased self-esteem, more sexual confidence, more insight into how one is with the opposite sex, a wisdom about relationships and a greater sense of autonomy. People sometimes feel that they grew while their marriages suffered. Yet others report that their own growth took place apart from their marriages and had no direct effect on them.

There are ample accounts of these effects, especially in literature and films. Much of the explosion of women's novels and films of the late sixties and early seventies focused on women's self-growth through affairs. *Diary of a Mad Housewife*, both a successful film and novel, is emblematic of this. Although her affair ended in bitterness, the heroine of Sue Kaufman's story used her experience in it to extricate herself from a stifling marriage. There are fewer stories of men's growth through affairs. Men's affairs are 'macho', 'sexual' or 'exploitative'. Nevertheless, some men report self-growth, their affairs affording them the chance to live out different sides of themselves. This is one way of saying that they learned something from affairs, as David did. Affairs can also bring men, like women, sexual affirmation, or make them feel liked and valued. David's affair with a business colleague was sexually affirming. Sam's with Ellen, in addition to the sex, made him feel valued.

However, there are two major gender differences. Firstly, more men than women describe affairs as 'just sexual'. This difference may be in part a linguistic one, but a linguistic one which underscores the different sexual approach of men and women. 'Just sexual' is more acceptable language for men. Women have different ways of saying it – such as, sex in the affair was the 'main point of interest' or satisfaction. But they also usually follow this with 'it was not just sex'. Given what we have described about the nature of their greater involvement, this difference is not surprising. For example, in Annie's first affair it was Joe's intense sexual interest in her which was his main attraction. However, Annie quickly points out that she liked Joe, he liked her; that she thought about him and his welfare from time to time in between seeing him; and she cared about the effects on him of their affair. She even cooked and washed his socks for him. Secondly, more often than men, women describe the consequences for others of their own self-growth. For example, Melissa reports that her affair made her feel 'sexy again after all those years of being primarily a mother – and mothers just aren't sexy. That was great – a real revelation for me. Just what I needed at that time. It was great fun. Because I felt so great I was a much better mother and wife during it and afterwards, too.' This is in contrast to Sam: 'I have had lots of affairs. I travel a lot. It probably has to do with the fact that I was not very confident in school – my family moved every few years and I never felt accepted in any school. I wasn't a particularly good athlete and I was smaller than most of the other boys since I was younger. So in a way I'm making up for lost time. I want to be able to feel that if I feel sexual with someone it is possible to have an affair.' Affairs are conduits to feeling for him and connections he makes with women. In contrast to Melissa, Sam does not mention effects on his wife – good or bad. As we have said, men are not as conscious of the web of effects, as they assume less responsibility for the feelings of others. Therefore, their own self-growth is seen more clearly in isolation from its effects on others. We are talking here, of course, about general, group differences, or tendencies for men and women. Particularly when men or women are not consumed by guilt, reports do seem to differ by gender.

It should be pointed out here, though, that many men feel terribly guilty about having had affairs. These are men, such as Simon, whose marriages are mainly in the marriage-is-for-everything model. But their guilt about having betrayed their marriages seems to cancel out any self-growth. The marriage-is-for-everything model also implies preoccupation with the effects of an affair on one's spouse and thus, by implication, on the affair partner, whom one has led astray, since one is supposed to be fully committed to one's marriage.

Affairs can also bring about a re-evaluation of what someone wants from a marriage, both in general and in his or her own marriage. Through affairs a redefinition of marriage can evolve as well as a re-evaluation of what is possible and desirable in one's own marriage. There can be any of these possible consequences: an affirmation that everything is fine as it is; a conclusion that something critical is missing in one's marriage and it is dead without it; a decision to accept the limitations of the marriage and an acceptance of affairs as compensatory; or a commitment to try to move the marriage closer to one's ideal.

Men and women differ in another respect. Women report more subtle effects on their relationships. Indeed, they seem to look for effects. Again, this is consistent with their socialisation. Women have the language for describing both feelings and the effects of those feelings on others. That is why Melissa, mentioned above, says that if she feels better that will affect her marriage, while Sam does not. Most women, even if they can segment their affairs off from their marriages, will find connections in indirect ways as Melissa did. Susannah, who is forty-eight, has had four affairs which she terms serious in twenty-three years of marriage. From a wealthy and privileged background in which both parents had affairs when she was growing up, Susannah owns her own interior-design business. Indeed, her main confidante is her seventy-five-year-old mother. Her husband is often away on business and her friendships with both men and women occupy much of her time and energy. She has felt 'something like love' in each of her affairs. In two she had long-standing friendships with her partners, both pre- and post-affair. Yet her feelings for her husband remain undented. She loves him above all. The spin-off for her marriage has been an increased freedom and a focus on its strengths rather than on what she lacks. She has re-evaluated and redefined her marriage. 'Why should Paul have to be everything for me? He is a terrific, dynamic man, a great provider; we share a sense of humour, tastes and a long history. I have never met a man I respect so much and find overall so interesting and attractive. We now have a relationship that works in most ways except his ability to give me time and attention and to be demonstrative. That's as much my problem as his. I solve it by not straining to fit him into the box I need but to look elsewhere for that. I think our marriage works.'

Both men and women say that affairs have revealed things they want to change in their marriages. But in trying to enact changes the results have been varied. For example, Nick, the academic with the 'second family', realised that he wanted more affection, more sexual experimentation and more talking with his wife. She was accommodating about more sexual experimentation. But she is a cool and distant woman for whom talking and demonstrativeness do not come easily. The marriage improved only slightly in those respects. However, Linda, who had the passionate affair with Jim, did press for more intimacy with her husband, John, and she was much more successful. Six years after her affair with Jim ended the couple is much closer and happier than ever before.

Finally, sometimes an affair illustrates so much that is wrong with the marriage that the marriage ends. Kate and Jonathan, who have now been married for fifteen years, are a case in point. Their affair crystallised for them both the idea that their previous respective marriages were dead.

Affairs also can ring changes in the network of other relationships, outside the immediate family and the affair partner. People in secret affairs often look for trusted, safe confidants but may find them in unlikely places. Or secrecy can breed silence, changing the nature of formerly intimate friendships, sometimes leading to isolation. Almost all of Linda's spare time was spent with Jim, while she had previously been very gregarious. Moreover, she suspected that her closest friends, to whom she might have confided her affair, might be judgemental because Jim was professionally involved with John, her husband. This led to silence and further isolation. In secret affairs both men and women often feel a pressure to confide, especially if an affair brings on new or confusing feelings. For example, Sam confided in an old friend when he was in love. Feeling unbalanced, he needed to sort out his feelings. He deliberately chose to do this with someone safely distant. Or Wendy, who had an affair with her father's business partner, told Emma about her affair, only to discover that Emma had been having an eleven-year affair with her (Emma's) husband's business partner. The double secrecy bound them like black-mail, intensifying their friendship.

People have commented, 'I really knew who my friends were during that time.' The configuration of friendships is often profoundly affected by an affair: certain people who cannot be told, with whom one might have been very close, are avoided, while others who can be told move into the inner circle.

Having an affair can also affect the network of relationships because the need for secrecy can be isolating. 'I wish I could have told people because having the affair really cut me off from my friends and made me lonely', says Linda, after her affair had ended. And, as she herself experienced, that very isolation can intensify the affair, making the affair partner even more special, important and needed. Although this can happen to both men and women, the reasons for why it happens to each differ. Men, finding it easier to confide in women, may find that the affair partner is the only person in whom they can confide – because of the secrecy. With these women they can then talk about feelings their affair stirs up. For women, the secrecy takes on an increased urgency: they need to protect not only their marriages but also their reputations. This can mean that a woman may feel that no one would accept her affair. This may drive her more profoundly into the affair, the only place she can talk about the feelings aroused by it. And because there is always a tendency for women to become too involved, too merged, the isolation which breeds further dependence on the affair can reinforce this tendency.

However, as women are more accustomed to talking about their feelings, they usually find someone in whom to confide. Indeed, their guilt about affairs may be compounded because they are concealing important feelings from their women friends, denying them the usual currency of female friendship. Again, this is consistent with the gender divide: women do tend to confide in a wider network of people, including their women friends, than men. If those avenues for confiding are cut off, as in Linda's case, they will feel deep isolation. For many men this isolation is not foreign. They would not have confided to friends in any case nor would isolation have driven them to cast their social net more widely in an attempt to find a safe confidant. For many women isolation intensifies the need to confide. Either the woman then turns to the affair partner, increasing his significance and centrality, or she looks for another (usually female) confidante.

Alternatively, she copes with the sense of isolation, with varying consequences. It should be noted that many people do not have the choice – they cannot confide in others. There may be no safe and suitable person in whom to confide. The person having the affair may choose to be isolated rather than to confide or may have no choice but to be isolated. But this Hobson's choice may be one reason why many people turn at this point to therapists. They are safe confidants.

One consequence of the isolation suffered by someone in a secret affair can be depression – particularly over one's marriage. Diana went on a two-week holiday to a tennis camp – her first gesture of independence in ten years. She was then thirty years old: engaged at eighteen, she had married at twenty, with her first child on the way at twenty-one. Throughout her marriage, Diana had been her husband's assistant, running the office of his successful architectural practice. After her youngest child had gone to school, she began to feel increasingly lethargic and discontented. When a friend asked her to accompany her to a tennis camp, Diana somewhat apathetically thought it 'might be a good idea'. Her husband, fed up with her listlessness, encouraged her to go. There she became sexually involved with her instructor. Although Diana thought of it at the time as 'only a fling' and did not expect to see this man after she went home, on her return her depression deepened. She could not confide in her husband about the source of her depression. Nor did she want to risk telling anyone else (even her friend who accompanied her to the camp did not know about the affair). Her isolation increased her depression and for many months her marriage was in an intensely painful state.

A strategy for dealing with the isolation which preoccupation with an affair may bring is to decrease the preoccupation. Men, being better at cutting off, are more successful at managing this than women. When women try to bound their affair from the start by specifying rules to their lovers, they are also trying to tell themselves not to let the affair spill over messily into the rest of their lives. They are trying to prevent thoughts and longings from taking over. Although women are increasingly able to compartmentalise by specifying and keeping to boundaries, men are better at it. The following story illustrates how neatly men can cut off or segment. Nick, who is an internationally renowned economist, has a regular meeting in Germany once a year. Ghisela, a Belgian economist, is always at this meeting. Both are married, with children. During this week-long meeting they sleep together, as they have been doing for the past ten years. Nick's wife knows about it, and tolerates it as long as it stays this compartmentalised. This is the extent of their relationship, and Nick assumes that it will continue in this way indefinitely. We do not know whether Ghisela is as blasé as Nick, although Nick's wife suspects that she is not, reporting that there are phone calls and letters between meetings, while Nick denies communicating himself.

However, another consequence of the isolation attendant upon an affair can be increased self-reliance. Particularly for women, having something that they manage on their own can feel like a real achievement. Christina's first affair was an example of this. It revealed to her her effectiveness. Partly through it she pushed back the limited frontiers of her life, a life that had come to be lived very much within her own four walls, as she was crippled from a dance injury and very much stuck in the house looking after small children. After a succesful operation which enabled her to move freely, she began to work her way back slowly into the dance world and, in doing so, to commute to London one day a week. Both her children were then in full-time school and her husband, who had changed jobs, was more available for childcare. The headiness of her expanding life made her particularly susceptible to the attentions of a former colleague and they began an affair. Among the other things, the actual management of the affair, demanding time and attention away from her family, as well as canny and cool management of the secrecy, taught her that she was much more organised and in control than she had imagined.

As well as effects on the marriage, there are also effects on the affair partner. When secret affairs are discovered the impact on affair partners is often similar to that on the spouses: jealousy, anger and possessiveness run riot. A sense of betrayal, for perhaps choosing the spouses or expressing divided loyalties is also aroused. And guilt for being in an affair often rises up keenly at this point, if it has not been around all along. In fact, Jessica spent a lot of time feeling guilty about her affair with Daniel, in part because she considered herself a feminist. 'How can I be a good feminist, a "sister" to Daniel's wife if I am having an affair with another woman's, her, husband?' In fact, she felt less guilty when the affair came to light than before.

Instead, she felt betrayed by Daniel who suddenly felt bound by loyalty to his wife when she showed how hurt and angry he had made her.

There is another side to the coin. Affair partners, particularly in long-term affairs, think (sometimes with some justification, but not always) that they are the chosen, loved, special ones. Lovers stick with wives and husbands out of habit, duty, history and because of the children. But love, sex, attraction and excitement draw the lover to the affair partner. Sometimes this is true. When Daniel's wife found out about Jessica and Daniel's affair, Daniel at first went back to his wife, after promising Jessica he would live with her. At that point he wrote to her, painfully, saying that he would always love her, would love no one as he had her. But he 'could not do this' to his children. He was not sure his wife would cope. He did not see how he could throw away all those years of marriage: that would not have been fair to his wife. Moreover his parents deeply disapproved of his leaving his family.

In other cases, habit and obligation support the continuance of the affair, just as they are supposed to be supporting the continuance of the marriage. Sharon carried on seeing her lover, who worked on the support staff in her office, in part because she felt she owed it to him. He expected to see her and to sleep with her and she did not want to hurt him or let him down. Looking after his feelings went a long way towards sustaining their affair.

Frequently, the affair partner stays because he or she thinks the affair will turn into a marriage. Nora met Max when she was twenty-three and he thirty-five. He was her first serious lover and he was married, with two children. Regularly, for ten years, they met two nights every week, and in summers they spent most of one month together, while his family stayed at their summer home and he worked in the city during the week. Nora truly believed Max would leave his wife and marry her when his children were old enough. She was prepared to wait. But ten years on she wanted children and with her biological clock ticking away she began pressurising him to divorce his wife. Max made vague promises, but nothing changed and Nora grew increasingly resentful. Max's children were preparing to leave home, but Max showed no signs of doing so himself. One day Nora met Max's wife in the lift of his office block. Tempted to confront her, she resisted the urge. But she was sure then that Max's wife knew who she was; something in her stare convinced her. Shortly afterwards his wife somehow discovered the affair – Nora thinks that seeing her made certain suspicions click and, with a little detective work, the affair was indeed uncovered. Although Nora thought this would surely be her chance, it worked out quite differently. Max broke off with her utterly. As in many stories of the 'other woman', Nora lost out completely. After ten years, now in her thirties, and wanting children badly, Nora was out in the heterosexual dating field, this time quite alone and bitter.

Some people do marry their affair partners. Kate and Jonathan married and have stayed married, happily, for fifteen years. In chapter 7 we will see that while in some cases affairs do go on to be marriages, in others affairs cannot manage the transition. In still others, like Nora's and Max's, the affairs never even get to the first stage of the transition from affair to marriage.

Other affair partners remain in affairs, not rocking the boat, because the limits of affairs suit them. This is especially true if they are married. Marie, a fifty-one-year-old psychologist, has had six affairs while married. In one she fell in love with someone who lived in a different country. The tendency to merge, the compulsion to think and talk about her affair partner, to guess his thoughts, and to wonder obsessively whether or not she was central to his, began to overtake her, rocking her stability and disturbing her. For this reason, she preferred, on balance, that her lover live far away rather than near, although she was unhappy about this as well. The fact that he, too, was married was both maddening, as it made her jealous and prevented access to him even further, and also comforting, as it helped preserve her own marriage.

As we have already mentioned, most women automatically

mention effects on affair partners when discussing the affairs they have been in. Witness the example of Susannah, the forty-eight-year-old interior designer mentioned earlier:

> I did feel I loved Colin in a way, and I let him know in what way: he was ever so much fun, and we had a great time in bed. I made sure that he knew this, but also that Paul was simply number one. It was always very clear *when* I could be available for Colin and for *what*, and that I would make myself available then – and only then. I often would think of him on his own, or with his wife, whom he loved in his way, too, although they had a dreadful sex life. I knew he was OK and that made me feel all right going off with Paul – I knew Colin was fine without me. I always made sure I understood what Colin wanted from me and when it looked as if he might want more I did start to cool it – I was not going to hurt him if at all possible. We finally ended it when Colin met someone who wanted him more than I did, and he felt ready to leave his wife, and this other woman was ready and waiting for him in a way I would never be. We're still good friends and there are absolutely no hard feelings. On the contrary, I think we both feel we gave each other a lot and were very straight and fair with each other.

Whether or not their assessments of the effects on their affair partners are accurate is not the issue (Colin's story which we have not got may be quite different). Women seem to be trying to incorporate, during their affairs, what their affair partners want into what they themselves want and expect from their affairs. Men do not think this way. As we have argued, they assume their lovers can think for themselves. This is not to say that these men do not anticipate what these effects may be, but rather that they are not preoccupied with them. They are able to cut off actions from feelings, and their needs from the effects of these needs, much more than women. Their self-respect does not depend as women's does on ensuring that they are caring for others sufficiently.

While men manage to conduct their affairs without giving much thought to the effects on their partners, they may well face them in its aftermath. David reported being surprised at first by the vitriolic reaction of one of his affair partners. Although David fell a little in love with this woman while they were away, the affair ended in his thoughts as well as actions when they set foot on British soil. The abruptness of the ending tells us much about David's defences against merging with a woman. His affairs can be intense, and often are, because they are boxed off by the rules of his open marriage. These rules actually prevent him from becoming merged, or 'too involved'. The affairs, in turn, because they can be intense, if brief and limited, protect him from becoming too merged with Ursula. He had neglected to telephone his affair partner after they had spent nearly every day together for two weeks on a business trip. 'She knew I was married, didn't she?' was his response. He acknowledged that he had not clearly stipulated his terms for the affair – that it was limited and that he never intended it to get in the way of his marriage to Ursula. In his affair partner's eyes it was his responsibility to spell this out. But in his she should have assumed responsibility herself for getting the rules clear. Men act: if they need facts, they get them. They do not expect someone else to lead them there.

Similarly, while Sam had had brief affairs during his eight-year marriage, the one with Ellen was different. He seriously contemplated leaving his wife for her. Ellen's marriage was faltering when they began to see each other, and she pressed him for a decision. Ellen had been supportive during a terrible time for Sam of watching his parents die. When they finally did die, within a year of each other, Sam felt at loose ends, while Ellen's marriage at the time was practically over. When Sam equivocated about leaving his wife, Ellen grew bitter. At first her bitterness baffled him: where was the supportive, understanding woman he had come to love? Nursing his pain for a long time he gradually accepted Ellen's rejection. Unfortunately for Ellen, Sam had a different view of marriage. His was not bad, although it was limited. History, affection and appreciation for her placidity bound him to his wife. When his grief and mourning began to abate, he grew more sure, rather than less, that he needed his serene and accepting wife. Years later he feels for

Ellen, regretting her pain. Sam, being a man, could cut off from Ellen at the time of their break-up, to do what he had to do. His wife's placidity meant she was not intrusive, Ellen's passion was, and Sam ran from the merged relationship Ellen would demand.

An even more striking example of this is John, who fell in love with his affair partner and intended to marry her. But John is a devout Catholic, whose faith in the end short-circuited his affair. Twenty-eight years old, a teacher, he was married for five years to a woman he has known since childhood when he met a fellow teacher, Caroline, on a counselling course. Caroline, divorced, was at the end of an affair 'going nowhere'. She was substantially older and more worldly than John and John saw her as a woman with a strong spiritual side badly treated by the men in her life. They were passionate as he had never been with his wife, whom he had married primarily out of a sense of responsibility. He and Caroline talked about marriage from the beginning and he was acutely aware of her need for a stable relationship. But when the time came, the reality of leaving his wife seemed impossible; more importantly, if he left her he did not see how he could continue in his faith. He did an about-face, rejecting Caroline completely. He refused to see her or contact her. Although he felt awful for her, he was dismayed that she, as such a deeply spiritual woman, could not accept the impossibility of their relationship. In the end Caroline was more horribly betrayed than ever since John was supposed to have been different. But John took his decision without reference to Caroline – to take it he had to cut off from his intense feelings for her and to erase thoughts of her reaction. Months after the affair was over, when he could consider his feelings from a distance, he contemplated Caroline's point of view and felt for her.

Cause and Effect and Back Again: The Synergy Between Marriage and Affairs

Quite apart from these specific effects there is also a synergistic relationship between affairs and marriage, both cause and effect at the same time. People live in marriages and affairs simultaneously. For some people living in each is like existing in two separate narratives. Christina's first affair was mostly like that, cut off in both time and place more or less regularly as it was. Nick's affair with Ghisela is another example of this. But even then these separate narratives reflect on each other. Christina's sex with her lover reflected the segmentation of her marriage that had taken place. Her children and domestic life showed what was missing from her affair. But for others having an extramarital affair is like living in one narrative, in which events in one inform events in the other. The quality of each is affected by the other and helps give each their meaning. For instance, coming back feeling wonderful about one's lover may deflate one's feeling about one's spouse. This was certainly true for Linda, who grew more and more distant, disenchanted and angry with John as she grew more involved with Jim. Or, as Melissa experienced, it can enhance one's feelings about one's spouse and domestic life. Feeling good in one can help make one feel good in the other.

For some people who have had affairs they have seen that marriage is like a membrane. It can change form and shape, sometimes incorporating affairs and becoming different in character while the affair exists, then changing again when it is over. They learn something profound about marriage, which is that it changes in quality as other events inform it, such as deaths, births, job changes, moves and also, it seems, affairs. People can no longer subscribe to the static, romanticised notion of marriage with which they began. But they often have a more profound respect for it as an institution, if it survives, as they watch it adapt.

The influence of marriage on affair and vice versa can also lead to the break-up of either the marriage or the affair. Demands from Ellen on Sam to divorce his wife made him end his affair with Ellen. Sexual excitement and intense intimacy with Daniel led Jessica to acquiesce in her husband's wish to separate.

From all these accounts it is clear that affairs have a range of effects on the marriage, from its improvement, through to its demise. Individuals themselves may develop markedly through their experiences in affairs, or they may remain largely unaffected by them. Still others, like Diana, may become emotionally unbalanced as a result of their affairs. There is no formula for predicting which way an affair will turn out. Strategies like bounding affairs so that they fill only a clearly marked place in people's lives are sometimes but not always successful. Christina's second affair began that way and ended by usurping her feelings for her husband. A large number of affairs do not wreck lives or marriages but certainly some do. The relationship between affairs and divorce is often assumed to be stronger than it probably is. In chapter 7 we will examine this relationship more fully.

The Impact on Children of Affairs

The common line about affairs is that they must affect children, and, like divorce, that children are affected adversely. But if an affair is kept secret and separate, and if people do manage to segment affairs and marriage, cutting off when they are not with their affair partners, why should children be affected? Indeed, there will be effects on children when affairs are associated with marital discord, or when the affair brings out depression (for example, either the depression of the spouse having the affair or the one discovering the existence of the spouse's affair). But in these cases it is not necessarily the affair, *per se*, but its damaging impact on the parent or threatening effects on the marriage which have an impact on children. In segmented marriages in which the affair is successfully kept secret, children may not be affected just as spouses may not. Melissa does report an indirect benefit from her affair to her children: 'I felt better about myself, therefore I was a more cheerful, resilient mother.'

There is the obvious point that children are upset by marital disharmony, by fighting, by seeing their parents unhappy with each other and in themselves, and by the lack of energy parents have for them when they are depressed or else preoccupied with the potential breakdown of their marriage. But sometimes children also have not liked to be around the affair partners even if they do not know that an affair is going on. This happens in cases in which they ascertain, either by witnessing some striking show of emotion or by the affair partner taking up too much of the parent's time or performing the other parent's functions, that someone is having an effect on their parent which rivals or detracts from that of their other parent. The children resent people of the opposite sex making that parent too happy or taking them away from their other parent. An example is that of Alexandra, an eight-year-old who lives with her mother now that her parents' marriage has ended. Alexandra has never been told the true story of her parentage, nor of the reasons for her parents' marital break-up. While her parents were married her mother began an affair with her boss and became pregnant. Unable to have an abortion because of religious convictions, she confessed her affair to her husband. Her husband agreed to accept the baby as his own if she would agree to leave her job and end the affair. When Alexandra was four her mother returned to work part time. Her work as a systems analyst brought her into renewed contact with her old lover, whom she began to see again, sometimes at home, since he expressed interest and curiosity in seeing Alexandra, his biological daughter. When her husband found out about the renewed affair he left her, although still recognising Alexandra as his own daughter, and with joint custody arrangements for her post-divorce. Alexandra has never liked her mother's lover, even though she has been told nothing of this story. She has been told only that, 'Daddy and Mummy stopped loving each other and could not get along together any more.' When her biological father comes into the room Alexandra says that she feels uncomfortable, changing seats if seated near him.

This discomfort sometimes develops when the climate at home changes. For example, Michele's ten-year-old son, Ethan, got along very well with her research colleague, Tom, whom he had known as long as he could remember, since his mother had always worked closely with him. Tom used to take him to sports events with his daughters, since Michele's husband, Paul, was often away, and was not much interested in sports anyway. When Michele and Paul began to have marital problems, which coincided with the break-up of Tom's marriage, Ethan began to act decidedly cool around Tom, and, moreover, became surly and difficult with his mother. This surliness would become aggravated whenever Ethan suspected that Michele had spent time with Tom. The fact was that Ethan was right to feel threatened by Tom, since he and Michele had, indeed, begun to have an affair soon after Tom's wife left him. Ethan was correctly picking up the shift in their relationship and the attendant one in his parents' – as well as the potential threat to that relationship. For Michele was racked by difficult decisions at that point. Her affair with Tom made her feel discontented with the level of intimacy and companionship she felt she and Paul had established. Her relationship with Paul became more distant and discordant. Ethan noticed this, but also noticed that his mother was cheerful around Tom and spending more time with him. These children are acting similarly to the children of divorced or separated parents, often resenting the new partner for stepping into the other parent's place.

Children also can feel during parental affairs that they are in the middle. Adolescents are particularly vulnerable to this triangulation. Because adolescents are like adults in many respects, needy parents may, often inappropriately, lean on them. When Karen's father was having an affair with his secretary he confided in her both about the affair and his intention to leave her mother when the 'time was right'. Loyal to her father, and afraid of upsetting her mother, Karen carried this secret. In the meantime, her mother suffered from myriad psychosomatic complaints, and the marriage, never good, further deteriorated. Karen withdrew from both parents and her schoolwork began to suffer. A year later her father told her that he had had a child with the other women. Ultimately, Karen left home, angry at her father, and also at her mother for not standing up to him.

Sally's mother drew her daughters around her like a blanket when her husband went off to France with another woman. He was 'shiftless', 'irresponsible', a 'hopeless romantic', while she was blameless, a model wife, treated badly by this fool. Her daughters, who had formerly adored him for he was fun-loving, affectionate and warm with them (entirely unlike their mother), viewed him with contempt. This was especially so when he returned a short time later, minus the other woman, begging to be taken back. Even now, thirty years later, his daughters side with their mother in the firm belief that he was 'shiftless', 'irresponsible', a 'hopeless romantic', while their mother was a poor victim of such a man. The daughters' loyalty to both parents was challenged and they lost one parent as a result. In Karen's case she lost both.

It is primarily what is associated with having the affair – be it depression, preoccupation, discord, loyalty struggles or a threat to the marriage's survival – which upsets children. Obviously, when a secret affair is discovered, a stage when a marriage may become deeply unstable, children are affected by the turmoil. When Richard's affair was discovered Polly told their two children. They supported her and were against Richard at first. Then, feeling left out by both parents as their parents fought each other bitterly, they both began to act out, getting into minor legal scrapes, failing in school. The effects on children of marriages in turmoil because of affairs varies with a child's age. Younger children will be affected in obvious ways by overt marital dysfunction. Their needs for time and attention are great and these may be subverted by their parents' marital dramas. Older, or adolescent children, more independent, will be affected in more subtle ways; their trust and belief in stable partnerships might be shaken, or their need for refuge in a relationship of their own creation might be forged at that point.

Moreover, adolescent children are probably more attuned to their parents' sexual relationship and to whether there are sexual undercurrents in their parents' other relationships. In addition, since they may also act as confidants to their parents, they may be drawn into their parents' marital dramas and affairs.

Even adult children can be or have been affected by their own parents having affairs. Of course, adult children are more likely to know about affairs because they are both more likely to notice and more likely to be told by their parents. Dennis was extremely upset by the fact that his mother had left his father after forty-two years of marriage, because, in part, she was 'fed up with his other women'. He had never known that his father, a well-known playwright, had been unfaithful. Now, forced to think about it, he realised that it was entirely possible that the intense friendships his parents had formed with certain actresses and women agents over the years, and one journalist in particular, were probably not as innocent as he had thought. These had been his father's girlfriends and his mother had known. He felt deceived, angry at both his parents, duped by them into thinking they had a kind of marriage which they did not. His unmarried sister came to live with his grief-stricken father. Sides were taken. Even his relationship with his sister became twisted through their respective anger and pain.

However, some people recount being unaffected by their parents' open affairs. Ted knew of his father's open affair with Camilla, a younger unmarried neighbour. His mother accepted it. His father's loyalty to the family was unquestioned. Eventually, the affair ended when the family moved away, and he thinks that Camilla finally married. It may be significant, however, that Ted's background is upper-crust, one in which affairs have figured in past marriages and generations. Fidelity is a peripheral value; sharing tastes, background and experiences, enjoying each other's company, and stable family life are far more central. Other adult children, however, report having had to take sides: 'It was selfish of him to do that – it hurt her', was the way Michael talked of his memory of his father's 'flings', as he called them.

Whether these children who are now grown-ups have affairs in their own marriages is influenced by this history, or their family scripts, as the psychiatrist and therapist John Byng-Hall has called them. But each script may call for a different denouement. Susannah, the child of a home in which affairs were openly tolerated, carries on 'discreet' affairs. Her model of marriage is very like that of her own parents, which survived over fifty years. Michael's feelings are more ambivalent. He has affairs and feels bad about them. For him secrecy is particuarly important if there are children in a marriage. Memories of having to comfort his mother when his father ran off with the nanny haunt him still.

Retrospective accounts such as these may be rewriting history. But we can speculate that children may feel confused by knowing about their parents' liaison with someone not their other parent. Certainly, if the child is caught in the middle, or forced to side with one parent over the other, as Michael was, affairs are going to be painful. But, on the other hand, if a child feels that the family is secure, perhaps he or she can indeed accept parental affairs with equanimity, as Susannah and Ted report.

Emotional Involvement and the Impact of Affairs

The impact of an affair also depends upon how strongly people feel about their affair partners. Christina's two affairs show this. When she was first interviewed for this book she was having an affair which barely affected her marriage. She enjoyed her affair partner but she loved her husband. A few years later, after that affair had ended relatively painlessly, she fell in love with her husband's best friend. Consumed by her feelings for him, she could barely focus on her husband. Even before she disastrously told him, her marriage had deteriorated under the impact of her passion for her lover.

Limited emotional involvement often means limited impact on the marriage, as Christina's first affair demonstrated. Perhaps she could have gone on having affairs if all had remained limited. But, as we mentioned in our discussion of risks in affairs, one risk is that people cannot always be sure that their feelings will remain in neat compartments, as Christina found out in her second affair.

Discovering a Secret Affair

The impact of discovering a secret affair, whether it be revealed through exposure or through a spouse's disclosure, is of a different order altogether. Any good effects up to that point can be vitiated. The impact of discovering that vows were broken, evidence hidden, often lies told and other deceits committed, is traumatic to any partnership, let alone to a marriage. For marriage is supposed to be built on honesty. It explicitly demands monogamy. Unless a marriage is open, its foundation of trust and its rules have been violated.

When a secret affair comes to light, no matter whether the impulse to tell has come from a desire to make the marriage better at one end of a continuum, or to end it at the other, a period of increased bad feeling ensues. This is more so if the affair has been exposed rather than disclosed. The spouse feels betrayed. The betrayed spouse, feeling fully justified as victim, heaps pain and anger upon the betrayer. But if the affair has ended, the spouse who had the affair is often grieving for its loss. If it is continuing, he or she feels caught horribly in the middle. Resentment of the spouse's pressurising can even precipitate a turning away from the spouse and towards the affair partner.

Even when an affair is revealed long after it has ended the spouse who had it usually remembers feeling, or even continues to feel, some attachment to the affair partner. There will often be something good to be remembered or cherished which lingers. The opposing positions in which spouses find themselves tend to become entrenched, exaggerated, distorted and deeply polarised. Pain divides rather than unites when one of the couple is the cause of it. Guilt drives the erring spouse defensively further away from the other. When this proceeds begins, when pain and guilt are thick between them, the couple enters a phase which Emily Brown has called obsession with the affair. It is a deeply divisive stage. Yet the mutual obsession joins the couple. They are stuck, the affair still dividing them, yet not yet providing the resolution of either divorce or reconciliation. For the injured spouse the obsession includes a preoccupation with the affair partner and the details of the affair which feels both perverse and gripping: is he/she better than I? Does this mean that my spouse is less than/more than the man/woman than I thought? What has my marriage meant? What have I meant to him/her? How could I have trusted him/her? How can I continue to do so? What else have I been betrayed about? What else do I not know about him/her? The marriage feels like a house of cards. For the spouse who has had the affair, it sometimes means defending the affair partner. This slows the ending of feelings for him or her as well as driving a further wedge between the couple. In this phase the spouse who had the affair often undergoes terrible self-doubt, feeling cruel and vile for inflicting such pain. This is so even when affairs had been valuable and important. Others can get caught up in the affair at this stage, too. For this is a phase when sides can get taken, children can become triangulated, and friendships can be severed.

Some couples never progress from this phase – the marriage is stuck in its quagmire, doomed to its pain. It is very difficult to move beyond it. Paradoxically, it seems, in trying to leave the affair couples can get stuck in its aftermath for the rest of their married life as have Richard and Polly, introduced in chapter 5. In many cases this aftermath is what ends marriages, rather than the affair itself. Thus, the impulse to confess, even though it may come from noble intentions and benign motivations, such as to relieve guilt or to clear the air, may certainly backfire. Revelation of a formerly secret affair leads to the most painful stage of the affair for the marriage.

This is not to say that disclosure in itself is destructive. It can be the catalyst for rebuilding, even strengthening, a marriage as it was for Susie and Simon. But this will depend in part on what model of marriage both partners desire: if one spouse wants to continue the segmented model with its attendant secrecy or to move to an open marriage while the other wants to return to marriage-is-for-everything, rebuilding is doomed. It also depends on whether in the aftermath of disclosure both spouses learn something from the affair, detach from it, and focus instead on new goals for their marriage.

There are other traumas a marriage undergoes in the aftermath of discovery. When an affair is discovered it usually becomes public. The spouse who discovers often confides in others. This can also mean that the one who had or is having the affair also turns to outsiders. Often these others are not impartial and reinforce one side against the other. Sides are taken, battle lines are drawn. Friendships change and are sometimes broken. Loyalties thicken and may not shift even if the couple put the affair behind them. For instance, when the recently unemployed Matthew left his wife and children to go around the world with his new lover, his wife, Caroline, confided in her mother. She knows that her mother would never forgive him. To take Matthew back would entail a breach with her mother.

If the publicity or uproar surrounds children, things grow even more complicated. Valerie's and Julian's eight- and eleven-year-old daughters felt like parcels bouncing back and forth between parents and various side-taking friends. Julian became very depressed on discovering Valerie's affair, while Valerie responded with self-righteous indignation, blaming him for driving her to it through his passivity and sexual indifference. From one day to the next they made plans to separate, first with Julian leaving, then Valerie. Each time they told the girls. Each time they changed their minds. Valerie would sketchily confide in the elder daughter and Julian would go to bed while the girls brought him cups of tea. The couple then tried reconciliation, taking a family holiday. Before long the two girls were avoiding going home, turning up on neighbours' doorsteps at dinner time, looking sad and bewildered. In this case neither child took sides. But in Richard's and Polly's they did. Both children are openly contemptuous of their father. His constant apologies remind them of his transgression and renew their mother's pain. They say, 'Anyone who has an affair is dirt.' Anger at the affair permits other older anger to surface: why was he so marginal? Why did he not care enough about them to take time with them when they were little? Together, mother and children continue to marginalise him through their contempt.

There is also lasting, if diminished pain even when marriages successfully survive the post-discovery phase. Susie will never forget her shock and insecurity. Like the death of a loved one, it lives in her memory, scarring her, a sadness she has buried but which she will not forget. It is possible to spark her pain, if harder these days than it was earlier.

Moreover, the model of their marriage is now fixed, rigid even: there are no affair jokes allowed. Rules are set. Marriages which have endured discovery and survived, mended, are usually marriages which feel as if they must stick to rules.

Discovery can yield either a real and important change in a marriage, or it can consign it to terrible pain, and even break it apart. In any case, it should be remembered that no matter what the outcome, it produces a difficult, unsettled and painful aftermath which cannot be avoided. And, it should also be remembered, despite everyone's best efforts, the risk in secret affairs (which are the most common sort) is that they will be discovered, although many, in fact, remain secret.

Guilt and Disclosure: the Desire to Tell

Some people disclose because of guilt. As we have said in chapter 4, the guilt may arise from the fact they are withholding something from the marriage which has been promised to, or acknowledged to belong to, the spouse, or from the imagined hurt that will result if the affair is discovered. But they also may feel guilty because the moral climate or their religious upbringing make it impossible to feel otherwise. No matter how beneficial they may feel the affair to be, as we saw in the case of Simon, they will feel guilty.

However, the impulse to disclose to relieve guilt most often backfires. Coupled with the desire for relief is too often the one for absolution. This presupposes that one's spouse will understand and will leave his or her own feelings behind. Accompanying this may be the naive wish that one's spouse will appreciate those qualities in the affair partner which were attractive in the first place. Another frequent component of the impulse to confess is that people think that if they are brave enough to do so then the spouse will appreciate their courage. The expectation is that this appreciation should be enough to mitigate the inevitable sense of betrayal. Of course, these expectations are usually misguided. When we turn to the spouse's reaction we shall see why this is so.

The impulse to confess puts women, particularly, in a double bind. They feel guiltier but they will suffer graver consequences if they confess. As Laura says of her policy of secrecy around her four affairs:

> I might want to have a closer relationship with my husband. But that is simply not what he is interested in. This kind of relationship that we have had now for almost twenty years is workable – I do not put pressure on him, the way I used to do, to make him talk to me more, or to do more 'sensitive' things with me. He is a good husband and father in many ways, but he is just not a confidant. So – you don't need it all in the same package, do you? I used to feel lonely a lot. Now I think the way we've worked it out is all right although it would not work if he found out. So sometimes I feel frightened that things might get found out, and everything would blow up. Or I sometimes feel sad that these affairs actually make me more distant from him, and they symbolise how I can't be close to him. I think *if* he found out I might feel guilty – for the secrecy, especially.

The 'if he found out' stops her telling: for if he did, she thinks her marriage would be over.

Men's confessions often engender quite different consequences. Indeed, some men confess because their affairs become too painful, and they actually turn to their wives for comfort. Since wives are usually their main and only confidantes, this is not that surprising. In contrast, wives may have talked to one of their many women confidantes. Sometimes men disclose for reasons other than guilt or pain, such as a desire to end the marriage. But whatever the motivation, the consequences of disclosure are not usually as severe for them. Women will not necessarily divorce them. And indeed, sometimes their wives will comfort them as they always have done.

This happened in Phillip's and Rachel's marriage. Married for ten years, Phillip began an affair with a younger woman with whom he worked on a political campaign. For most of their marriage Phillip had exalted Rachel, an accomplished and charming woman. In contrast, Phillip was marginally successful, tentative and unsure of himself. Rachel organised their social life, kept their finances and was responsible for housework and major purchases. She had also brought her own independent and more substantial income to the marriage. In his political work Phillip met someone who in turn idolised him and, of course, flattered, he fell completely. For two years he kept the affair secret. In time his lover met someone else and ended their affair. Despondent, he turned to Rachel. Her response was to mother him – she says that she had to put jealousy and betrayal to one side until she was sure he would be all right. They spent many tortured weeks until he began to stabilise. Only then did she permit her own pain to surface. She never thought seriously of divorce.

As we have seen, women are more likely to leave or to be thrown out of marriages after disclosure or exposure. Those men who stay on find themselves suffering a different consequence – marginalisation within the family, even scapegoating. Men, already usually more peripheral to their children than are their wives (even if both are working) may be further marginalised as a result of their wives' anger and pain, as they gather their children to them for support. Sometimes they turn their children explicitly against their father. Barbara, a thirty-three-year-old teacher and mother of three, told of how she and her younger sister grew up distant from their father, whom they adored, because he had had an affair when she was ten and her sister eight. Although he left home for a few months, he did return after ending his affair. Her mother never forgave him. One way this was demonstrated was by her mother's pointed exclusion of him from family activities. Mother organised their social life and outside activities. Most of these revolved around things which excluded men, such as sewing, baking or decorating. If Sunday walks were ever suggested by her father her mother usually prevented these by diverting the girls to other more pressing projects or duties. Women, because of the emotional power and control they have within the family are able to marginalise their husbands, while husbands, usually without that power, cannot do the same.

People may disclose an affair when they want their marriages to end. In those cases it is painful but straightforward. Not everyone chooses this strategy. A great number of people construe divorce as something separate from their affairs, so they think confessing an affair clouds the issue of ending their marriage. However, many see the decision to end as inextricable with the desire for the lover and so present it that way to their spouses.

Kate is now happily married to her former affair partner with whom she has two children. She says, 'I think both Jonathan [her present husband] and I both really knew that our marriages were over when we met each other.' They had worked together for a while. Gradually they realised that they were falling in love. Kate felt that her marriage had been a mistake from the beginning. Jonathan had become deeply unhappy with his wife. When they fell in love it became clear what each was going to do – that is, each was going to end their respective marriages. As Kate says, 'Luckily there were no children involved on either side. It was pretty messy for a while, but we both left our spouses.' They think that it was quite clear from the start that they did the right thing. They have been married now for almost fifteen years.

Others decide to tell because they want their spouse to know what they have learned from their affairs. For instance, if in an affair someone learns that he or she can be uninhibited in bed while their sex life at home is dull and constrained, there may be a great temptation to say, 'Look, this isn't my fault. I found that out in bed with so and so.' Linda was greatly tempted to tell John about Jim's passion in bed as well as about his intense interest in her ideas because John dismissed as idealistic her wish that he be more attentive and passionate. She resisted the impulse to tell, but not everybody does.

Even people in segmented-marriage models can feel the pressure to tell in this way, in a belief that if only they could show their spouse, with evidence, then the spouse might change. The marriage would not have to be segmented any more. Sam sometimes wishes that he could tell his wife about his more passionate sex with other women or about the fact that because Ellen was more spikey, spirited and independent this made her more attractive to him. Then maybe his wife could change. Again, Sam does not tell because he knows that his wife would not change and would only be hurt.

Sometimes people confess affairs because they want to end a state of indecision. Daniel, whose affair with Jessica was discussed in chapter 4, wanted to tell his wife about their affair partly because he hoped that she would throw him out and he would then not have to make the decision to leave himself. But he had not predicted the power of her fury, and when, enraged, she did indeed throw him out, he backtracked, horrified at what he had provoked. Sometimes people tell because they think in doing so they will find out whether their spouses really care deeply for them after all. When Annie told her husband about her last affair, she was shocked but gratified by her husband's deep hurt. From the depth of his pain she realised that he cared far more than she had imagined. For a moment it looked as if there might be hope for her marriage. Unfortunately, this was not to be. His rage was so enormous that he moved out and began divorce proceedings almost immediately.

People also reveal their affairs when they want either revenge or to equalise a relationship after their spouses have had affairs. The desire to pay back or to rebalance the marriage emotionally can brew over many years. A few years after Ian, a fifty-year-old physicist, found out that his wife had had an affair which she had claimed was 'insignificant', he had an affair – again 'insignificant' – with one of their acquaintances. It was necessary for him to tell his wife. Both understood that it had made something equal again in their marriage, putting an end to something which his wife had begun with her earlier affair. Equality of power is a central, explicit issue in their marriage: it comes out over many other things, such as the time each allots to his or her career, or over negotiations over who does what with their children. Thus, it is not surprising that it was a major dimension in the aftermath of his wife's affair. The story of Ian and his wife is unusual. The retaliatory or spiteful affair more often results in a tremendous emotional mess. Often, when disclosed, such quid pro quo affairs end with a lot of bad feeling, including the affair partner feeling exploited or a pawn in a marital game, without achieving the desired effect – the sharply targeted suffering of the spouse who had the original affair. Too often other things suffer, including the quality of the marriage as well as the person who had the retaliatory affair. The process of guilt, betrayal, hurt and insecurity just begins again. Now the retaliator becomes the guilty one (sometimes doubly so, since he or she should have *known* how it feels).

Exposure

Sometimes an affair is discovered even though people have resolutely decided that they will not tell. This occurs through exposure, which is usually the most explosive way for any affair to be revealed. If a spouse chooses to tell about his or her affair at least he or she is partially prepared for the drama which is likely to ensue. This is not the case in exposure. Exposure is a shock to both spouses and so can destabilise a marriage far more. It underscores the deception element of an affair, emphasising the potential for feeling betrayed. The revelation is unmitigated by an attempt at honesty.

Exposure can occur through a third party's actions (either witting or unwitting). Or it can occur through the spouse who is not having the affair finding evidence. Or it can happen through the spouse who is having an affair leaving evidence more or less accidentally for the other to discover. Sometimes it can come through the devices of the affair partner.

Joe, a defence engineer, was supposed to be working on a consulting job overnight when he got taken ill and immediately turned back and came home. He found his wife in bed with one of her co-workers; this began the end of their marriage. Linda's affair was almost unwittingly exposed through a friend's mentioning in John's presence that she had seen Linda riding with Jim around town on a day when she had told John she would be away with college friends. Linda managed to recover with a semi-plausible story and John never knew the truth. Susannah's lover threatened to tell her husband in a blackmailing attempt to get Susannah to continue their relationship. The knowledge that she had the power to retaliate by blackening his name in his profession made it possible for Susannah to call his bluff and so stop the exposure. George had numerous affairs in this thirteen-year marriage to Dottie. In the first Dottie surprised George in bed with a friend of hers, in much the same way as Joe had surprised his wife. After that she became sensitive to clues. Itemised phone and credit card bills have left trails which she has followed usually to discover that her suspicions have been correct.

Exposure, like disclosure, but more so, can be a precursor to a marital dissolution. It can so rock a marriage, and the aftermath of it be so painful and ugly, that no matter how stable and good the marriage was before or how unimportant the affair, or how beneficial the affair might have seemed, exposure can destroy a marriage. On the other hand, some marriages survive, often with help. In Dottie's case religious conviction kept her married, in the belief that to divorce was a sin.

The Spouse's Reaction: Betrayal, Jealousy, Insecurity and Rage

Because marital ideology proscribes both secrecy and affairs, there is no way to avoid a spouse reacting with fury, betrayal, jealousy and insecurity. Both men and women feel them. However, their gender means that they will express them differently.

Husbands do not act the hurt, rejected victim as easily as wives do. Instead, they smoulder with anger, put fists in walls, threaten to kill people. This is even true for gentle, forbearing men. For instance, Henry, a social worker, was shy and retiring, while Alicia, his wife, was extrovert, flamboyant and assertive. Alicia had had a history of abusive, tortured relationships, including with her father, while Henry's was a relatively stable background. In consequence, Henry did a lot of looking after Alicia, calming her often ruffled nerves and quick temper. When Alicia had an affair and confessed it to Henry, to relieve her misery since she had been rejected by her lover, instead of his comforting her, he got so angry he smacked her, another abusive experience banked in her already large account. While men, like women, do feel hurt, betrayed, insecure and jealous (indeed, this was the reason Henry gave for hitting Alicia – he had felt betrayed) they act on these feelings, angrily. There is cultural support for a man's anger. In contrast, despondence detracts from his sexuality, his manliness. Rob and Maria are a case in point. After thirteen years of marriage with no children but a history of emotional distance and unsatisfactory sex, Maria left Rob for another man. When this affair began to go sour Maria tried to return to Rob. However, Rob had moped around, depressed, unmotivated, his self-esteem hitting rock bottom, for the entire seven months of her affair. At its end he was still stuck in the pit of despondency. He had never shown anger. Maria realised that she could no longer respond to Rob sexually. All she could feel was pity, a feeling which left her uncomfortably turned off by her former husband.

On the other hand, women, while also being furious ('hell hath no fury like a woman scorned') are more generally despondent and hurt rather than angry. This is consistent with their gender role and cultural expectations. Indeed, we are less tolerant of a woman angrily divorcing on grounds of adultery – except when the affair is still continuing. Shouldn't she be thinking of her children? The family's stability? Won't she give him another chance? Unlike men, she is supposed to consider family welfare first, rather than to act in hasty anger. Part of the fascination of the film, *Fatal Attraction*, was the role reversal: the murderous jealousy came from a woman rather than from a man. On the other hand, a woman hurt gets mountains of sympathy, and her husband is supposed to repent and repay. We have already referred to Richard's and Polly's marriage, stuck in the guilty aftermath of Richard's affair. Although Polly, and their two teenage children, were enraged, her main feeling was that she had been immeasurably hurt. She has been on antidepressants for four years. For four years Richard has been the repenter. He phones several times a day to see how she is doing; he buys his family expensive vacations and toys, and in general sees that his duty is to woo his wife out of her pain. He has become the family scapegoat and he acccepts this role as his penance.

Of course, wives who discover their husbands' affairs are usually also angry. But if they show too much anger the tide of support may turn away from them and roll towards their husbands. When Eric's affair with one of his ex-students was discovered by his wife, Mary, Mary went to town with her revenge. She began persecuting the former girlfriend through letters and phone calls. She phoned her repeatedly at work, leaving messages explicitly calling attention to her affair with a married man. When Mary began exposing Eric at his department, the tide of sympathy turned surely and steadily against her. In contrast, when Hugh, also an academic, publicly humiliated his wife and her lover, sympathy ran with him. Hugh suddenly punched her former lover at a drinks party in front of his wife's entire department. Although the party spirit may have been dampened, Hugh's reputation remained undiminished. In contrast, Mary was deemed 'deranged', and 'unhinged'.

The revelation of a secret affair obviously has the potential for this sort of destructiveness. As we said in chapter 4, secrecy can both breathe life and bring death to an affair. We have focused on how its revelation can threaten or even kill a marriage. But it is also important to realise that while the revelation of a secret affair may always rock a marriage, it also can signal its reconstruction as well.

Managing Marital Change After Discovery

Despite these traumas the exposure of an affair can be constructive in the end for many marriages. If the affair is well and truly over, if both husband and wife want to preserve the marriage, and if they both want to dissect it, looking for avenues towards change, the prognosis is better. It is also enhanced if there was voluntary disclosure of the affair, rather than exposure. Prognosis is often even better if there is marital therapy.

After Susie found out about Simon's affair the couple endured an extremely painful few months. Susie lost weight; both lost sleep, were unproductive and cried copiously. Both recoiled from divorce. This shared horror enabled them to realise that they would have to try to get over the affair. While not in therapy, they turned to supportive friends, who fortunately did not take sides. Susie's constant questioning 'why' pressurised Simon to find an explanation both for Susie and for himself. He found that the overwhelming appeal of the affair was that it removed him from Susie's inordinate dependence on him. Although Susie was as highly trained as her husband, she had trained under him. In the early stages of her career this had not been a problem, but with middle age coming upon them, Simon was clearly moving far ahead of her. Susie remained too identified, too merged, with him and as his confidence grew hers diminished. For Susie this did not feel a problem but for Simon it did. In other ways, too, she had woven her life around him. Although a naturally gregarious person, her friendships slowly attenuated, especially after having children. Galvanised by the crisis in her marriage Susie joined an exercise class, began to see more of her friends and eventually set up her own office. The quality of her life improved, and, perhaps of greater note to their marriage, Simon was more passionate and demonstrative with her. A few years post-discovery their marriage had transformed. No longer did they jump from arguments, usually initiated by Susie who was feeling neglected, to reunions to arguments again.

The example of Susie and Simon illustrates four points in the recovery period after an affair has been discovered. The first is that they used the affair to initiate changes in their relationship, rather than allowing it to control their marriage. As a consequence, the affair receded as the marriage changed. Secondly, they chose commitment to their marriage. Third, they indicated appropriate areas of manageable change and initiated actions to change. Fourth, they restated their mutual commitment to a clear model of marriage, in this case to the marriage-is-for-everything model.

But in the aftermath of discovery of his affairs Nick's marriage changed to an open one. He and his wife now have a clearly agreed contract of what kind of affair is permissible and under what conditions. This is because Nick firmly believes that his resentment would crush his marriage if he were forced to be monogamous. His wife rather begrudgingly capitulated. The statement of a clear marital model is central to recovery. If a spouse wants a monogamous marriage, he or she needs reassurance that there will never be another affair again. Thus the marriage must move to a marriage-is-for-everything model. In Nick's case his wife could live with affairs as long as she was assured Nick would not prefer another woman. Her reassurance was not about sexual but emotional fidelity. Nick is now explicitly bounded to affairs of brief duration, little intensity and with women who live at a distance.

There is no place for the segmented model, with its secrecy

about affairs, in the recovery process. The issues of trust, betrayal and insecurity which surface need to be settled; only then, calmed, is there space enough in a marriage for a couple to reflect upon it and renew their commitment. The spouse who has felt betrayed needs reassurance through increased intimacy, something at odds with the segmented model, which emphasises autonomy at the discretion of only one of the spouses. The spouse who has felt betrayed needs to carry on protecting him or herself so there is a keen alertness to evidence of any subsequent betrayals. Consequently, any subsequent affairs are much more likely to be discovered. Most marriages will not survive further discoveries. But certainly there are marriages which do. Keith had eleven affairs which Sandy knew about in their fifteen years of marriage. But Sandy was a staunch Catholic who took her vows so seriously she preferred to remain married, suffering anew each time she smelled another affair.

Marital Therapy and Managing Marital Change

People turn to therapy in crises. As we have already said, people who feel upset by affairs may engage a therapist because they find no other safe person in whom to confide. It is not surprising then that when a secret affair is discovered people turn to marriage therapists. Moving out of the obsession stage, away from the debilitating pain, is very difficult for a couple to manage on its own. That is in part why outsiders often get pulled in. Therapists, because supposedly unbiased and devoted to analysing sources of problems, may offer the calm and reflection the couple need.

A couple may weather the post-discovery phase without therapy, but it is tricky. Christina and her husband did not get professional help, and their marriage survives, but there are still rough days, two years after discovery. The marital rules are clear, they have moved to a marriage-is-for-everything model, but Christina occasionally feels empty, her husband's pain is still palpable, and she is extremely careful around him. The atmosphere at home is often tense. Yet they feel they have created clear rules for their marriage through the discovery of the affair.

From what has been said up to now it might seem obvious that marital therapy can sometimes make the difference between a marriage's survival and its death after discovery. Because betrayal, insecurity, jealousy and guilt are powerful and gripping emotions, couples often cannot loosen that grip alone. A therapist is likely to be an outsider, seen in an arena unsullied by past painful associations. Moreover, having therapy means that the couple is committed in principle to spending regular amounts of time and energy in trying to understand at least the motivation towards the affair and its effect on the marriage. Of course, not every therapist provides the dispassion, wisdom or proper judgement and tact necessary to the process. And not every member of a couple wishes to heal his or her marriage in therapy.

In addition, most marital therapy operates from the marriage-is-for-everything model, and therefore emphasises intimacy over autonomy. Because of the prevalence of this model, much therapeutic work devotes itself both to moving couples towards monogamy and also to encouraging disclosure, which promotes intimacy, although there is some disagreement about the degree – how much detail is it healthy to hear? To permit secrecy discourages intimacy, the line goes. Openness and honesty are promoted. Intimacy is increased if the couple suffers through the trauma of the affair together, rather like mourning a painful loss together draws people closer. Moreover, there is a strong feeling among many therapists that they should not keep marital secrets told them by one member of the couple if they are treating the marriage as a whole. For technical and ethical reasons this is often a sensible stand to take. If the secret comes out and the therapist is discovered to be party to it, the spouse who feels betrayed also feels betrayed by the therapist. This can undo any past or future work. But as we have seen, disclosure is sometimes the very thing which itself wrecks the marriage. In addition, pressuring to disclose can hasten the end of therapy. When Clark and Lydia were in therapy the therapist suspected that Lydia was having an affair. He scheduled separate sessions for the spouses, in the hope of encouraging Lydia's confession in Clark's absence. Because Lydia suspected this she cancelled both sessions and therapy ended.

This is clearly a particular view of the function of marital therapy. As we have said, most marital therapy starts from the view that 'marriage should be for everything', and an affair is a symptom of something wrong with the marriage. Consequently, whatever the person got from an affair should probably be got in the marriage. The task for the therapy is to get the couple to work on getting it in the marriage. So, in the case of Richard and Polly, the task is to develop more intimacy, co-operation, shared activities and interest in each other, as the affair pointed up the enormous isolation between Richard and the rest of his family.

In Nick's case, therapy which promotes monogamy, or the marriage-is-for-everything model would not have worked. His undemonstrative wife felt awkward having cosy, intimate fire-side talks every night, or throwing her arms around him in public. This was one of the reasons he felt drawn to affairs, as they renewed his connections with women. The couple's compromise was to accept that their marriage is limited, working out a marital agreement bounding but allowing extra-marital affairs. In fact, therapy helped them reach this agreement. The emphasis in marital therapy on the importance of intimacy in a marriage does not acknowledge the competing need for autonomy. Both Nick and his wife had different autonomous needs. His wife wanted to be left alone some nights, unpressured to be demonstrative, just as Nick wanted sexual freedom.

In addition to seeing affairs as pathological, or symptomatic of something wrong with a marriage which therapy has to set right, there are therapists such as Frank Pittman (see page 7), who take a strong position against affairs on moral grounds. In his view affairs are a 'sickness' in a 'sick' marriage.

Other therapists take a different position. They see their

brief as to help the couple decide whether they want to stay together or not and, if they do, to identify realistic, appropriate and manageable negotiations which they must achieve in order to do this. The model of marriage is up to the couple to decide. Disclosure is not an aim in itself, because it can lead to destruction. If it occurs, it produces a crisis which therapy must manage. Instead, in this view, therapists must weigh up the pros and cons of disclosure should they suspect an affair, and decide as the professional helping the marriage whether they should encourage or discourage disclosure.

When Linda and John went into marital therapy, as Linda was trying to end her affair with Jim, their therapist knew about the affair from an individual session with Linda. She decided against encouraging Linda to confess. Instead, she encouraged Linda to bring what she had learned from her experience with Jim – that she wanted more intimacy, time and demonstrative-ness from a man – to the therapy sessions. Linda never mentioned Jim. The therapist helped John to accommodate to Linda's now clarified desires. The therapy was successful, using the affair without ever confessing to it.

In order for a therapist to make an adequate assessment of whether to permit or encourage disclosure, or what model of marriage towards which to move a couple, we think the therapist needs to try to analyse the affair along specific dimensions first. What is the context of the affair – the life cycle, personal history or family-script issues and the history of vulnerability in the particular marriage? What model of mar-riage has each member of this couple been operating from? And finally, the gender issues which we have tried to highlight throughout this book need to be underscored when treating the marriage. In trying to get the couple to understand their respective reactions to the affair itself and its aftermath, men and women will use different language and constructs to describe their feelings, motivations and the impact of the affair. The therapist must be a 'gender broker', in the phrase coined by the American feminist therapist, Virginia Goldner. He or she must interpret each spouse's experience to the other, trying to take each member of the couple over the gender divide, encouraging empathy with the spouse's experience. It is difficult and not always successful work, but therapy sometimes offers the chance for a wounded marriage to recover.

7 Marriage, Affairs and Divorce: Old Beginnings and New Endings

All three women are equally upset, equally desperate. All three men involved have double vision. All seek the conveniences of marriage and the freedom of the sexual chase. All three women want sexual joy and security to be combined in the same person: their image of men is an integrated one. Therefore the desires of men and women are incompatible. Not because the man's desire is for the woman and the woman's desire is for the desire of the man, but because women can't find in men whole human beings, and the whole human beings women are are not what men have been led to believe they want.

Ann Oakley
Taking it like a woman, 1984

It is often taken for granted that affairs cause the break-up of marriages; or if they are not the cause, that they are at least a symptom of a decaying relationship and so represent a step on an inevitable path to a divorce. In this chapter we will examine connections between affairs and divorce. We conclude that the consequences of affairs for marriages are not as straightforward and obvious as many believe.

From the picture of modern marriage that we painted in chapter 1, it follows that an affair will now be much more threatening to the survival of a marriage than it would have been in the past. As marriage has become more exclusive and the value placed on open communication, intimacy and a shared sexuality between the couple has grown, other sexual relationships represent a much more potent betrayal and threat. This conflict may be further increased if an extramarital relationship shares some of the very same companionate features of modern marriage. An affair may make its own demands for exclusive-ness and sharing between the partners. But do affairs, like the excitable games we were warned about as children, always lead to tears? Clearly, they do in some cases.

Affairs and Remarriage

Some affair partners become new spouses through divorce and remarriage. But the journey from one partner to another is only very rarely a simple one. Quite apart from the financial, emotional and practical difficulties that divorce always brings, as well as the immense upheavals for children, the ending of a marriage will always put great strain on the affair relationship as the new couple try to convert it into an exclusive marriage. As we have emphasised throughout, there is always a degree of interdependence between an affair and a marriage, so that the ending of one is bound to have implications for the other. The very secrecy of the affair may have been a major element in its attraction. The couple's limited time together and the usually very restricted circumstances in which they can meet may help to give the relationship its special excitement and intensity. Everyday life and all its routineness are excluded; the couple are there solely to be together. It's all prime time and, as one of our interviewees remarked, 'you don't have to stay to do the washing up'. Affairs are often fed by a sense of what might be. The secrecy and the competing demands of the couple's marriages inevitably mean that there are many things they cannot do together. Not least among these may be idealised features of a marriage, such as quiet evenings together with nothing particular to do. Once an affair becomes a marriage, romantically imagined futures become present realities and not all relationships can stand the transformation. The couple may be too dependent on the limitations within which most affairs exist. The imagined possibilities that were always beyond reach may not be quite so wonderful when they become everyday life. For these reasons, when many affairs become public and the couple begin to extricate themselves from their old marriages to move into a new one, the relationship does not survive. Others may get as far as remarriage or cohabitation before the relationship collapses. As has been well demonstrated in surveys from many countries, second marriages are less long-lasting than those of couples on their first time round.

A second marriage that grows out of an affair always has to face an uncomfortable truth at its heart: as both partners commit themselves to a new exclusive relationship they know that one or both of them have been through that very same process before and that exclusiveness was betrayed. But, of course, they will always hope and try to convince themselves that this time it will be completely different and hope will surely triumph over experience. The fear may not always be expressed openly but it can provide a strong stimulus to rewrite history and to reach an understanding of the earlier marriage which leaves the new partners in the clear. Often, the new story will be that the earlier partner has some quirk of character or behaviour which made living with them impossible, despite all the best efforts of their spouse, or that the marriage was already dead when the affair began. Indeed, a solution to these difficulties of transformation which was found by one man was simply to exchange the roles of wife and mistress.

Charles was a successful professional in his early thirties. After seven years of marriage he had become involved with a single woman at his place of work. The affair blossomed in secret for a couple of years but as time passed Charles came under increasing pressure from his new partner to leave his wife and set up home with her. He resisted, not least because of his two children and because he felt unable to face telling his own family, who had initially rather disapproved of his marriage. His mother, in particular, had not been happy with his choice of bride, but she had seemed to be won round, particularly after the birth of the first grandchild. It was his mother's death that provided the key for Charles to change his situation. Within a few months of it he told his wife about his affair and said he wanted to leave. She was very shocked but gradually came to accept the situation, perhaps more in sadness than anger. Within a few months Charles was established in a new home with his new partner and, as soon as the divorce was finalised, they married.

Charles was very keen to maintain links with his children. As well as having them over at weekends he would drop in to see them during the week. There seemed a lot to discuss about the children and he would arrive before they got back from school so there was time to talk things over with his ex-wife. Gradually these talks became rather more intimate and the couple restarted their sexual relationship. When we last had news of Charles he was two years into his new marriage and had a new daughter. He was also eighteen months into his affair with his ex-wife which at that time was unknown to his new partner.

People may be convinced that they are right to leave their marriages for their lovers, but they may miscalculate, or the affair may fail to weather the transformation phase. The affair and the needs of those involved may have been too dependent on its limitations. Marina, who left her husband after twenty years of marriage for a man who then became her business partner, found that she had traded a life of predictability and security for one of constant turmoil, instability, financial ruin and emotional abuse. Before she left her husband she had found her lover exciting, interesting and challenging. She had seen herself to be growing through her relationship with him, changing from a middle-class, middle-aged, rather dull woman into a more unpredictable, questioning and sexually uninhibited one. For this man she had left her job and marriage and invested a good deal of her capital in their shared business venture. Whether she wants to return to her marriage is a moot question; her husband is not waiting with open arms. But what is clear is that she does not feel prepared to stand on her own, which she is now forced to do. She had left her husband for a new relationship with her lover. She had not left her marriage to be on her own.

Betty's is another story of misjudgement about the durability of an affair when it transforms into the central and exclusive relationship. Betty had been married to Steve for eighteen years. They had two children, now young teenagers. Steve, a highly controlling and charismatic man, had been the main player in the marriage. Betty had pushed aside education and career plans, and felt that she had lived in Steve's rather long-cast shadow throughout their marriage. She had become highly dependent on him and had received much reflected glory as his wife. When she met and fell in love with Mark, a teacher, she felt enormous relief. She did not have to compete with Mark, nor to prove to him that she was bright or interesting. Within months of their affair Betty had left home, leaving her children with Steve. Enormous rows ensued. Betty needed a lot of support and attention. Mark was exhausted by it and clearly out of his depth. He felt her children intruded on their relationship, he resented Steve and his anger and was impatient with Betty's depression. Betty, for her part, felt let down and pathetic, and had trouble accepting her loss of status, no longer being the wife of a highly successful, respected pillar of their community. Soon Mark was also getting angry at Betty for disturbing the peace of his former life. Betty's and Mark's affair had worked because it was limited. But it did not work as a marriage: Mark was emotionally limited and Betty was lost without someone of Steve's dependability, emotional stamina and powerful position.

Matthew, having lost his job, met a woman who had recently ended her third marriage. Their intense affair, involving his dropping out and travelling for a year, completely estranged him from his family. The family, shocked and grieving, managed to consolidate around his wife, and soon adjusted to being without him. His lover, intensely jealous of his wife and children, blocked contact with them. After about one year together his lover began to show bizarre, disturbing behaviour, throwing furniture out of windows, staging fist fights in public, and threatening both murder and suicide. The affair ended in dramatic arguments and violent fights. But without it Matthew was both without moorings and alienated from his family. In the cold light of its aftermath his affair looked very like an escape hatch from depression over both job loss and inability to confront years of marital dissatisfaction. Without his marriage the affair had become too intense and unstable. Without his affair he had nothing, except the original depression, arising from issues left still unsettled.

So, as we see, the transformation of an affair into an exclusive relationship is a very difficult process. What may make an exciting relationship within the limits of an affair is very different from the kind of relationship needed to sustain the everyday life of a marriage. Stories like those of Betty, Matthew and Charles underline the difficulties. When the secrecy and excitement are gone, there is too little left to sustain a joint life.

Do Affairs Cause Divorce?

We do not know how important affairs are as a cause of divorce. It would be too simplistic to count those divorces where an affair is cited as the grounds for the divorce. This, of course, would leave out of the account other divorces where there may have been affairs but the couple chose other grounds on which to base the legal proceedings, quite apart from all those marriages that persist and remain, despite or because of the affairs that one or other spouse may have had. Even where there has been an affair with a divorce following, and the affair partners set up home together, it may be quite misleading to say that the affair has caused the marriage to end. Perhaps the affair was simply the stimulus to end an already dead or dying marriage. But none of this is to deny that affairs can end marriages.

The fact that a majority of petitions for divorce are initiated by women is consistent with the idea that the decision to leave a marriage is most often taken by a woman. Studies both in Britain and Australia show that it is divorced husbands who are much more likely to regret the ending of their marriages than their ex-spouses. However, the choice of the legal grounds used to seek a divorce is probably not a very good guide to the reasons why a marriage has ended and has more to do with attitudes among solicitors and the way the legal system works. In Britain adultery and 'unreasonable behaviour' are the grounds that can be used to get a relatively quick divorce. Together these grounds are used in about two-thirds of all divorces but men who initiate proceedings are much more likely to cite adultery while women use unreasonable behaviour. Adultery is much more often cited by upper- and middle-class couples while working-class couples more frequently use unreasonable behaviour. It has been suggested that this, rather than indicating an upper- and middle-class predilection for adultery, represents a concern among these couples and their legal advisers to avoid the more socially unacceptable grounds of unreasonable behaviour. There are also local differences in the practices in different courts. Or at least this seems the most plausible explanation for the fact that petitions citing adultery are, for example, twice as common in Yeovil compared with Cardiff. There is certainly no independent evidence to suggest that affairs are particularly prevalent in Somerset or especially infrequent in South Wales. As some of the researchers who looked carefully at grounds used at divorce concluded, 'whatever the client's reason for wanting divorce, the lawyer's function is to discover grounds'. Given that, it would be unwise to try and deduce anything about the frequency of affairs – or affairs as a cause of marriage breakdown – from the grounds used in legal proceedings.

The experience of another relationship can convince a spouse that their marriage is so unsatisfactory that they should leave it. So even secret affairs can lead to divorce, as we noted in chapter 6. And, of course, when some affairs become known the other spouse may find the betrayal and pain unacceptable and decides to leave.

Gender is all-important. Just as sociologists like Jessie Bernard, who have analysed marriage, have found the experience of men and women so different that they talk of his and her marriage, so we need to consider his and her divorce. The circumstances in which men and women leave their marriages are often different as are the consequences of divorce for each. When it is the man who takes the active step to leave, it is usually because he has someone else to go to, while for women it is the quality of their marriage and the feeling that it cannot improve that so often persuades them to leave. Even when they do have someone else, it is the impossibility of creating a better marriage with the current partner that is their main motive.

In Britain the majority of petitions for divorce are brought by women. It would be a little simplistic to suggest that whoever makes the first legal move is always the leaver. It might be of course that, having more concerns about the house and children, women are more often in a position where they need to sort out the legal situation and so feel impelled to make the first legal move. However, in surveys of satisfaction with marriage, men and women's complaints about it are consistent with the idea that levels of dissatisfaction are generally much higher among women than men. But, on the other hand, in practical and financial terms women usually have much more to lose at divorce than men. Just as within marriage they are the homemakers and carers of children, so it is after divorce. The woman will almost always continue to care for and support her children after a marriage ends but with the difference that economic support will be reduced and she is even more likely to be juggling childcare with a job. While men may lose their housekeeper and emotional support at a separation, financially they are usually much less hard hit. Indeed, some American studies have suggested that men actually gain financially at divorce as maintenance payments may be a good deal less than they were paying to support their wife and children in the joint home.

Given that childcare is unlikely to be their major preoccupation after divorce, men, unlike their ex-wives, are usually much freer to pursue other relationships. Given that the picture we have of the lives of single parents is often a bleak one with a great deal of unremitting struggle, it is perhaps surprising that so many women choose this, rather than remaining in their unsatisfactory marriages. But that some do leave is a testament to the female commitment to a close, sharing and intimate relationship – a relationship of a kind that many women fail to find in their marriages. This is clearly indicated in studies of the complaints that ex-spouses have of their marriages. Those which are uppermost for women concern the emotional and social quality of the marriage. They say that their spouse was distant, not close emotionally that they could not talk to him, that he was not open and would not share his feelings. They did not feel understood or emotionally supported. These features seem much more important than a good sexual relationship for many women. Indeed, some women value sexual intercourse not least because it can bring moments of emotional closeness and sharing. While some complain of their husband's unfaithfulness, this is much lower on most women's list of complaints than the emotional tone of their marriages. Men's lists of dissatisfactions are typically much shorter. It is issues like nagging and bickering, together with their wives' other relationships – including some which are not sexual – that are the important issues for husbands.

These are, of course, complaints from men and women whose marriages have ended. They are marriages where, for whatever reason, spouses have been unable to settle their differences and produce a relationship that meets at least some of their needs. We have described the historical rise of modern marriage and the high ideals of what it should provide (see chapter 1). In the early honeymoon years the ideals of intimacy, companionship, shared time and an exciting sexual relationship are usually easy to sustain but as time passes a process of renegotiation will gradually come into play. This negotiation may be seen as a readjustment of the balance between intimacy and autonomy. At first the balance is strongly tipped towards intimacy while individual autonomy tends to be pushed aside. But as the first rosy glow begins to fade, other outside interests begin to reassert themselves. There will be things each will want to do separately, people to see, relatives to visit, leisure interests and perhaps above all the world of work which, of course, will usually be chiefly a male preoccupation. This process of renegotiation does not always go smoothly and, as one might expect, marriages are particularly vulnerable at this stage with the highest rates of divorce coming in the early early years of marriage. Things will be further complicated if either spouse has an affair during this phase of renegotiation. Because a marriage may feel a draining and disappointing experience at such a time, an affair may feel particularly rewarding. So not only is the contrast between the two relationships likely to be particularly strong, but the energy that goes into the affair is likely to impede or inhibit the process of renegotiation of the marriage. That can spell the beginning of the end of the marriage. However, in other cases the affair, provided it does not become too engrossing, can form a stimulus to the renegotiation process. We found cases where this has happened but it is clearly a high-risk strategy.

Recent surveys have pointed to a list of common-sense factors which are related to marriages foundering at this early stage. These factors are related, all else being equal, to the likelihood of a couple successfully renegotiating their marriage relationship. Those who have known each other for a reasonable length of time and have not rushed into marriage are least likely to divorce, as are those whose marriages have the approval, and so presumably the help and support, of the family on both sides.

Age too seems important. Those marrying for the first time when aged less then twenty and more than thirty-five are the most vulnerable but the reasons are probably different at the two ends of the age spectrum. The young are most likely to be working-class couples who may well lack adequate material resources and housing for a reasonable start for their marriages. And, of course, their experience of relationships of any kind will be more limited than for those who delay marriage. While we should hesitate to use the term emotional immaturity for all those who marry young, there can be little doubt that many young couples still have a lot to learn about the conduct of social relationships. These marriages are often complicated by the early arrival of children so that, long before the couple have worked out a satisfactory way of living together, they are coping with pregnancy and childcare. Middle-class couples are much more likely to delay marriage until their education is complete

– in itself a longer drawn-out process – and careers have been launched. Not only does this mean that economically things will be much more secure for them but of course they are likely to have had a great deal more experience of varied relationships. But delaying marriage too long brings its hazards. This is usually because of reasons which are opposite to those of the very young; those who have lived on their own for a long time are likely to have developed strong patterns of autonomy and individual need which they find difficult to give up and so it is hard for them to create the required intimacy to sustain a marriage. It causes too much upheaval in long-established patterns of living.

The coming of children brings a whole new set of issues for any couple because not only do they intrude on the ideal of intimacy but they also force a division of labour which may run counter to a couple's notion of a shared domestic life. But although satisfaction with a marriage typically falls after the birth of the first child, couples do not necessarily become more prone to separate, as children tend to hold couples together. This may be less a conscious decision that they should stay together for the sake of the children, than a feeling that leaving a family with children is something that should only be contemplated if things become very desperate and serious. Increasingly couples are aware of all the problems that divorce may bring, especially when children are involved.

Adjustments in what were once the ideals for the marriage may bring compromises. Men may make their work the centre of their lives and develop more of a social world for themselves around this. Others will put their time and emotional energies into leisure activities. The obsessional quality that men demonstrate in their hobbies, whether it be collecting 1950s seventy-eight records, sealed knot reconstructions of Civil War battles or growing leeks on the allotment, gives some indication of the emotional energies that may be invested in these activities as a flight from domestic intimacy.

Typically, women make a virtue of necessity and preoccupy themselves with their children. But the cost of the lost ideals of the marriage can be very high as is indicated by the very high prevalence of depression among married women, especially those at home with children. Very significantly, the research has demonstrated that depression is much more likely to develop where women lack a close and confiding relationship with their husband. There seem to be links, too, back to the earliest relationship in childhood. Those who become depressed are much more likely to say that they had a difficult relationship with their own mother or that this relationship was disrupted for some reason. As we suggested earlier, these early relationships play a basic role in forming our capacity to build and sustain close emotional relationship in adulthood.

Affairs, Divorce and the Maturity of Marriage

To understand the possible link between divorce and affairs we need to examine the consequences of affairs in the context of the maturing pattern of marriage. Our difficulty here is not only that we have so little detailed knowledge about who chooses to have affairs, but also that affairs are such a varied phenomena, pursued for such varied motives, that it is hard to discern patterns. However, there seems little doubt that those who are having difficulties in renegotiating their marriages after the initial phase may be particularly vulnerable. It is easy to suggest that the pattern is a simple one: that when all is not well at home there may be a temptation to seek consolation elsewhere. Doubtless this happens, but the circumstances are usually a little more complex.

For some people, the experience of building a close and confiding relationship has always been in a sexual one. So when intimacy begins to fade within the marriage, and is developed elsewhere, the pattern is repeated and a sexual relationship begins as a way of creating a new intimacy. Men are particularly at risk here as they choose women as confidants. Confidants may become lovers. Women, on the other hand, turn to other women. Or it may simply be difficult to break old patterns. If the experience and convention before marriage was that most, if not all, intimate relationships become sexual ones, it may be hard to change the pattern when close relationships are formed after marriage. We know that those who have many sexual relationships before marriage are most likely to have them outside marriage too.

There is also the question of opportunity. As the marriage matures and the couple begin to spend less of their time together, there are more possibilities to meet and spend time with possible affair partners. Opportunity and the phase of the marriage may coincide. The summer schools of the Open University are a notorious example here – at least by reputation. The Open University provides degree courses for mature students which are often seen as a way back into a career by women who have been preoccupied by marriage and children. Typically, they reach a turning point in their marriage when they decide to reassert their autonomy and seek a route back into employment via some further education. Men, too, may be using the education to make a change of course in their lives. Such changes may place people in settings where they meet new people and they, like those they meet, are in a mood for change and re-examination of relationships.

There is some suggestion that in recent decades the length of a marriage before a spouse has an affair is getting shorter. Annette Lawson found that those who responded to her questionnaire about affairs, who had been married before 1960, had on average been married for fifteen years before their first affair. This fell to eight years for those married during the 1960s and four years for more recent marriages. But, of course, these figures may be somewhat biased because anyone in the recent decades who was 'postponing' their affair would be outside the sample as the survey only covered people who already had had an affair.

While women may be catching up a bit, there is a general belief that men have more affairs than women. We have already discussed some of the reasons why this may be so. A further reason may be that men's affairs are less likely to end their marriages than those of women. We make that statement not simply on the grounds that a continuing double standard may make their affairs more acceptable than those of their wives, but because of some of the typical features of the male affair and how these relate to their marriages. Because of their emotional and sexual development, men are usually much more successful than women in creating compartments in their lives which allow their affairs and marriage to exist alongside each other with little apparent connection. Both the way that male emotional development involves a necessary separation from the first love relationship, that with the mother, and that their sexuality is formed outside of a social relationship, mean that splitting off an affair and a marriage is more possible for them.

It is frequently said that wives can always tell when their husbands are straying, but our interviews suggest that this may well be a myth and is not surprising given men's ability to compartmentalise their lives. We have all heard stories of a chance discovery that has uncovered an affair that has been continuing for months or years without any suspicion at all. In occasional dramatic cases a husband has established a second home complete with children, a car and a mortgage without arousing suspicion. In interviews with wives who have suddenly discovered their husband's infidelity, we have been struck by the fact that what often hurts and perplexes them most is that they could not tell that their husband was having an affair.

Jane had a typical story. The chance discovery of a letter led to the uncovering of a two-year-old affair.

> Alistair [her husband] has been working hard for some months and his work took him away from time to time – or so I thought – but that seemed quite natural at this point in his career. I remember thinking one day after hearing about the break-up of a friend's marriage how lucky we were. We still enjoyed each other and liked to do things together. And he could be so warm and loving. It is very hard now looking back on it to know that all through that time he was seeing someone else . . . I think in many ways it would be easy to accept now if I *had* suspected. If I could have told something from the way he was with me.

The pattern of men's lives, more often than women's, split between home and a world of work, encourage and reinforce the patterns of separate compartments. Here we mean more than that work provides opportunities to meet others and excuses to be away from home. It can be through work that men may become practised in living in two separate social worlds and will often learn to keep them apart. This can mean that they may feel relatively comfortable about the coexistence of an affair and marriage. If this argument is correct we would expect there to be many more men's affairs that remain secret and undiscovered, continuing alongside a marriage without disturbing it. Most of these are likely to be affairs which will not lead to divorce, unless they are discovered and the wife decides it is time to leave the marriage. But difficulties can arise if there is a discrepancy and there are pressures from the affair partner to make things more permanent.

Malcolm was an academic nearing the end of a long and not undistinguished career. He had been married for over thirty years and his three children had all left home. His wife, Patricia, worked part time in a library and led a full and apparently satisfying life with many activities and an active social life. They were beginning to talk of retirement and moving to a smaller house in the same city. Three years earlier Malcolm had met Deborah while travelling to a meeting abroad. She was some ten years younger, a journalist who wrote features for a quality paper. She too was married with two children, the youngest of whom was soon to complete her education. Malcolm had had earlier affairs, including one which his wife had discovered, but this one was much more important to him. He felt immediately drawn to Deborah and found it easy to talk to her and to be close. They shared many interests. The affair prospered. Although they lived hundreds of miles apart, the nature of their occupations made it relatively easy for them to meet from time to time. About once a year they managed a week away together.

After about a year they both began to talk of leaving their marriages and setting up together. Malcolm agreed but as he began to consider the consequences for all the parts of his life he became more doubtful and kept postponing the final decision. Deborah was ready to tell her husband about the affair and to leave as soon as Malcolm agreed to a date. At this point Malcolm's wife discovered the affair through a friend's chance meeting with Malcolm and Deborah. When confronted by his wife, Malcolm admitted to the relationship but said that, although it had been going on for some time, it was not serious. Patricia was not so sure and did see Deborah as a threat to her marriage. She wanted the marriage to survive and set about making sure that Malcolm would stay. She played on his guilt. In as many ways as she could she tried to show him how much he would be giving up if he left and how uncertain his future life would be with Deborah. But Deborah fought back and for several months the two women, in their different ways, pushed their cases. More than anything, Malcolm wished to preserve the status quo of before the discovery. Slowly and painfully he came to realise that he could not give up his marriage and all the life that surrounded it but, to preserve it, he would have to end the affair. It took him a long time to get to that point. Patricia knew that time, and history, were on her side.

Because wives are indeed part of the status quo and will usually be the emotional and social housekeepers, as well as the providers of bed and board, men find it hard to leave marriages even when their relationship with their wives has become very unsatisfactory. But through compartmentalisation and splitting they can find intimacy and more satisfying sex and love elsewhere. Women, on the other hand, find this more difficult because for them splitting is much harder. Despite the much greater practical difficulties for them of leaving a marriage, for them an affair may be a more serious threat to a marriage. But as we have already noted, this does not necessarily mean that they will leave a marriage for an affair partner. Perhaps more commonly, the affair begins a process of evaluation which eventually leads to them leaving their marriage. As we have pointed out, they are likely to be dissatisfied with more things in their marriage.

Jane, a doctor's wife, had been married for nearly fifteen years. The youngest of her three children was now safely established in primary school and Jane was back working part time in a design studio. At that point she said she felt 'OK' about her marriage. Her husband Dick was a little distant from her at times and she did not particularly like to spend time with his work colleagues. But he was good with the children and they seemed to function well as a family. Through her work Jane met another designer who was visiting the town for a few weeks. Dick happened to be away for part of this period and she and her designer colleague spent a lot of time together.

> I liked him. He was easy to talk to and was interested in my work – something that I don't think was true for Dick. After spending an evening with him, we slept together. It wasn't great passion. I think I was interested to see what it would be like more than anything. But it was lovely to be with someone who seemed to care for me and wanted me.

They kept in touch – 'more friends than lovers, I think' – but distance made it hard for them to meet.

Some months later Jane began a second affair with a colleague at the studio where she worked. 'This time it was real passion' and it was not long before James, her new partner, was asking her to leave her marriage and set up home with him. 'I was certainly tempted but it seemed an impossible step to take.' She continued to hesitate but decided to tell her husband what was happening.

> The whole thing exploded and within a couple of weeks the affair was definitely over. James's wife was told and on one awful evening we all met together. James quickly decided that he wanted to stay put. The way he behaved then certainly reinforced my doubts about him. Dick and I spent hundreds of hours talking. He was angry of course and I don't think he ever understood how I felt. He saw it all as a need to rejig our domestic routines while I wanted the basis of how we were together to change.

Jane described how these discussions, at least in retrospect, were the beginning of the end of her marriage. It was nearly two years before they separated. Now she lives on her own with her children. 'I am a new woman now. It's been hard and painful, especially for the children, but most of the time I am sure I did the right thing.'

We may have come a long way since the attitudes of the last century regarding infidelity, but double standards do persist and, in general, women remain more tolerant of their husbands than husbands do of their wives. Some wives may be fairly certain that their husbands have had an affair but, provided it has been discreet and it does not impinge on their marriage, she is not going to ask and he is not going to tell. For a few there is a more or less tacit agreement, not an open marriage in the sense we discussed earlier, but an acknowledgement that if he is away and he sleeps with someone that is acceptable. And perhaps surprisingly, the advent of AIDS does not seem to have had much influence on these attitudes. Indeed, we should note more generally that the advent of the HIV virus, as yet at least, seems to have had no impact at all on affairs.

Male tolerance of their wives' affairs is much more limited. Where there are agreements, tacit or explicit, the motives are not always reciprocal. Men who do enter such agreements seem to do so as a necessary price they have to pay for their own sexual freedom. They still feel sexual jealousy very acutely. Some marriages are stuck in a kind of frozen distance where the husband harbours a continuing unspoken resentment and hostility because their wives have slept with someone else. Retaliatory affairs may be part of this male pattern but these are often kept secret as this both avoids confrontation and anger and because knowledge of them would detract from the power that the husband feels he gains from the deception. While we have examples of this pattern where it is a wife who feels resentful about her husband's affair, the patterns seem much more common the other way round.

The continuing double standard and the power of male

sexual jealousy mean that there are usually greater dangers to a marriage when wives' affairs become known than those of husbands. It is probable that their affairs become known more often because they are less practised in splitting off the two relationships. Also, because their lives are more home based and they may not have the convenience of excuses related to work, they may run more risks of discovery. Wives' affairs are more prominent among the issues that men bring up at divorce. Once again we must emphasise that it is not possible to say exactly what role they play as causes of divorce. While affairs may certainly be seen as breaking points, it is our impression that the affairs of women, like those of men, are not in themselves the major cause of divorce.

The popular myth is, of course, that love conquers all: that married people (less often, married men) may, if they meet the right person, fall in love, and, in spite of their spouses, children and home, are forced by uncontrollable passion to give up everything to be with their lover. This view regards love as a kind of external affliction which, unannounced and unexpectedly, can cause people to take leave of their senses and behave in abnormal ways. It is certainly not difficult to find people who have left a marriage to be with someone else, who speak in these kinds of terms.

As social scientists we would not wish to deny the experience of feelings that our trade has so singularly failed to analyse or understand very deeply. However, love has come to be seen as the justification for relationships in our culture. It has come to represent something even more powerful than marriage. Not only is love now a required condition for marriage, but it can also be a justified reason for leaving it. Indeed, we come back once again to the contradiction of our ideal of the companionate marriage. Love is regarded as a sudden unpredictable state that overtakes people and leads them into marriage. Unless the state of matrimony inoculates against any subsequent attack, it may strike again. Following its imperative will lead people from one marriage to another.

But our rather more prosaic view is that for most, those who leave their marriages for others do so because they have failed to find what they wanted and they hope they may do better with someone else.

8 Conclusions

A marriage, so free, so spontaneous, that it
would allow of wide excursions of the pair from
each other, in common or even in separate
objects of work and interest, and yet would
hold them all the time in the bond of absolute
sympathy, would by its very freedom be all the
more poignantly attractive, and by its very
scope and breadth all the richer and more vital
– would be in a sense indestructible, like the
relation of two suns which, revolving in fluent
and rebounding curves, only to recede from
each other in order to return again with
renewed swiftness into close proximity – and
which together blend their rays in the glory of
one double star.

It has been the inability to see and understand this very simple truth that has largely
contributed to the failure of the monogamic
union.

Edward Carpenter,
Love's Coming-of-Age, 1896

Since the nineteenth century many reformers have argued, like
Edward Carpenter, that monogamous marriage is a prison
which stunts love and the human spirit, especially for women.
The early critics were responding to the rise of companionate
marriage which they saw as damaging as it reduced the
autonomy of the spouses for the sake of the ideals of their
shared life. For some of these reformers, although they did not
always argue the point directly, sexual exclusiveness was part of
what they objected to. They saw the Church and the State as
the enemies that forced monogamous marriage on the population – through marriage and divorce laws, denial of sex
education to young people, censorship of information about
sexuality, banning of contraceptives and an educational system

and economy which made women economically dependent on men. It was this compulsion towards monogamous marriage that these critics disagreed with, rather than monogamy itself. Indeed, their claim was that if unions could be freely entered into, love would blossom and long-term relationships would remain mutually satisfying perhaps over an entire lifetime.

Some also emphasised the need for easier divorce so that when marriages did go wrong, or were entered into without sufficient consideration, the couple could be free to try again. Beyond that, they felt that if divorce was possible it would improve the quality of marriage.

> If people could divorce themselves at will and without publicity, they would be as careful to preserve each other's esteem after, as they were before marriage. We should then seldom see what so frequently happens now; the charming, neat, obliging, fiancée, developing into the giddy, careless, slatternly, and disobliging wife, or the ardent and devoted lover cooling down into the neglectful and heartless husband. Those truly married would continue to do all they could to please each other, and those superficially united would practice the outward decencies of married life from mutual and self interests. Marriage would cease to be the grave of love, and the sum total of human happiness would be immensely increased. Possession during good behaviour is far better for our weak human nature than possession absolute. (From *Wrongs of Married Men. Essays on Social Topics*, Lady Cook, *c.* 1900)

What would these Victorian critics make of present-day marriage? The elements that they saw as essential for satisfactory marriage have now been more or less achieved. We have divorce on demand; contraception and abortion are freely available, as is information of all kinds about sexuality. Economic pressures on women to marry no longer exist, at least in the sense they did at the beginning of the century. There is freedom to pursue sexual relationships before marriage and to cohabit without it. But have we achieved those ideal marriages the early reformers hoped for? Has the loving fulfilment they argue for replaced the prison they so eloquently criticised? At the Sexual Reform Congress in London in 1929 – a large gathering of the great and good of marriage reform – the writer Vera Britten argued that 'the non-observance of monogamy [is] due, not to a surplus but to an insufficiency of freedom'. In a limited sense there is an element of truth in what she said, as prostitution has declined with the rise of sexual freedom. However, despite the high ideals with which many now begin their marriages, monogamy may not even characterise the majority of them, as affairs are commonplace. So history has not borne out Vera Britten's belief. Why have the visions of these reformers proved false? Why has the removal of the evils that they described as the bane of marriage in the early part of this century not led to the blossoming of love they hoped for?

Throughout the present century, while the external pressure for marriage and the constraints on it have declined, paradoxically the institution has grown in power. It is no longer the Church and State that strive to maintain standards for marriage but couples themselves who set their own ideals for an exclusive, loving, companionate marriage. As sexual relationships before marriage have become general and accepted, not just between those intending to marry but for all, there has been a growing need for couples to mark off marriage as a very special kind of relationship. This has been done by putting an increased emphasis on the wedding itself, as well as elevating the ideal of the exclusive monogamous marriage. In a sense then, the historical shifts in marriage are a consequence of changes in relationships outside, and especially before, marriage.

The freedoms provided by the new attitudes and the availability of contraception have made sex part of many more kinds of adult relationships. These have pushed marriage away from the open model envisaged by the early reformers and towards the closed exclusive ideal that we find today. It is that situation that gives present-day marriage the contradiction that lies at the heart of this book. It is the contradiction that is displayed issue by issue in magazines like *Cosmopolitan* and *Marie-Claire*, but without acknowledgement or any attempt at its resolution. Side by side these magazines print articles about such topics as 'When is sex right?' or 'Should you sleep with him on the first date?' for the unmarried, with others that chart the consequences and difficulties of affairs for the married. The clear message is that while sex is fine for the unmarried with a variety of partners, to stray from the conjugal bed is fraught with dangers. And to confuse matters further, these magazines, unlike the turn-of-century marriage-manual authors, advocate openness and honesty in all matters in marriage while we know that most affairs remain a secret.

There is little sign that we are moving towards any resolution of this basic contradiction. Throughout the period in which companionate marriage has grown and become the norm, there always have been advocates of open marriage but, despite well-publicised examples, the model has never extended beyond a very small minority. Many people do not want to give up their aspirations for marriage. They want to hold on to the romantic ideal and the security they hope that monogamy will bring. Open marriage seldom receives institutional support from the marriage gurus – the counsellors and therapists. Indeed, we may see these as groups that operate very strongly to uphold the contradictions of the exclusive companionate marriage. The marriage menders promote monogamy and regard affairs as a problem, if not a sign of pathology, which must be removed to bring the couple back to the straight, narrow and healthy. Secrets are not to their liking and many refuse to work with a couple if one member has disclosed to them an affair which has not been revealed to the spouse. Indeed, the relationship between therapist or counsellor and client shares many of the characteristics and contradictions that are seen in the marriage relationship itself.

While it would be unfair to accuse all those in these professions as promoters of current contradictions, there is little sign that they are close to devising constructive solutions to present dilemmas. But with or without their help, open marriage seems all too fragile. Perhaps we are stuck with the model of exclusiveness as long as this same characteristic remains the basis of our first love relationship – that with our mothers. Earlier in the book we pointed to the connections between the pattern of mother–child attachment and that of marriage. There are a few signs that the exclusiveness and 'monogamy' of mothers' relationships with their infants in our society has been diluted a little, and children are beginning to experience a richer variety of relationships, but changes are still minimal. While we would not wish to suggest that these early patterns determine all that follow and, in that sense, adult relationships are unchangeable, we do want to draw attention to the close historical and cross-cultural parallels between the exclusiveness of mother–baby attachments and the ideal for adult heterosexual relationships.

One recent shift in behaviour which can be interpreted as a response to the contradictions of modern marriage is to avoid marriage altogether. As compared with Victorian England, the twentieth century has been a time when more of the population married and at an earlier age. But since the 1970s these trends have reversed. Age at marriage is now rising and the marriage rate is falling. These changes are partly explained by the rise in cohabitation and partly because more people are living on their own. Cohabitation began to be a significant phenomenon in the late 1960s. Then, as now, it was largely a phenomenon found before and after marriage. Most of those who cohabited eventually married, although not necessarily the person they first cohabited with. Or they were divorcees, but this group, too, often married in the end. A common pattern was for cohabiting couples to marry when they had children. But this link has weakened and an increasing number of children are born to cohabiting couples. Approaching a third of all births are now to unmarried parents. In the majority of cases these births are registered by both parents, suggesting that these are cohabiting couples. So we could say that, at least to some extent, cohabitation is coming to replace marriage. This seems particularly true for the previously married. Perhaps for this latter group at least, experience has begun to triumph over hope. These trends towards cohabitation have gone much further in Scandinavia where marriage is rapidly becoming a minority preoccupation and almost as many children are born outside marriage as within it. Adults living as single represent another response to the contradictions of marriage, if we assume, as seems reasonable, that most of them have sexual relationships.

How far does cohabitation represent an attempt to rewrite the rules of marriage and so avoid some of the contradications? Here we are stuck for lack of information. Despite its prevalence, we have no large scale studies of cohabitation.* But such indications as there are do not suggest that, in general, the rules for cohabitation are very different from marriage. Ideals for exclusiveness are high and, although doubtless there are cohabiting couples that have negotiated rules for other relationships, the general patterns seems to be of a monogamy indistinguishable from marriage. This, of course, raises the question of why these couples do not marry or, alternatively, why others do.

There seem two main pressures that lead cohabitees towards marriage. The first comes from their families. Attitudes towards marriage are more traditional among the older generation, and the young may feel strong pressures to get married. And to 'do it for the parents' may allow the couple to maintain their stance of organising their own lives in their own way without being seen to bow to societal pressures. It is more a case of pleasing their close kin than conforming to an expectation of society. The second pressure comes from the couple themselves. The evidence continues to suggest that marriage is viewed as a demonstration of a greater commitment. So for many, cohabi-

---

* A signal failure of the social science research community in Britain and especially bodies like the government-funded Economic and Social Research Council, has been to promote research on any of the important aspects of contemporary family life in Britain. To take but three topics that are central not only to this book, but to life in Britain today, cohabitation, the development of sexuality and affairs, we find an absence of relevant research that is so complete as to suggest a positive policy of avoiding research on such matters of public interest.

tation remains a prelude to marriage, albeit one that may last for several years. While marriage clearly maintains its symbolic importance, in legal terms its power has gone. We now have what is effectively divorce on demand. Indeed, one could argue that the legal processes of divorce provide a simpler way out of a relationship and a means of settling disputes about property and children which is largely denied to those who cohabit.

At what point does a cohabiting couple decide to marry? Obviously situations are very varied but often the marriage will follow a change in the couple's life; a pregnancy, or a move and a new house. For others it may come as an attempt to resolve a problem in their relationship. A number of the couples we have talked to got married in the aftermath of an affair. They saw the commitment of the marriage as a way of avoiding such problems in the future. But it seems more likely that such a tactic will lead to a postponement of problems rather than their avoidance.

A striking feature of the accounts of affairs given by many married people is that they claim that they still believe in monogamy. This is particularly true for women. It seems less a case that they are saying that they would like to be monogamous but do not find themselves able to live up to it, but rather that they are claiming that their affair does not break their commitment to remain faithful or at least to stay in their marriage. These are affairs which are not intended to threaten the marriage and because of this are almost always kept secret. Sometimes they are explained away in terms which suggest that they do not really count: 'It was just sex'; 'It's not real life, it's like going to the cinema'. This seems another way of squaring the circle of modern marriage and it could be seen as a particular strategy of the segmented marriage that we described in chapter 4.

Another strategy some adopt is to turn the affair into a marriage. Serial monogamy, albeit with a little overlap at the beginning and end of each relationship, becomes a way of resolving the contradictions. But this strategy carries huge emotional and financial costs, especially if there are children involved. While the growth of new ways of sorting out the practical consequences of divorce, such as conciliation, may reduce some of the trauma, they can never abolish the upheavals and problems that any change in a live-in relationship will bring. But despite these all too obvious difficulties, there is a small group of people who marry and divorce repeatedly.

Already in this chapter we have suggested that people may have strong needs for an exclusive, all-embracing marriage relationship as a result of their early experiences with their mothers. Are there ways in which these needs may be modified so that patterns of marriage are less demanding? If we expected less of marriage perhaps some of its contradictions could be reduced. While many young people are very thoughtful about marriage and the way they may want to live their lives, the belief in an exclusive, marriage-should-be-more-or-less-for-everything model, remains very strong. One group which one might expect to have rather different views is young people who have had the experience of seeing their parents divorce. More than most, one might expect this group to use their experience to avoid some of the pitfalls they will have seen for themselves. Up to a point, surveys of the attitudes of the children of divorce suggest this is true. These young people often begin with a whole range of reservations about marriage. They will say you have to be very sure before you commit yourself, or that you should wait until you are older and have had the experience of several relationships. But what people say and what they do are not always the same, and this seems to be often the case for the children of divorced parents. Looking at the eventual patterns of marriage of these young people, we see what appears to be a contradiction. While they often express more caution about marriage than those whose parents did not divorce, they marry at an earlier age and, perhaps because of this, they are more likely to divorce in the early years of their marriages.

The explanation for this apparently contradictory behaviour is that this group tends to begin their sexual and cohabiting relationships at an earlier age than those whose parents remain married. This seems to be because they leave home at a younger age and end their education earlier – both of these are factors associated with an earlier start to sexual relationships. Once having got into relationships and then into cohabitation they are 'at risk' of marriage. The pressures are on them to convert their cohabitation into a marriage, so they end up married earlier than those who begin their relationships later. All their good intentions about caution seem to be set aside once they get into a serious relationship. Perhaps that is the very situation that lies at the heart of our central contradiction in marriage. In the heat of passion and love, it is easy to promise everything and mean it. The model of the exclusive 'until death do us part' is ever present and how can you offer a lover less? But patterns can change.

As we have described in this book, the marriage of today that causes us so much pain and difficulty is little more than a century old and it does not rule everywhere. Not so far away in southern Europe and the Middle East we can find different patterns of marriage that are a lot more stable than ours. In many of these societies, marriage is much more of a deal between two families and, for the couple themselves, may not constitute their closest confiding relationship. These are societies in which the divide of gender cuts even deeper than in our own and close confiding relationships usually remain within one's own gender – a wife with her mother, sister, mother-in-law or aunt and a husband with his male friends and relatives. It would be silly to suggest that we can transport a marriage pattern out of the society of which it is part into our own. But by looking elsewhere at how marriages work, we can build a base from which to reflect on our own society. And reflection is needed, if we are to solve our current problems.

Western companionate marriage is very far from a universal of humans; it is a recent invention which appears to offer security and support in a fleeting and uncertain world. For many, its initial promise is short-lived. Some are able to renegotiate and create a more sustainable alternative, while others falter and seek the same illusions elsewhere. Affairs are as old as marriage. But when marriage becomes companionate and based on romantic love their power to erode becomes greater. It is that bittersweet model of modern marriage that lies at the heart of our difficulties.

References and Further Reading

Affairs

Block, J. *The Other Man, The Other Woman* N.Y.: Grosset & Dunlap, 1978.

Brown, E. *Patterns of Infidelity and Their Treatment*. N.Y.: Brunner/Mazel, 1991.

Eskapa, S. *Woman vs. Woman*. London: Heinemann, 1984.

Lake, T. and Hills, A. *Affairs: The Anatomy of Extramarital Relationships*. London: Open Books, 1979.

Lawson, A. *Adultery. An Analysis of Love and Betrayal*. New York: Basic Books, 1988.

Moultrip, D. *Husbands, Wives, and Lovers: The Emotional System of the Extramarital Affair*. N.Y.: The Guildford Press, 1990.

Pittman, F. *Private Lies. Infidelity and the Betrayal of Intimacy*. New York: Norton, 1990.

Richardson, L. *The New Other Woman: Contemporary Single Women in Affairs with Married Men*. N.Y.: The Free Press, 1985.

Strean, H.S. *The Extra-marital Affair*. New York: The Free Press, 1980.

Van Sommers, P. *Jealousy: What Is It and Who Feels It?* London: Penguin Books, 1988.

Wolfe, L. *Playing Around: Women and Extramarital Sex*. N.Y.: William Morrow, 1975.

Divorce and Remarriage

Burgoyne, J., Ormrod, R. and Richards, M.P.M. *Divorce Matters*. Harmondsworth: Penguin Books, 1987.

Davis, G. and Murch, M. *Grounds for Divorce*. Oxford: Clarendon Press, 1988.

Franks, H. *Remarriage. What Makes It. What Breaks It*. London: The Bodley Head, 1988.

Hetherington, E.M. and Araste, J.D. (Eds.) *Impact of Divorce, Single Parenting, and Step Parenting on Children*. Hillsdale, N.J.: Lawrence Erlbaum, 1988.

Ihinger-Tallman, M. and Pasley, K. *Remarriage*. Newbury Park, Calif.: Sage Publications, 1987.

Law Commission. *The Grounds for Divorce*. Law Commission No. 192. London, HMSO 1990.

MacLean, M. *Surviving Divorce. Women's Resources after Separation*. London: Macmillan, 1991.

Phillips, R. *Putting Asunder. A History of Divorce in Western Society*. Cambridge: Cambridge University Press, 1988.

Vaughan, D. *Uncoupling. Turning Points in Intimate Relationships*. London: Methuen, 1987.

Wallerstein, J. and Kelley, J. *Surviving the Break-Up*. N.Y.: Basic Books, 1980.

Weiss, R. *Marital Separation*. N.Y.: Basic Books, 1975.

Emotional Development and Relationships

Atwood, Margaret. *Cat's Eye*. London: Virago Press, 1990.

Belenky, M., Clinchy, B., Goldberger, N. and Tarule, J. *Women's Ways of Knowing*. N.Y.: Basic Books, 1986.

Carter, E. and McGoldrick, M. (Eds). *The Family Life Cycle: A Framework for Family Therapy*. N.Y.: Gardner Press, Inc., 1980.

Cartledge, S. and Ryan, J. *Sex and Love: New Thoughts on Old Contradictions*. London: The Women's Press, 1983.

Chodorow, N. *The Reproduction of Mothering*. Berkeley: University of California Press, 1978.

Douglas, J.D. and Atwell, F.C. *Love, Intimacy and Sex*. Newbury Park, Calif. Sage, 1988.

Ehrenreich, B., Hess, E. and Jacobs, G. *Re-making Love. The Feminization of Sex*. London: Fontana/Collins, 1987.

Eichenbaum, L. and Orbach, S. *Understanding Women*. London: Penguin Books, 1988.

Freud, S. *A General Introduction to Psychoanalysis*. N.Y.: Boni and Liveright, 1916–1917.

Gilligan, C. *In a Different Voice. Psychological Theory and Women's Development*. Cambridge Mass.: Harvard University Press, 1982.

Lazarre, J. *On Loving Men*. Virago Press, 1981.

Lerner, H.G. *The Dance of Intimacy*. N.Y.: Harper and Row, 1989.

Miller, J.B. *Toward a New Psychology of Women*. Boston: Beacon Press, 1986.

Oakley, A. *Taking it Like a Woman*. London: Jonathan Cape, 1984.

Person, E.S. *Dreams of Love and Fateful Encounters: The Power of Romantic Persuasion*. London: Pengiun Books, 1988.

Sarsby, J. *Romantic Love and Society: Its Place in the Modern World*. Harmondsworth: Pengiun Books, 1983.

Willis, P.E. *Learning to Labour: How Working Class Kids Get Working Class Jobs*. Westmead: Saxon House, 1977.

Winnicott, D.W. *The Maturational Process and the Facilitating Environment*. N.Y.: International University Press, 1945.

Marriage and Domestic Life

Askham, J. *Identity and Stability in Marriage*. Cambridge: Cambridge University Press, 1984.

Bernard, J. *The Future of Marriage*. Harmondsworth: Penguin Books, 1976 (1972).

Blood, R. and Wolfe, D.M. *Husbands and Wives*. Glencoe, III: Free Press, 1960.

Blumstein P. and Schwartz, P. *American Couples*. N.Y.: McGraw-Hill, 1983.

Botwin, C. *Is There Sex after Marriage?* Boston: Little, Brown & Co., 1985.

Braby M.C. *Modern Marriage and How to Bear It*. London: Werner Laurie, (c. 1910).

Brittain V. *Halcyon or The Future of Monogamy*. London: Regan Paul, Trench, Trubner, 1929.

Carpenter, E. *Love's Coming-of-Age*. London: Methuen, 1986.

Clark, D. (ed.) *Marriage, Domestic Life and Social Change: Writings for Jacqueline Burgoyne*. Routledge, 1991.

Clulow, C. and Mattison, J. *Marriage Inside Out*. London: Penguin Books, 1989.

Chesser, E. *The Sexual, Marital and Family Relationships of the English Woman*. London: Hutchinson's Medical Publications, 1956.

Cook, Lady N.D. *Essays on Social and Other Topics*, Vol. I. London: Roxburghe Press, (c. 1900).

Davidoff, L. and Hall, C. *Family Fortunes: Men and Women of the English Middle Class 1780–1850*. London: Hutchinson, 1987.

Dicks, H. *Marital Tensions: Clinical Studies Towards a Psychological Theory of Interaction*. N.Y.: Basic Books, 1967.

Finch, J. *Family, Obligations and Social Change*. Cambridge: Polity Press, 1990.

Gillis, J.R. *For Better, For Worse, British Marriages, 1600 to the Present*. N.Y. Oxford University Press, 1985.

Gittins, D. *Fair Sex. Family Size and Structure 1900–1939*. London: Hutchinson, 1982.

Gorer, G. *Exploring English Character*. London: Cresset Press, 1955.

Gorer, G. *Sex and Marriage in England Today*. London: Nelson, 1971.

Haughton, W.E. *The Victorian Frame of Mind*. New Haven: Yale University Press, 1957.

Hewer. *From Bud to Blossom*. London: privately printed, 1922.

Jackson, B. *Working Class Community*. London: Routledge and Kegan Paul, 1968.

Jeffreys, S. *The Spinster and Her Enemies. Feminism and Sexuality, 1900–1930*. London: Pandora Press, 1988.

Kanter, R.M. *Commitment and Community: Commune and Utopias in Sociological Perspective*. Cambridge Mass.: Harvard University Press, 1972.

Lasch, C. *Haven in a Heartless World*. N.Y.: Basic Books, 1977.

Leonard, D. *Sex and Generation: a Study of Courtship and Weddings*. London: Tavistock, 1980.

Lewis, J. *Women in England, 1870–1950: Sexual Divisions and Social Change*. Brighton: Wheatsheaf, 1984.

Lindsey, B.B. and Evans, W. *The Companionate Marriage*. London: Brentanos Ltd, 1928.

Mansfield, P. and Colland, J. *The Beginning of the Rest of Your Life*. London: Macmillan Press, 1988.

Minuchin, S. *Families and Family Therapy*. London: Tavistock, 1974.

Newson, J. and Newson, E. *Infant Care in an Urban Community*. London: Allen & Unwin, 1963.

O'Neill, N. and O'Neill, G. *Open Marriage*. N.Y.: Avon Books, 1972.

Rapoport, R. and Rapoport, R.N. *Dual Career Families*. London: Robertson, 1971.

Rapoport, R. and Rapoport, R.N. *Dual Career Families Re-Examined*. London: Robertson, 1976.

Richards, M.P.M. and Elliott, B.J. 'Sex and Marriage in the 1960s and 1970s' in Clark, D. (ed.) *Marriage, Domestic Life and Social Change: Writings for Jacqueline Burgoyne*. Routledge, 1991.

Roberts, E. *A Woman's Place. An Oral History of Working-Class Women 1890–1940*. Oxford: Basil Blackwell, 1984.

Rubin, L. *Intimate Strangers*. London: Fontana, 1985.

Scarf, M. *Intimate Partners: Patterns in Love and Marriage*. London: Century, 1987.

Skolnick, A. *The Intimate Environment. Exploring Marriage and the Family*. Boston: Little, Brown, 1983.

Walkowitz, J.R. *Prostitution and Victorian Society. Women, Class and the State*. Cambridge: Cambridge University Press, 1980.

Vicinus, M. (ed). *A Widening Sphere: Changing Roles of Victorian Women*. Bloomington: Indiana University Press, 1977.

Young and Wilmott. *Family and Kinship in East London*. London: Routledge & Kegan Paul, 1957.

Sexuality and Sexual Development

Acton, W. *The Functions and Disorders of the Reproduction Organs in Youth, Adult Age and Advanced Life, considered in their Physiological, Social and Psychological Relations*. London: John Churchhill, 1857.

Barbach, L. *For Yourself*. N.Y.: Anchor Press/Doubleday, 1974.

Caplan, P. (ed). *The Cultural Construction of Sexuality*. London: Tavistock, 1987.

Chesser, E. *The Sexual, Marital and Family Relationships of the English Woman*. London: Hutchinson's Medical Publications, 1956.

Comfort, A. *The Joy of Sex*. London: Quartet, 1972.

Comfort, A. *More Joy: A Lovemaking Companion to the Joy of Sex*. N.Y.: Crown Publishers, 1987.

Dinnersteen, D. *The Mermaid and the Minotaur. Sexual Arrangements and Human Malaise*. N.Y.: Harper and Row, 1976.

Ellis, H. *Studies in The Psychology of Sex. Vol. VI, Sex in Relation to Society*. Philadelphia: E. A. Davies, 1910.

Feminist Review. *Sexuality: A Reader*. London: Virago, 1987.

Ford, C.S. and Beach, F.A. *Patterns of Sexual Behaviour*. London: Eyre and Spottiswood, 1952.

Foucault, M. *The History of Sexuality. Vol. I. An Introduction*. London: Allen Lane, 1979.

Friday, N. *My Secret Garden*. New York: Pocket Books, 1974.

Friday, N. *Men in Love*. New York: Delacorte, 1980.

Gagnon, J.H. and Simon, W. *Sexual Conduct: The Social Science of Human Sexuality*. Chicago: Aldine (Hutchinson, 1974), 1973.

Hall, L.A. *Hidden Anxieties: Male Sexuality 1900–1950*. Cambridge: Polity Press, 1991.

Hass, A. *Teenage Sexuality*. New York: Macmillan, 1979.

Hite, S. *The Hite Report on Male Sexuality*. N.Y.: Knopf, 1984.

Hite, S. *Women and Love: A Cultural Revolution in Progress*. London: Penguin Books, 1987.

Humphries, S. *A Secret World of Sex. Forbidden Fruit: The British Experience 1900–1950*. London: Sidgwick & Jackson, 1988.

Hunt, M. *Sexual Behavior in the Seventies*. Chicago: Playboy Press, 1974.

Jackson, S. *Childhood and Sexuality*. Oxford: Basil Blackwell, 1982.

Kinsey, A.C., Pomeroy, W.B. and Martin, C.E. *Sexual Behavior in the Human Male*. Philadelphia: Saunders, 1948.

Kinsey, A.C., Pomeroy, W.B., Martin, C.E. and Gebhard, P.H. *Sexual Behavior in the Human Female*. Philadelphia: Saunders, 1953.

Kitzinger, S. *Woman's Experience of Sex*. London: Dorling Kindersley (Penguin 1985), 1983.

Masters, W.H., Johnson, V.E. and Kolodney, R.C. *Human Sexuality*. 3rd ed. Glenview, Ill: Scott, Foresman, 1988.

Masters, W.H. and Johnson, V.E. *Human Sexual Response*. Boston, Mass.: Little, Brown & Co., 1966.

Mort, F. *Dangerous Sexualities: Medico-Moral Politics in England Since 1830*. London: Routledge and Kegan Paul, 1987.

Pietropinto, A. and Simenaur, J. *Beyond the Male Myth: What Women Want to Know about Male Sexuality*. N.Y.: Times Books, 1977.

Reinisch, J. and Beasley, R. *The Kinsey Institute New Report on Sex*. London: Penguin Books, 1991.

Rusbridge, A. *A Concise History of the Sex Manual 1886–1986*. London: Faber & Faber, 1986.

Sanders, D. *The Woman Book of Love and Sex*. London: Sphere Books Ltd., 1985.

Schofield, M. *The Sexual Behaviour of Young People*. London: Longman, 1965 (Penguin Books, 1968).

Schofield, M. *The Sexual Behaviour of Young Adults*. London: Allen Lane, 1973.

Stopes, M. *Married Love: A New Contribution to the Solution of Sex Difficulties*. London: A.C. Fifield, 1918.

Van de Velde, T.H. *Ideal Marriage. Its Physiology and Technique*. London: Heinemann Medical Books, 1928.

Weeks, J. *Sex, Politics and Society: The Regulation of Sexuality Since 1800*. London: Longmans, 1981.

Wight, D. *The Impact of HIV/AIDS on Young People's Heterosexual Behaviour in Britain: A Literature Review*. MRC Medical Sociology Unit, Glasgow: Working Paper No. 20, 1990.

Wolfe, L. *The Cosmo Report: Women and Sex in the '80s*. N.Y.: Bantam, 1982.

World League of Sexual Reform. Sexual Reform Congress, London 1929. *Proceedings*. London: Kegan Paul, Trench, Trubner & Co., 1930.

Wright, H. *The Sex Factor in Marriage: A Book for Those Who Are or About To Be Married*. London: Williams and Norgate, 1930.

Wyatt, G.E. & Powell, G.J. *Lasting Effects of Child Sexual Abuse*.
    Newbury Park: Sage Publications, 1988.
Zubin, J. and Money, J. (Eds). *Contemporary Sexual Behavior. Critical
    Issues in the 1970s*. Baltimore: John Hopkins University Press,
    1973.

Index

A Selected List of Non-Fiction Titles Available from Mandarin

While every effort is made to keep prices low, it is sometimes necessary to increase prices at short notice. Mandarin Paperbacks reserves the right to show new retail prices on covers which may differ from those previously advertised in the text or elsewhere.

The prices shown below were correct at the time of going to press.

☐	7493 0961 X	**Stick it up Your Punter**	Chippendale & Horrib	£4.99
☐	7493 0988 1	**Desert Island Discussions**	Sue Lawley	£4.99
☐	7493 0938 5	**The Courage to Heal**	Ellen Bass and Laura Davis	£7.99
☐	7493 0637 8	**The Hollywood Story**	Joel Finler	£9.99
☐	7493 1032 4	**How to Meet Interesting Men**	Gizelle Howard	£5.99
☐	7493 0586 X	**The New Small Garden**	C. E. Lucas-Phillips	£5.99
☐	7493 1172 X	**You'll Never Eat Lunch in This Town Again**	Julia Phillips	£5.99

All these books are available at your bookshop or newsagent, or can be ordered direct from the publisher. Just tick the titles you want and fill in the form below.

Mandarin Paperbacks, Cash Sales Department, PO Box 11, Falmouth, Cornwall TR10 9EN.

Please send cheque or postal order, no currency, for purchase price quoted and allow the following for postage and packing:

UK including BFPO   £1.00 for the first book, 50p for the second and 30p for each additional book ordered to a maximum charge of £3.00.

Overseas including Eire   £2 for the first book, £1.00 for the second and 50p for each additional book thereafter.

NAME (Block letters) ....

ADDRESS...

....

☐ I enclose my remittance for ....

☐ I wish to pay by Access/Visa Card Number

Expiry Date